Saving Face

Families in Focus

Series Editors

Naomi R. Gerstel, University of Massachusetts, Amherst
Karen V. Hansen, Brandeis University
Rosanna Hertz, Wellesley College
Margaret K. Nelson, Middlebury College

Saving Face

The Emotional Costs of the Asian
Immigrant Family Myth

ANGIE Y. CHUNG

RUTGERS UNIVERSITY PRESS

NEW BRUNSWICK, NEW JERSEY, AND LONDON

Library of Congress Cataloging-in-Publication Data

Names: Chung, Angie Y., 1973– author.
Title: Saving face : the emotional costs of the Asian immigrant family myth / Angie Y. Chung.
Description: New Brunswick, New Jersey : Rutgers University Press, [2016] I Series: Families in focus I Includes bibliographical references and index.
Identifiers: LCCN 2015047296I ISBN 9780813569826 (hardcover : alk. paper) I ISBN 9780813569819 (pbk. : alk. paper) I ISBN 9780813569833 (e-book (web pdf)) I ISBN 9780813572819 (e-book (epub))
Subjects: LCSH: Asians—United States. I Asian Americans. I Asian American families. I Model minority stereotype—United States. I Immigrants—Cultural assimilation—United States. I Immigrant families—United States.
Classification: LCC E184.A75 C5165 2016 I DDC 973/.0495—dc23
LC record available at http://lccn.loc.gov/2015047296

A British Cataloging-in-Publication record for this book is available from the British Library.

Visit our website: http://rutgerspress.rutgers.edu

Manufactured in the United States of America

To Sofie and Marisol

Contents

Preface and Acknowledgments

Around the time I began drafting the outline of this book, there was a great deal of public commotion over a controversial book related to Asian American families written by law professor Amy Chua. The book, *Battle Hymn of the Tiger Mother*, is a memoir describing the draconian-like parenting methods Chua had supposedly adopted from her Chinese parents that she used to raise two highly accomplished daughters. As an American-born daughter to Chinese immigrant parents, she talks about the ups and downs of trying to enforce her own rendition of Chinese parenting, which involved strictly managing her daughters' schedules around schoolwork and music lessons, forbidding them from attending sleepovers or parties, and showering them with criticism and threats as opposed to praise and encouragement if they did not earn a perfect A.

Putting aside the question of whether or not such rigid parenting strategies indeed explain Asian American "success"—a subject that has been well disputed by numerous research studies, I was interested in understanding the powerful psychology and culturally rooted emotions that shape these parent-child relationships and how they affect Asian Americans as they come of age. My interviews suggest that Chua's strong view on parenting and family among Asian Americans does stereotype and exaggerate the diverse experiences of second-generation Asian Americans I myself encountered in the New York metropolitan area, many of whom did not relate to the kind of extreme, authoritarian parenting approach she claimed to have experienced in her own family. This is not to say that traditional values on education and discipline did not surface in the accounts of second-generation adults I interviewed. Indeed, intergenerational struggles over academics and friends and lack of verbal affirmation and affection from their parents also formatively shaped the views of many Korean and Chinese Americans I met as they made critical decisions on marriage and family in their own lives.

However, the memories of their childhood and the emotional tone of their relationships with their parents varied widely depending on family roles, histories, and background. I found that Chua's one-dimensional interpretation of these "Chinese parenting strategies" only scratched the surface of these parent-child relationships and obscured the more complex interaction of emotions, sacrifice, and loving devotion parents expressed to their children in diverse ways. Most important, she failed to emphasize the larger structural context of immigrant hardship, discrimination, and nostalgia that characterizes Asian American lives and causes even immigrants to reinterpret the cultural systems they carry over from their homelands.

At the same time that I strongly disagreed with her view of parenting as signifying the values of the "culturally superior Asian American family," I also sympathized with Chua's need to find meaning in her life by crafting a worldview that reconciled the memories of racial harassment and strict parental upbringing she reported experiencing throughout her childhood. Granted, one can argue Chua bears some responsibility because she is in a position of power that allows her the privilege of perpetuating stereotypes and myths that serve only to legitimize systems of racial inequality through such controversial and highly visible books. However, for Chua (and others like her), raising her children with this approach, interpreting her experiences as "culturally superior" (a theme that she returns to in a follow-up book called *The Triple Package*), and even writing these books as a testament to her family's success were ways of managing the wellspring of emotions that her experiences most likely unleashed. I was fortunate to have been raised by two parents with whom I did occasionally have bitter clashes over generational and gender differences but for the most part had faith in my and my brother's ability to succeed on our own when it came to our education and careers. However, I have also met other second-generation Asian Americans through both my research and my professional life whose lives were strictly controlled by their parents and who do relate to some of the beliefs Chua propagated about her parents' culture. As this book reveals, the emotional responses of second-generation Asian Americans toward their families are filled with as much profound loneliness, resentment, and regret as indescribable gratitude, affection, and devotion.

It is with this understanding that I set out on a personal and professional journey to make sense of my family experiences and my role as the oldest daughter of Korean immigrant parents by discovering how other Asian Americans made sense of theirs. Throughout the research process, I was quite surprised to realize that one of the biggest struggles was not so much the challenge of discussing the parental abuse and neglect, racial and sexual harassment, social ostracism, and depression that occasionally surfaced in the narratives of Asian Americans I met. I would hope that making that emotional connection with a sympathetic listener and offering this therapeutic outlet made the experience valuable for both parties. The struggle for me instead lay in what should come naturally in my profession—that is, categorizing the complex lived experiences of Asian Americans whose lives have been continuously squeezed into academic checkboxes of "whiteness" and "blackness" that simply do not capture their sense of in-betweenness.

Indeed, one thing that did resonate throughout all these experiences was the emotional complexity with which Asian Americans perceived their relationships with family that did not fit properly within the Western binary framework we had been taught between what was right and what was wrong, of being Korean/Chinese or being American, of experiencing oppression and pursuing liberation, and of being loved and feeling abandoned. Having also been interviewed once by a student journalist about a personal issue in my life, I also understand the natural human tendency to resist an outsider's simplistic rendition of our complex and deeply personal feelings. At the same time, one of the most common sentiments emerging from all of these narratives was a deep yearning to hear more about the experiences of other second-generation Asian Americans and make sense of their immigrant parents' worldviews. I hope that this outside interpretation of these narratives can help both those who were involved with this study and those who were not find meaning behind their experiences, recognize that they are not alone, and feel a sense of social and emotional connectedness with Asian Americans they may have never met.

This book was made possible with the help, feedback, and support of many people at different stages of the process. In order to be able to target hard-to-reach populations, I relied on the assistance of Frank Mok, who recruited and interviewed LGBTQ and married Asian Americans with children. In addition, former graduate assistant and now faculty member Joseph Gibbons recruited and interviewed many of the second-generation white Americans in this study. A big thanks to Trivina Kang for letting me develop her article and coauthor with her Chapter 2, on the educational aspirations of second-generation Asian Americans.

I am grateful for the various colleagues from my department at the University at Albany who were generous enough to read different versions of these book chapters and provide detailed feedback, including Christine Bose, Richard Lachmann, Richard Alba, James Zetka, Nancy Denton, and Glenn Deane. In addition to these colleagues, Min Zhou, Pyong Gap Min, John

Logan, Glenna Spitze, Zai Liang, and Philip Kasinitz provided me with invaluable guidance on navigating the ups and downs of the publishing process and my career. I also thank the different members of my Junior Faculty Reading Group (you know who you are), who let me pretend I was a junior faculty and provided both detailed comments on book chapters and badly needed study breaks throughout the process. In addition, I received some very helpful comments from Bandana Purkayastha and Pyong Gap Min on different conference panels. Thanks to the Research Center for Korean Community at CUNY Queens, Asian American/Asian Research Institute, CUNY Graduate Center, and the Sociology Department at Korea University for inviting me to conferences and forums where I could present my work and receive more feedback.

Of course, I could not have shared this labor of love with the rest of the world without the constant guidance and enthusiastic support of Peter Mickulas, Naomi Gerstel, and the entire staff at Rutgers University Press. I have been so impressed with my experience working with this professional editorial team, who have given me the kind of push, advice, and encouragement every author seeks in a press. My thanks to Peter for replying to all my emails, expediting the publication process, and providing sage advice every step of the way. As the reviewers for this book, both Naomi Gerstel and Nazli Kibria were enormously helpful in providing very detailed and insightful feedback that helped me to focus, streamline, and package this book in a compelling way.

In terms of funding, I owe many thanks to the Dr. Nuala McGann Drescher Affirmative Action/Diversity Leave Program, which allowed me to take a paid leave of absence so that I could complete my last book manuscript while jumpstarting the interviews for this project. I also received invaluable support from several sources at the University at Albany, including the Initiatives for Women (IFW) Award, the Faculty Research Award Program B (FRAP B), and seed money from the Department of Sociology, which covered expenses like research assistantships, subject payment, and indexing costs.

Of course, the inspiration to write a book about family could not have happened without the love and support of my dear family. This includes both my parents Connie and Dale Chung, who taught me everything I need to know about the meaning of parental love through their unsaid sacrifices and support throughout my life. This book forms my message to them that their love and sacrifice were not left unheard and will never be forgotten. I also give thanks to Eric Hwang, whose love, feedback, and patience have helped to broaden my perspective on both cultures and keep me grounded throughout the process. I am also indebted to Sejin Kim for feeding and caring for our family while I worked on this manuscript and showing all of us the true meaning of grace, selflessness, and kindness. And of course this book is especially dedicated to my two daughters, Sofie and Marisol, whom I will tell every day how much I love them the American way and show how much I love them the Korean way. May this book give you a sense of emotional connection and belonging to our family history someday.

—

Saving Face

CHAPTER 1

The Asian Immigrant
Family Myth

In 1995, *New York Magazine* published as its cover story a piece on Korean immigrants and their American-born children titled "The Overachievers." In the article, the reporter Jeffrey Goldberg compares the historical evolution of Koreans and Jewish immigration and generational change in the United States, concluding that "Korean history in New York reads like an abridged version of the Jewish [by] skipping whole chapters as they suburbanize and assimilate."[1] His comparison centers on the two groups' propensity to raise well-educated and talented children, their entrepreneurial conflicts with black consumers, and an overall sense of racial and class marginalization in America. In addition, Goldberg remarks on similar ambitions among Korean immigrants to use entrepreneurship as a way to achieve the American Dream and have their children replicate their extraordinary educational achievements without losing their ethnic ancestral heritage, as did Jewish immigrants before them.

In presenting Koreans as the next immigrant success story, the mythical narrative that Goldberg constructs in this article signifies a broader shift in the racial visibility and positioning of Asian Americans in the post–civil rights era. The caption on Goldberg's cover page proclaims that "the city's super-immigrants slaved and scraped to give their children the American Dream. There's only one catch—the kids are turning into Americans."[2] Although the comparison is focused primarily on Korean and Jewish immigrants, the general racial imagery it evokes has many parallels with other Asian model minority figures in feature stories throughout this era, such as the Japanese success story, the Chinese American whiz kids, and, more recently, the South Asian Indian national spelling bee winners. The overall impression is that immigrant parents may have encountered many hardships in coming to America, but this sacrifice has enabled their children to succeed—perhaps even a little too well—in school.

What makes Goldberg's article particularly intriguing and arguably nuanced from other similar media coverage of the time is the way he touches on the mixed emotional context of the Korean immigrant family experience as they rigorously pursue the American Dream. The article offers an interesting starting point for discussing the emotional experiences of Asian American families in several ways: On the one hand, it highlights the ways in which many Korean immigrants seem to view their situation as comparable with white immigrants before them based on similar immigrant ideologies about hard work and success. Despite the many challenges, disappointments, and failures they may have endured, reaffirming these values and having faith in the American Dream allow immigrants to justify everything they have lost in voluntarily coming to the United States. Thus, it should come as no surprise that Koreans want to express their emotional affinity with Jewish immigrants, who they believe used the same tools of education, entrepreneurship, and religion to achieve similar goals of educational success without losing their ethnic roots. Although media pundits tend to associate optimism with success, these similarities in norms and values do not necessarily mean that both Jewish and Asian immigrants and their American-born children face the same challenges and achieve the same outcomes; however, they do show how immigrants emotionally process their hardships and seek social connectedness with others' experiences in order to make sense of their life decisions.

Goldberg suggests that despite their many achievements, Koreans seem to harbor a profound sense of unease and self-consciousness as a result of their struggles that ironically intensifies their "dependency" on the mere idea of a "Jewish success story." Beneath all these outward expressions of hope, optimism, and faith in the American Dream, Goldberg also sensed a deep and growing doubt and anxiety among Korean immigrant parents. He notes, "This sudden vulnerability is causing some first generation Koreans to register a more fundamental anxiety: Why are they here at all? Many Koreans say that they feel essentially powerless; powerless in their own homes, as they watch America turn their children into people they don't fully understand— that is, Americans; powerless outside their homes, in the unnavigable world of coalition politics; and powerless in their own businesses, where they find they don't control the largest levers of economic success."[3] In many ways, the struggles, aspirations, and self-consciousness among Korean immigrants also pervade the worldview and experiences of other immigrant groups, who voluntarily leave all that they know back in the homeland in the hopes of a better life in America with all its real and overidealized expectations. The costs are magnified in the case of racial minority groups who must navigate not only the harsh realities of immigrant life but also the obstacles that come with racial marginalization.

Jeffrey Goldberg is an Israeli American, but he picks up on a comparison that is often made among Asian immigrants and their American children. As I will discuss, references to the "Jewish American experience" regularly emerge throughout the narratives of Korean and Chinese Americans in this study. As a youth, I remember overhearing similar discussions among my relatives excitedly discussing their commonalities and differences from Jewish Americans and what Koreans needed to do to follow the Jewish path to success. Like many other Korean immigrants who took over businesses formerly owned by Jews, my father also got his start at his own firm by learning the business model from Jewish acquaintances in the lighting industry. He eventually became a successful entrepreneur, building what began as a small import-export business into a large nationally recognized company. Through the imperfect medium of family gossip, I also get the sense that despite pride in his achievements, he feels some remorse over what this success cost him in terms of his family life.

Of course Goldberg focuses on the first generation of immigrants, who arrived with little English proficiency, nontransferable educational credentials, and the hopes of a better life through entrepreneurship. He says much less about the emotional conflicts of second-generation Korean Americans, who appear as one-dimensional caricatures of the model minority.[4] As the potential carriers for their parents' dreams, the American-born children of immigrants face a very different social terrain marked by its own opportunities and challenges. Does the emotional context of their parents' migration have any influence on the worldviews of the American-born children who are expected to carry the weight of their parents' sacrifices and attain the American Dream? If the pressures and burdens that immigrant families face have changed in this new economic era, then have they also shaped how immigrants and their children perceive sentimental attachments, negotiate the emotional dynamics of parent-child relationships, and communicate across generational barriers? How do second-generation Korean and Chinese Americans use emotion work to navigate and make sense of the responsibilities and expectations of these shifting family roles within the context of their public lives? And in the processes of engaging and managing these feelings, how have second-generation Asian Americans viewed and carried on their ethnic identity and parents' ancestral culture as they reach adulthood?

This book establishes the family as the site for both the production and the enactment of emotion work, while situating these processes within broader social and economic contexts. The main goal of this book is to understand how different types of intimate relationships and emotion work between parent and child have informed the way these American-born children view and practice ethnicity and culture in their own adult lives. Challenging the mainstream portrayal of Asian immigrant families as cold, homogeneous, and timeless relics of the past, I explore how emotions are managed and expressed in adaptation to family roles and structural constraints, the way they are conveyed across generational and cultural differences, and how they condition the ethnic worldviews of the second generation. I also discuss how second-generation Korean and Chinese Americans negotiate the social costs and benefits of being both valorized and dehumanized by the racial imagery of the model minority family. In the end, the book seeks to problematize the notion of the one-dimensional "Asian American family experience" and reconsider how these complex experiences have influenced the ethnic identities of second-generation Korean and Chinese Americans.

The Myth of the Model Minority Family

The time period and social context within which Goldberg's article was published are particularly salient in that the stereotypical image of Asian Americans as the "model minority" was by then firmly entrenched in the American racial imaginary. At the core of the myth is the claim that Asian Americans use hard work, strong cultural and family values, and entrepreneurial thrift to overcome racial barriers and achieve extraordinary success in America, just like Jewish immigrants before them. As evidence of this, scholars and pundits point to the high educational attainment levels of Asian Americans as a whole and their increasing presence in prestigious universities and well-paying white-collar professions.[5] First coined by sociologist William Petersen in a 1966 feature story on Japanese Americans in *New York Times Magazine*,[6] the image of Asian Americans as good citizens and obedient workers offered a suggestive and deliberate contrast to America's "problem minority"—African Americans—months after the passage of the 1965 Voting Rights Act and the outbreak of rioting in inner-city black ghettoes.[7] Within a year of Petersen's publication, *U.S. News & World Report* more pointedly stated, "At a time when it is being proposed that hundreds of billions be spent to uplift Negroes and other minorities, the nation's 300,000 Chinese Americans are moving ahead on their own—with no help from anyone."[8]

Supporting the idea that poverty is the result of culture, not discrimination, the term "model minority" has since been broadened to include Jewish Americans and other Asian Americans (mainly Chinese and Koreans) and has caught on like wildfire in media circuits and among scholarly debates as resounding proof of the American Dream. The model minority myth image of Asian American success persists today in the mainstream media, political discourses, and academic circles. Public fascination—and repulsion—with the model minority has also driven the popularity of books such as Chua and Rubenfeld's book *The Triple Package* on the cultural superiority of such ethnic groups as Chinese and Jews,[9] as well as TV shows that highlight the intelligence, competitiveness, passivity, and emotionless rationality of their Asian American characters such as Sandra Oh as the type-A Dr. Cristina Yang from *Grey's Anatomy* or B. D. Wong as the soft-spoken forensic scientist George Huang in *Law & Order: Special Victims Unit*.

Family and the cultural values they pass onto their children are central to this myth. Right before the model minority myth first emerged, Assistant Secretary of Labor Daniel Moynihan published a 1965 report on *Negro Families*, in which he turned the public spotlight on the growing plight of African American in inner-city ghettoes.[10] Moynihan attributed the poverty, crime, and welfare dependency among African Americans to the general "deterioration of the Negro family" as signified by growing black male unemployment, single-female-headed households, and illegitimate births. Although he described this "dysfunctional" family structure as a legacy of slavery and discrimination in the United States, Moynihan painted a picture of black families as culturally flawed and socially unstable, which he argued contributed to their ultimate self-destruction.

Moynihan was not the only one to perpetuate the image of inner-city black families as culturally deficient. The so-called cultural pathology of poor matriarch-oriented black families has been and continues to be a pervasive theme, including in studies of early twentieth-century scholars like Lloyd Warner, E. Franklin Frazier, and Talcott Parsons and in work by contemporary social scientists like William Julius Wilson and Thomas Sowell. Unlike voluntary immigrants who arrive with intact cultural systems that help to organize family and communal life, native-born African American families are often portrayed as lacking the resources, community support, and cultural value systems to promote the educational achievement and upward mobility of their children, as a result of the long legacy of slavery, segregation, and discrimination that has undermined the foundations of families and communities.[11] This cultural explanation for black poverty is used to justify increasing restrictions on financial aid and social services to poor black mothers (e.g., welfare) and inner-city ghettoes.

As a corrective to this approach, Carol Stack argues that black families do not lack social organization and stability but are resilient enough to adapt their family structures to the realities of poverty and racism by relying more heavily on associational networks composed of extended kin.[12] These studies nevertheless agree on the enduring impact of racial discrimination on the family structures of racial minorities. In the United States, immigrant families who are racially profiled as "black" must negotiate their ethnic resources within this restrictive racial environment. Mary Waters finds that "assimilation to America for the second generation black immigrant is complicated by race and class and their interaction, with upwardly mobile second generation youngsters maintaining ethnic ties to their parents' national origins and with poor inner city youngsters assimilating to the black American peer culture that surrounds them."[13]

In stark contrast to the stereotypical black family, the model Asian family is viewed as providing the moral training ground and main support system for the unsurpassed educational achievements and social mobility of the children of Asian immigrants. Research studies have consistently shown evidence for the relative cohesion and stability of Asian families based on their higher percentage of traditional one-earner married-couple households, their lower divorce rates, and their lower percentage of children born out of wedlock as compared with most other racial groups.[14] Drawing on these figures, pundits attribute the "success" of second-generation Asian Americans to a deeply rooted Confucian-based culture that emphasizes strong family values, marital stability, filial piety, and reverence for tradition and hard work. They argue that though culturally distinct and foreign, Asian Americans share certain norms and values that complement the middle-class white Protestant work ethic, including "group membership and honor, fear of shame, respect for authority," and the "suppression of their real emotional feelings, particularly desires of physical aggressiveness," all of which enable them to achieve success.[15] In response to the wave of criticism that followed his report, Moynihan pointed to the case of Japanese Americans, whose "singularly stable, cohesive, and enlightened family life," he argued, should "inspire hope in all Americans for the possibility of eradicating black people's 'tangle of pathology.'"[16] By demonstrating that traditional family values and hard work can help ethnic minorities overcome all obstacles, the model minority myth validates not only the meritocracy of America, but also the normativity of (white) heterosexual nuclear families; it also implicitly blames the root of all social problems to "deviant" or "culturally pathological" family structures among poor, black, and gay/lesbian households.

There are however two sides to the Asian immigrant family myth: the first praises Asian families for upholding the traditional heteronormative structure and ideal of the "normal (white) American family" based on a hardworking male breadwinner and a family-devoted wife/mother who raises obedient children with proper family values. At the other end of the spectrum, rising economic competition from the Pacific Rim and educational competition with Asian Americans at home have also fueled hostility, fear, and condemnation over these same mythical qualities. The myth presents Asian immigrant parents and their children as objects of societal ridicule and criticism about the dangers of excessive parenting, oppressive hierarchies, and emotionless pragmatism in a monolithic Asian culture. In this portrayal, the sexist oppression of the Asian patriarch and the education-/discipline-obsessed Asian Tiger Mom create an emotionally stifling family environment that causes their children to reject their parents' ancestral culture and seek to liberate themselves by assimilating into a progressive American society. Although one celebrates and the other disparages Asian immigrant families, both stereotypes essentially achieve the same purpose of highlighting the racial foreignness of Asian Americans against the normativity of the "traditional American family"—one that is presumably white, middle-class, heterosexual, and nuclear-oriented.

A growing area of scholarship has disputed the research used to support the model minority myth, pointing to the faulty methodological assumptions of the data and disregard for the effects of discrimination, poverty, and hardship on a heterogeneous population. For example, a report from the National Commission on Asian American and Pacific Islander Research in Education and College Board points out that the perception that Asian Americans are flooding elite private colleges and universities across the nation is flawed in that it conflates groups from different ethnic and class backgrounds along with international students and overlooks the fact that compared to other racial groups, they are concentrated in a smaller range of schools including public two- and four-year colleges.[17] Critics argue that the model minority myth uses the so-called cultural exceptionalism of Asian Americans to justify the racial privileges of white Americans by stigmatizing the overachieving obsession of Asian Americans and the cultural pathology of African Americans. Challenging the idea that their stellar records indicate faith in American equality and meritocracy, Sue and Okazaki show how the educational achievements and concentration of Asian Americans in a narrow range of profit-making professions may actually reflect the fact that immigrant parents perceive fewer avenues for mobility in noneducational occupations such as entertainment and politics because of social discrimination and language barriers.[18] More central to this book, numerous sociology and psychology studies have put forth strong evidence of the discrimination and negative sociopsychological damage that this so-called positive stereotype has inflicted on Asian Americans by implying they are good workers but weak leaders, setting the bar much higher for Asian American students and workers, and portraying them as devoid of other social, creative, and humanistic qualities. Among other things, these assumptions have been used to justify discrimination in college admissions, to deny promotions into managerial and leadership positions, and to ignore the educational, psychological, and social service needs of all Asian Americans regardless of background.[19]

Critics have pointed to some of the limitations of this cultural deterministic approach—that is, "the presupposition in these debates that black families are either 'better' or 'worse' organized, and that it is either culture or structure that shapes family organization."[20] Yet despite this recognition, few studies have employed a more synthetic approach to minority and immigrant families. In addition, these models promote a static, homogeneous, and decontextualized view of immigrant families that neglects both the internal heterogeneity of Asian American populations and the diverse social and historical contexts within which they develop.[21] The Asian population in the United States includes over thirty different ethnicities and nationalities, and even within a single nationality there are a wide range of regional origins, dialects, religions, classes, and generations. Post-1965 Asian immigration is characterized by its wide class polarization and diverse migration contexts, including poor Vietnamese refugees fleeing war and political instability, highly educated South Asian Indian professionals in the tech industry, and undocumented Chinese laborers employed by more resource-endowed coethnic business owners. Within the Korean, Chinese, and Taiwanese populations alone, some immigrants come from rural areas with little education and capital, while others migrate with stellar educational credentials and substantial financial resources from the booming cities of Seoul, Hong Kong, and Taipei. As opposed to treating families as antiquated relics from the homeland country, scholars have examined how Korean and Chinese families face different structural barriers depending on their backgrounds and are differently equipped to adapt to the pressures of economic survival, discrimination, and shifting household structures.[22] However, less has been said about how these structural constraints shape the emotional environment of American-born children and lead to different ways of viewing ethnicity and practicing family culture among the next generation.

THE CHANGING CONTEXT OF THE ASIAN IMMIGRANT FAMILY

One of the main problems with the model minority myth is its overemphasis on the cultural exceptionalism of Asian Americans with little thought to the different social and economic challenges that children of Asian immigrant families are facing today. Ever since immigrants first arrived en masse from Europe at the beginning of the twentieth century, immigrant families have been considered the institutional mainstay for ethnicity and culture among the American-born generation. During the industrial era, immigrant families served as a temporary sanctuary where parents could preserve the traditional cultural norms of the Old World against the competing influence of modern capitalism and individualism within American society.[23] By carrying over the cultural values, ethnic networks, and social institutions of their ancestral homeland, European parents were able to maintain a sense of stability in their uprooted lives and ease the adaptation of their families into the social structures of American society.

To some extent, the same can be said about most immigrant families today. Bonded by a web of affection, trust, and obligation, immigrant families are powerful institutions that can help to mediate the processes of adaptation by pooling together the labor and resources of its members, providing an intimate space for socializing, nurturing, and monitoring children, and mediating interactions with the host society. For minority families facing racial and economic uncertainty, family members can provide a strong network of support, a buffer against outside racial discrimination, and a means to preserve cultural values. As a result, Rumbaut finds that "cohesive families with low levels of parent-child conflict and disparagement are significantly advantaged with respect to youths' educational achievement and aspiration, as well as their level of effort, social support, and psychological well-being."[24]

On the other hand, studies on immigrant and minority families have shown how, historically, people of color have long had to adapt to racial and economic barriers by creating alternative family arrangements and caregiving practices that depart from the traditional Western nuclear family ideal.[25] In general, immigrants have a competitive edge over native-born workers only if they are willing to work for lower wages under unfavorable working conditions. Immigrants of color receive even fewer economic returns on their education and work experience, forcing them to adapt by pursuing different family strategies and household structures that deviate from the middle-class white norm. Espiritu points out that a combination of capitalist interests and social exclusion has historically depressed the wages of Asian male immigrants in relation to those of white laborers, pushing immigrant women to enter the workforce in order to contribute to family income.[26] Even as more immigrants are lured by the promises of the American Dream, their lived experiences are shaped by their persistent racial and legal exclusion from the social citizenry of the dominant mainstream.[27]

In addition, the economic structure that early European immigrants navigated at the height of industrialization is not the same as the one immigrants encounter today. Pressured by uneven development caused by the capitalist penetration of peripheral and intermediary nations, many Asian and Latino families are pushed to diversify their household incomes by exporting their labor to highly industrialized nations like the United States, where capital and job opportunities are increasingly concentrated.[28] Sassen argues that in global cities such as New York, the class polarization of economic structures around high-paying white-collar professions and downgraded low-skilled service work has widened the gap between the rich and the poor and has decreased opportunities for upward mobility among immigrants and racial minorities concentrated at the bottom.[29] The rising competitiveness of the global economy has put pressure on families to restructure their households to ensure their children's economic future. Sometimes, this means working apart from family members for long periods of time to take advantage of work or educational opportunities overseas.

These economic shifts have disrupted the social stability of immigrant households and changed the emotional dynamics of family relationships. Structural vulnerabilities within the family and poverty in the neighborhood community can aggravate these tensions. For one, many American-born children of such families have difficulties communicating with their immigrant parents as a result of cultural and language barriers and must straddle the typical pressures of childhood with the weight of parental expectations and obligations. Without proper supervision, today's children are also susceptible to the negative effects of racial and class segregation within poor urban neighborhoods afflicted by chronic poverty, inferior schooling, youth gang activity, and high crime rates.[30] Among children of color, racial discrimination and weak social support systems can contribute to depression, low racial self-esteem, and alienation from their families.[31]

Within this context, Asian immigrant families must be reexamined not only as a site of harmony, discipline, and reciprocity but also as a site fraught with multiple contradictions, tensions, and conflicts that have been growing with the rise of the global economy. Immigrant parents and young children who are physically separated in this manner often struggle with feelings of guilt, emotional estrangement, and resentment toward their absentee parents. Even among family members who live together, strains caused by periodic separation or alienation from overworked parents evoke feelings of anxiety, depression, and loneliness. The growing visibility of women in the low-wage labor force and the family's increasing reliance on children for adult responsibilities have changed the power dynamics and emotive ties between not only husband and wife, but also parent and child.[32]

Both parents and children adapt to these social dislocations in their own strategic ways. For example, Parrenas shows how mothers in Filipino immigrant families who are separated from their children across national borders try to compensate for their absence by sending remittances, micromanaging their children's daily activities, making frequent phone calls, and sending care packages.[33] Song finds that Asian immigrant parents who own labor-intensive family businesses use financial compensation to assuage parental guilt over the extra responsibilities shouldered by their children, who in turn find ways to "reverse guilt-trip" their parents.[34] Immigrant parents try to mask the shifting power dynamics within the family and preserve the integrity of their culture against outside racism through nostalgic references to homeland culture and the preservation of traditional gender roles.[35] However, this defensive strategy has the negative effect of reinforcing the patriarchal order and exacerbating intergenerational tensions with both daughters and sons.

Beyond the Generation Gap

The inherent paradox of the model minority myth lies in its dual claim that, on one hand, Asian immigrant parents are able to promote the educational achievement and ultimate assimilation of their children by preserving Confucian values of hard work, obedience, and family unity; yet this Asian fixation on education, competition, discipline, frugality, and conformity makes them perpetual foreigners. Books like Amy Chua's *Battle Hymn of the Tiger Mother* and the public frenzy over the "cheating epidemic" among Asian American students help to feed the misguided perception that Asian Americans, like their immigrant parents, lack any redeeming individualistic humanistic qualities like emotions, morals, and creativity because of this obsession to succeed.[36] According to model minority myth proponents, Confucian values may help Asian Americans to succeed because they align with the (white) Protestant ethic, but the only way for second-generation Asian Americans to become completely "normal" is to shed the backward ways of their immigrant parents and integrate fully into a middle-class white American core. It is clear that the myth proclaims that assimilation is attainable in a color-blind American society, but whether or not Asian Americans can achieve true parity with native-born white Americans has yet to be resolved.

Robert E. Park, one of the first scholars to systematically explain assimilation processes, described race relations as a cycle in which different ethnic groups come into contact and then undergo conflict, accommodation, and eventually assimilation.[37] Based mostly on the experiences of early twentieth-century European immigrants, traditional assimilationists believe that there is a tendency for ethnic differences to fade with each passing generation that acculturates and intermingles with Americans.[38] As social contact with other racial and ethnic groups and intermarriage rates increase, the family becomes a less effective institutional medium for promoting ethnicity and cultural values across generations.[39] In those cases when future generations do choose to preserve their ethnicity, it is primarily a symbolic and superficial display of cultural and social belonging that rarely impacts the social relationships and daily lives of most Americans.[40] In the context of U.S. race relations, however, the flexibility with which individuals can choose their identities depends on their racial phenotype and status within power structures. As Nagel points out, "European Americans and black Americans represents two ends of an ethnic ascription continuum, in which whites are always free to remember their ancestry and blacks are never free to forget theirs."[41]

Within this context, the generation gap serves as the marker of this transition from the racial other to American democracy and freedom. The Asian immigrant family myth characterizes this generational divide as a binary between the traditional, nostalgic, and antiquated ethnic worldview of immigrant parents and the supposedly more modern, Americanized culture that children encounter outside the home. On the one hand are those traditional parents who demand respect and obedience to elders, hard work and discipline, and fulfillment of family obligations over individual needs, and on the other hand are their children who are drawn toward an American culture that values independence, critical and free expression, and democratic egalitarianism. The greater the divide between these two cultures, the more likely children are to experience internal identity conflict and reject their parents' ancestral heritage.

The problem with most theories that have examined the generation gap is that they assume that immigrant families play static roles in conveying traditional values from the Old World that the second generation will simply discard or readapt to their American surroundings. Despite increasing diversity in family structures, the predominant approach has been to describe Asian immigrant families as unchanging repositories of old traditions ultimately fighting a losing battle against the modern, liberating forces of

American culture and society. Although I acknowledge the need to address intergenerational tensions, this book problematizes the way this divide is racially portrayed and reified as a binary between Eastern antiquity and Western civility, between authoritarianism and egalitarian democracy, and between static tradition and dynamic modernity. As Zontini notes, this classic assimilation view of immigrants and their children as transitioning along a continuum "from tradition to modern or from ethnic to mainstream" elides the fact that "traditional itself is under constant change and negotiation."[42] These studies do not consider how shifts in economic production and persistent barriers to social acceptance have substantively altered the cultural and emotional fabric of Asian immigrant families and made their mark on the ethnic worldviews of second-generation Americans. Indeed, the advent of the postindustrial era has made the classic assimilationist emphasis on the decline or persistence of ethnicity within the American framework insufficient in explaining how contemporary immigrant families have adapted to the complex emotional strains of modern American society. More important, Lowe points out that "the reduction of the cultural politics of racialized ethnic groups, like Asian Americans, to first generation/second generation struggles displaces social differences into a privatized familial opposition."[43] By blaming immigrant parents for their inability to adjust to their new surroundings, it absolves American citizens and institutions of the responsibility to rectify the unequal practices, myths, and resource distribution responsible for aggravating these cultural differences.

Most studies on immigrant families also assume that the social standings of all young family members are the same, disregard the active role children play in shaping family culture during the adaptation process, and overlook the different social and emotional context within which each child understands his or her parents' experiences. Researchers suggest that children within the same family can adopt different racial and ethnic identities, speak different languages, and affiliate with different peer networks. For example, Stevens and Ishizawa find that compared to their younger siblings, older children are more likely to speak a non-English language, partly because of their age at migration but also their role as translators for their immigrant parents.[44] In her study on children of Korean and Vietnamese immigrant families, Karen Pyke argues that eldest siblings tend to take on more traditional obligations and roles as cultural preservers and family disciplinarians, which helps them to empathize more with their parents but creates cultural tensions with their more Americanized younger siblings.[45] Although much has been said about variations across ethnic groups, scholars have yet to explain the underlying mechanisms and processes that cause some children to be more receptive to the positive influences of ethnic community than their siblings even though they are raised within the same family and neighborhood context.

Challenging the concept of immigrant families as unified households, studies on gender and immigration point out that the values, needs, and interests of individual family members do not always align with those of other family members or even with the greater good of the household.[46] Because of the ways in which gender constrains and organizes the lives of women and men, certain family members have greater access to family resources to pursue individual goals or may be motivated by different concerns. Boys and girls are socialized differently about their obligations to the family from birth to adulthood, and the way they are taught to practice cultural values and protect family honor has significant bearing on their later views on ethnicity and culture. Regardless of birth order, daughters generally struggle with a wider range of emotionally intimate and conflict-ridden family roles and obligations than do sons, which Dion and Dion suggest may also shape their ethnic identities in different ways.[47] This study calls for a more flexible and nuanced understanding of how the generational divide between parent and child plays out at the intersections of race, class, and gender inequality. It also recognizes the ways second-generation adults are able to play an active role in negotiating these cultural differences in ways they may not have been capable of doing as youth.

The Presentation of the Asian American Self

In light of the many challenges immigrant families face, emotions and emotion work have everything to do with how adult-age children of Korean and Chinese immigrants view and reproduce ethnicity and culture in their day-to-day lives. In this sense, the binary mainstream characterization of Asian immigrant families either as "normal" or "dysfunctional" misses the emotional complexity of children's very human relationships with their parents—both connected by an unsaid understanding of their sacrifice and love but distanced by their inability to communicate as a result of socioeconomic constraints and generational barriers. Sociological approaches to emotion have emphasized the need to "look beneath the surface appearance of emotion to focus on the way emotions are culturally constructed and shaped by social norms." These include "what people feel, how they make sense of their feelings, how their feelings affect their actions, how they manage their feelings, and how they display the appropriate feelings in given situations."[48] This inner struggle is related to what Arlie Hochschild calls "emotion work," or the process of trying to manage feelings in order to preserve the stability and well-being of a social relationship and, in the case of immigrant families, the sanctity of a worldview.[49] Emotions are culturally constructed, but the way women and men in families perceive sentiment, make sense of their feelings, and manage their emotions in front of others can have concrete effects on not only the stability of the family but also their socioeconomic livelihood.

These feelings are also deeply intertwined with both the societal values and economic structure of the time. Since the late 1960s, women of all backgrounds have entered the paid labor force in large numbers, yet workplace wages, benefits, and policies have failed to keep pace with the expensive yet time-constrained realities of dual-wage-earning households. Faced with increasing demands on their time and labor, outdated workplace policies, and declining public assistance for children and families, Hochschild argues that the typical dual-earner couple has come to view home as a site of negative and emotionally draining experiences that rely on women to juggle multiple duties as mother, wife, and wage earner.[50] In the face of these many responsibilities and expectations, women are forced to actively negotiate and manage a conflicting range of emotions in order to preserve family stability. This so-called time-bind has had far-reaching effects on gender and family roles, as well as the dynamics of caregiving.[51]

The concept of emotion work can also help us understand how second-generation Asian Americans process and make sense of ethnicity and family culture, given the various tensions and constraints they face in their day-to-day lives. Despite an environment of pervasive commercialism and utilitarianism, emotions based on nonquantifiable feelings of attachment, intimacy, gratitude, and empathy alongside feelings of neglect, loneliness, envy, and resentment still play a central role in structuring the relationship between Asian immigrant parents and their American-born children. In their study on Korean American adults, Yoo and Kim find that the willingness of children to help their parents is driven not only by pragmatic need, obligation, and guilt, but also by the affective bonds of intimacy, respect, and empathy in line with their shared emotional circumstances as an Asian family.[52] As I embarked on this study, the intense effects of emotion work became quite evident to me as participants—even those who resented their parents—burst into tears, glowed with respect and appreciation, and sighed deeply in resignation over the mere memory of their family's sacrifices and burdens.

Culturally, Korean and Chinese immigrant families engage in all kinds of emotion work as they adapt and respond to their changing social environment. For example, the Asian practice of "saving face"—or maintaining one's dignity and reputation by hiding and avoiding humiliating or embarrassing situations—involves not only molding one's behavior in front of others but also reigning in feelings of anger, shame, and disappointment that they fear may undermine their self-integrity. Emotion work in this case is partly shaped by the general struggles of the immigration experience, but I propose that in the case of Asian Americans, it is also precipitated by the difficulties and contradictions of normalizing their family's racial difference as well as juggling unusual family roles and responsibilities amid shrinking resources. All of this leads to a wellspring of conflicting emotions that they must learn to reconcile or manage in order to make sense of their own adult lives.

In the processes of mediating the multiple demands and affective gaps within these parent-child relationships, the children of immigrants find ethnic ties and cultural values anywhere from instrumental to obtrusive in helping them to deal with these emotions in different ways. Much of this depends on the children's position within the family pecking order, but one that is shaped by complex situations and conditions that go well beyond those of gender and birth order. It is true that as a result of Asian traditions, daughters may endure greater restrictions on their mobility, independence, and sexuality than do sons—a conflict that many assume will lead to a greater desire among daughters to relinquish their parents' culture. Based on the moving stories of participants in this study, I propose that the ethnic identities of sons and daughters are informed by the complex ways they are emotionally integrated into different roles within the family, depending on not only gendered expectations and birth order but also class and education, sibling composition, diverse immigration experiences, and specific parent-child relationship dynamics. Altogether, these forces can cause daughters and sons to blur traditional gender boundaries, alternate gender roles, and shift gender relations over the life cycle. In this sense, while gender clearly shapes and constrains the lives of daughters and sons, the emotional responses they evoke (and hence, the ethnic outcomes to which these lead) both intersect with and transcend multiple social identities.

Readers may note that while the experiences of the second-generation Korean and Chinese Americans appear diverse, ambiguous, multilayered, and dynamic, the language they use to explain them often sounds deceivingly simple and invokes traditional themes on family values, Asian American masculinities/femininities, racial stereotypes, the model minority myth, and the American Dream. In order to explain this apparent contradiction, it is important to distinguish between the public persona individuals may project and the root emotions that they need to manage in constructing that persona. Part of the immigrant story is articulated through what Goffman refers to as the "presentation of self," or the rational and calculated ways people manage their public image and exhibit a certain demeanor to others in order to achieve some social objective.[53] Thus, when immigrant parents brag about the educational achievements of their children, they are attempting to prove to others that their hard work and sacrifice have enabled their children to achieve the American Dream. They are in other words saving face.

However, this is only one aspect of human behavior that does not explain the deeper feelings and sentimental attachments that cause, guide, and even contradict the public self.[54] While outwardly expressing pride and happiness, these parents also restrain feelings of doubt, regret, and disappointment with the very same American Dream in order to give meaning to their life decisions and allow their children to succeed where they could not. How much of this American-born children are able to grasp depends on intergenerational communication. Thus, traditional theorists have been misguided in analyzing Asian American families based only on their outward presentation of self instead of delving deeper into the emotional and thought processes that help inform these diverse ethnic outcomes. The narratives of Korean and Chinese American children in this study bring to light the multiple contradictions that exist between the feeling rules that guide their external expressions and behaviors and the emotional dynamics that underlie their experiences both within the family.

Although rooted in nostalgic generalizations that obscure Asian American diversity, these Westernized ideologies offer a stabilizing reference point that helps second-generation Asian Americans make sense of the many sacrifices, failed dreams, and unsaid burdens their immigrant parents shouldered. I examine how in the processes of managing these emotions, second-generation Korean and Chinese Americans use these binary vocabularies and safe frameworks that belie the complexity of their actual behaviors and experiences because they help reconcile the difficult and convoluted emotions of being Asian American and offer what Kim describes as a "safe and acceptable form of expressing ethnic difference."[55] Characterizing America as racist and the American Dream as a failure would serve only to demean the sacrifices their parents made to secure their children's success and highlight racial differences that would reinforce their exclusion from American society.

METHODS

The book is mainly based on in-depth, semistructured, hour-and-a-half interviews with sixty-one second-generation Korean, Chinese and Taiwanese American men and women between the ages of twenty-five and thirty-eight who have lived in the New York–New Jersey metropolitan area for at least three years.[56] I targeted interviewees from this age range because it encompasses the prime age of marriage in the United States and the developmental stage of early adulthood when identities are more stable and adults contemplate issues of marriage, family, and career. The age range of twenty-five to forty is the general time period within which Americans typically make decisions to marry or have children, develop adult relationships with parents and extended kin, pursue career aspirations, and think more deeply about the values they want to embrace in their adult lives.[57] The study seeks to understand how adults make sense of their family upbringing in negotiating their present-day struggles with marriage, children, career, and culture.

I also chose to study East Asian Americans,[58] namely Korean and Chinese Americans along with Taiwanese Americans,[59] because as so-called model minorities, they are often held up as exemplary minority groups whose traditional family values have presumably helped them to excel in school and assimilate successfully into American society. Given the multiple dynamics that operate within different immigrant families, this study questions the uniform portrayal of Asian American families and its effect on ethnic outcomes. In addition to their depiction as the model minority, Korean and Chinese Americans relative to other Asian immigrants exhibit the most similarities in terms of their family traits (reliance on extended kinship, cultural similarities rooted in Confucian traditions and Chinese historical influence in Asia), the context of their immigration status and reception by the U.S. government, their comparable socioeconomic distribution and demographic characteristics on the local and national level, and their community context (presence of a visible, concentrated foreign-born community in the New York–New Jersey metropolitan area).[60]

As the main site of the study, the New York–New Jersey metropolitan area has stood out as the global nexus and historical gateway for immigration in the nineteenth and twentieth centuries. According to the 2010 census, the New York–New Jersey metropolitan area is also home to one of the largest Korean and Chinese populations in the United States (second only to California) with 14.9 percent of Korean Americans and 19.1 percent of Chinese Americans living in the metropolitan area. I chose to include New Jersey because it is considered the most important suburban outpost for Asian Americans who work in New York, especially for Korean Americans who have formed their own growing suburban communities in northern New Jersey. Because of their socially progressive, urban cosmopolitan culture, New Yorkers are more open to nontraditional family structures, and the area thus offers more options to Asians who want to stay connected with their ethnic, panethnic, American, or even global identities. Most of the interviews with Asian Americans were conducted between 2004 and 2008, after the

September 11 terrorist attacks in 2001 and before the 2008 global housing recession.

As shown in Appendix B, the median age of the Asian American sample is twenty-nine, with a higher percentage of females (roughly two-thirds of the sample) than males. A little over half (53 percent) of the participants identified as Chinese, about 10 percent as Taiwanese and 36 percent as Korean, and one person as mixed Chinese-Taiwanese ancestral origins. In terms of current class status and family status growing up, there is a relatively good mix of working-class and middle-class participants, although a slightly heavier representation of those currently from the middle- to upper-class categories. The highest percentage of participants (44.1 percent) were the oldest sibling in the family, the second highest were the youngest sibling (28.8 percent), and the lowest percentages were for the middle child (16.9 percent) and only child (10.2 percent). The majority of participants were unmarried heterosexuals without children, but I did include six self-reported LGBTQ, fifteen married, two divorced individuals, in addition to eight participants who were pregnant or had children.[61]

Although the book's focus is on Asian Americans, I also refer to interviews I conducted with fifteen American-born children of white immigrants between 2008 and 2010 in order to provide a reference point for understanding racial differences in family and identity in Chapter 6. For this chapter, I chose to focus largely on Jewish Americans—mostly Russian and Ukrainian from Reform or nondenominational backgrounds—because of parallels in their struggle to mediate cultural preservation and assimilation, as we see among Korean and Chinese Americans. The classic assimilationist narrative trumpets the extraordinary achievements of Jewish Americans as a testament to the enduring legacy of the American Dream and often draws on them as a comparison group for understanding why certain ethnic groups in the United States assimilate while others fail. Despite having struggled against a long history of institutionalized anti-Semitism, Jewish Americans have drawn on their familial solidarity and tightly knit ethnic networks and resources to achieve rapid socioeconomic mobility and lay the foundations for the complete assimilation of their American-born children. The educational achievements, entrepreneurial successes, family solidarity, and rising intermarriage rates among Asian Americans—particularly Korean Americans—have often been said to reflect the earlier stages of assimilation among Jews, seemingly lending more credence to the model minority myth. I argue however that parallels in the immigrant ideology can also obscure the racial nuances of Asian American experiences. The narratives of second-generation Jews thus provide an important frame of reference for interpreting and contextualizing the statements of Korean and Chinese Americans as the so-called newer model minority. I also included five additional interviews with whites from other European backgrounds to offer a broader perspective on how whiteness plays out across ethnic boundaries. Given the limitations of the second-generation white sample, I use these interviews not to provide a direct comparison of white and Asian Americans but to provide a general frame of reference for contextualizing the narratives of Korean and Chinese Americans.[62]

In the face of social isolation, lack of mentorship, and verbally uncommunicative parents, many participants became emotional during the interview, so I had to stop the recorder at times and ensure they were willing to continue. It may be that both my insider status as an Asian American as well as my outsider status as a stranger may actually have provided the right level of anonymity and empathy to make people feel open about their private lives. Many of the participants commented on the therapeutic value of talking through these issues with someone they did not know. A few even mentioned that they had never told anyone some of the things they divulged during our session and confirmed that everything was confidential. As a second-generation Korean American woman who was single and in her late thirties when I started the book and married with children in her early forties when it was published, I identified with many of the experiences, emotions, and values that participants openly revealed about their private lives and inner thought processes— things to which even their own families had never been privy. Throughout the interview, they would often ask me if I related to their stories and if my personal experience was at all similar to theirs. In order to show how my own story as an interviewer is interwoven with the perspectives of my participants, I occasionally make references to my personal experiences throughout this book.

However, given that family experiences range widely and Asian American identities are also multidimensional, there were also aspects of people's experiences and viewpoints with which I was not as familiar. For example, my status as a middle-class heterosexual woman and my role as a researcher may have had some effect on the degree of openness some participants felt in discussing personal or family issues, although surprisingly I seldom sensed any distrust or hesitation, with one exception.[63] This difference may have had some bearing in the case of gay men and white American participants. I did have some difficulty recruiting gay male participants, a weakness I addressed by training a gay male research assistant to recruit and conduct some of these interviewees. In order to minimize discomfort in discussing issues of race, I also hired a native-born white graduate assistant to recruit and conduct nine of the interviews with second-generation whites; I conducted the rest of the interviews.

With some regret, this book does not include the perspectives of immigrant parents because the goal is to understand how the American-born children of Korean and Chinese immigrants reconstruct their childhood memories of family in order to make sense of their lives. This means that their interpretation of family may be distorted by their selective reconstruction of memories that are fragmented by time, culturally rooted biases, and personal emotions. Wherever I did include analyses on immigrant perspectives or Asian culture, I drew from other research studies that used reliable interview or survey data. This does not weaken the validity of my conclusions because, as mentioned, the primary goal of this book is to understand how they reinterpret their family relationships as part of their sense-making processes.

Guide to the Book

Each chapter revisits different components of the Asian immigrant family myth as it relates to emotion work among the children of Korean and Chinese immigrant families. This includes the emotional responses to educational and socioeconomic mobility, love and communication in parent-child relations, the emotional context of children's different family roles, the emotional management of gendered expectations, and the racial negotiation of the Asian immigrant family myth.

Chapter 2 begins by revisiting one of the central premises of the model minority myth: the triumph of American meritocracy and the American Dream in driving the educational achievement of Korean and Chinese Americans. Focused primarily on my interviews, the chapter highlights and expands on parallel findings from a study on Chinese Americans in New York conducted by Trivina Kang in 2001. The chapter shows how children of Asian immigrants retrospectively interpret their parents' immigration experiences and the impact of the social meanings they attach to education and material success, which in turn shape their educational aspirations and career decisions. Even though Asian immigrant parents might possess similar educational qualifications and income, their children construct different meanings of academic success based on their family relationships and responsibilities, as well as the specific migration struggles of their immigrant parents. In particular, three ideal-type perspectives emerge from these narratives—namely, the views that education is a form of filial duty, that education is a passport to material success and the American Dream, and that education itself is a means of self-empowerment and liberation. The findings challenge the narrow ways scholars and the media have interpreted the diverse meanings of education, success, and the American Dream for Asian Americans.

In order to accentuate their cultural foreignness, the model minority myth depicts Asian immigrant families as one-dimensional cooperatives of rational actors, stripped of all human emotions, romance, physical affection, and verbal conflict resolution that are characteristic of the "typical American family." Chapter 3 challenges this dehumanized and stoic representation of spousal, parent-child, and extended kin relationships and reveals how emotion work in fact enables American-born children to connect with and understand their parents and families in more nuanced ways. I begin by looking at the ways in which second-generation Korean and Chinese Americans make sense of the emotional turmoil and stresses that arose in the marital lives of their parents and their own relationship with their families throughout childhood. I show how these participants, without the means to communicate across cultural barriers, find new ways of assessing their parents' marital relationship that do not neatly align with Western views of romance and parental love. The chapter explains how bridging this emotional gap despite cultural differences requires piecing together and reinterpreting family histories, relying on intergenerational mediators whenever they are available, and empathizing with their parents through their family roles. By compartmentalizing and channeling emotions around available networks, the children of immigrants are able to come to terms with some of the difficult, ambiguous, and contradictory aspects of growing up in an Asian immigrant family.

The image of the cohesive Asian family unit also masks the diverse socioeconomic situations that Korean and Chinese families face in a changing economy and the enormous burdens on some children in helping to hold their families together. As more immigrants struggle to adapt to the needs and demands of the new global economy, many families are turning to alternative caregiving arrangements that significantly impact the emotional environment and long-term ethnic identities of second-generation Americans. Chapter 4 considers how adult-age children of immigrants negotiate the emotional disconnects created by these varying contexts of care depending on their individual role within the family and how it shapes their views on ethnicity and culture in their own adult lives. The chapter focuses on three ideal-type family roles and responsibilities assumed by my participants: cultural brokers, familial dependents, and autonomous caretakers. Because of their intense engagement with family, cultural brokers describe their ethnic-centered experiences as evoking feelings of reciprocated empathy, whereas, on the other end, autonomous caretakers associate their parents' ancestral culture with ethnocentric exclusion. Depending on how they are able to negotiate the cultural divide, familial dependents generally view their parents' culture and immigrant experiences through the hierarchical lens of emulation.

In Asian American families, as in most American families, gender structures relationships between parent and child in a way that conditions second-generation perspectives on ethnicity and culture yet challenges the traditional assimilationist narrative on Oriental sexism versus Western egalitarianism. Chapter 5 explores the gendered ways in which adult-age sons and daughters navigate unequal family roles and responsibilities associated with gender and birth order and how this impacts the ways they approach ethnicity and family culture in their adult lives. Daughters and sons interpret their gendered family roles in complex ways, depending on their relationship with siblings and their position within the overall family structure. As youth, sons are generally taught to emulate the cultural values of sacrifice, patrilineage, and leadership depicted by the father figure. Daughters, on the other hand, are taught to practice family culture by preserving family honor, acting as family caretakers, and juggling multiple responsibilities. However, different family structures, class constraints, and social circumstances may also lead to blurred gender roles, role switching, and role shifting over the life cycle. Because of the specific ways they are integrated into family culture, sons practice ethnicity through relatively orthodox and nonengaging practices that allow them to carry on the family name and blood lineage. Because they face greater conflicts between the benefits of family values and the pressures of gender inequality, adult-age daughters are likely to re-create more subtle, self-empowering, and emotionally engaging ways of interpreting and preserving their parents' expectations on family, culture, and career.

In the traditional scholarship and popular media, the myth of the "Asian Family" is often invoked as a symbol of Asian American assimilation and the racial meritocracy of American society. Chapter 6 compares the diverse cultural perspectives and social experiences of second-generation Asian and white immigrant families and how they are negotiated within the context of racial power structures. Themes on family values, parental sacrifice, intergenerational conflict, gender inequality, and structural change also resonate in the passages of Jewish American participants, underscoring some parallels in the immigration experience. However, within the context of U.S. race relations, second-generation Americans who are viewed as "white" are more easily able to select aspects of their family culture and ethnic roots that allow them to downplay their racial privilege and blend into the cosmopolitan culture of the New York–New Jersey metropolitan region with a relatively muted sense of conflict or contradiction. Positioned as neither black nor white in an era of "color-blind" racism, Asian Americans have difficulties articulating the nature of their racial marginalization despite citing clear examples of experiencing institutional discrimination and racial microaggressions, especially in terms of work and romantic relationships. As a result, participants rely on mainstream themes of the American Dream, family values, masculinities/femininities, and the model minority myth that allow them to emotionally navigate these racial terrains and preserve valued aspects of their ethnicity without highlighting their racial Otherness.

Chapter 7 presents a summary of emergent themes throughout the book and considers the broader theoretical implications of these findings for contemporary immigrant families. The chapter reflects on the indomitable hold of the Asian immigrant family myth in the U.S. racial imaginary despite the tremendous progress scholars in gender and family studies have made in challenging monolithic images of the American family. I discuss how the findings illuminate the growing emotional pains and burdens of immigrant families attempting to adapt to the pressures of increasing economic competition and rising educational standards in the new global economy. In the case of Korean and Chinese immigrant families, I argue that most are resourceful enough to overcome some of these structural challenges by expanding family responsibilities while preserving a traditional cultural core, but this often comes at a considerable social and emotional cost to family members. The chapter also discusses the complex and nuanced ways race and racism inform the lives of second-generation Asian Americans at the crossroads of race, ethnicity, and nationality and what this means for how we study the "racial liminality" of new minority immigrant groups in the post–civil rights era. I conclude by noting some new developments in the family values and structures of Korea, China, and Taiwan and consider the shifting geopolitical context of U.S. racial ideologies, but also explore how future research can understand emotion work in mediating these new social contexts.

CHAPTER 2

Education, Sacrifice,
and the "American Dream"

(with Trivina Kang)

In an essay published in the *Wall Street Journal*, Amy Chua, author of *Battle Hymn of the Tiger Mother*, explains how the different parenting philosophies of Chinese and Western parents enable the Chinese to raise obedient, high-achieving children: "Western parents try to respect their children's individuality, encouraging them to pursue their true passions, supporting their choices, and providing positive reinforcement and a nurturing environment. By contrast, the Chinese believe that the best way to protect their children is by preparing them for the future, letting them see what they're capable of, and arming them with skills, work habits and inner confidence that no one can ever take away." She speculates that the reason why "Chinese parents believe that their kids owe them everything," may have to do with a Confucian culture based on filial piety and the sacrifices they made for their children. However, she narrowly interprets parental sacrifice as the time and emotional investments mothers make "tutoring, training, interrogating, and spying on their kids" to facilitate their educational development and has less to say about the larger context of their parents' past histories, migration struggles, and educational competition in the homeland.[1]

Scholars have long debated how culture plays a part in shaping the educational aspirations of immigrant and racial minority youth. Supporting the cultural assumptions of the model minority myth, some of the earliest works by anthropologists and sociologists argued that "Asian values"—particularly those rooted in Confucianism—best explain differences in the aspirations and behavior of parents and children in ways that determine economic success. The argument is that Asian American youth are more motivated to succeed in the American school system because they adopt Confucian-based values like meritocracy, emphasis on education, filial piety, and family honor learned from their immigrant parents.[2] In *The Story of the Chinese in America*, sociologist Betty Lee Sung argues, "Chinese respect for learning and for the scholar is a cultural heritage. Even when a college degree led to no more than a waiter's job, the Chinese continued to pursue the best education they could get so that when opportunities developed, the Chinese were qualified and capable of handling their jobs. Other minorities have not had the benefit of this reverence for learning. For minority groups, it is always more convenient to shout discrimination."[3] One of the strongest proponents of cultural determinism theory, Thomas Sowell, an economist and social theorist, argues that differences in wealth and power across racial and nationality groups can be largely explained by divergent cultural attitudes on education, business, and labor: "Differences in work habits, savings propensities, organizational skills personal hygiene, attitudes, and self-discipline all influence end results, both economic and social. Differences in all these respects influence economic and social outcomes among different groups within a given country, as well as among the nations of the world."[4]

Some social scientists argue that variances in the cultural values of racial minority groups can be attributed to the different contexts within which they migrate and integrate into American society. Ogbu and Simons propose that because the very context of their parents' migration is based on the dream of upward mobility, children of migrants who come here voluntarily are more optimistic about their prospects and place more trust and value in the U.S. educational system and its ability to promote their future success. Those minority groups that were brought over involuntarily as slaves and historically have been excluded from full citizenship—namely, African Americans—do poorly in school because poverty and discrimination have eaten away at their faith in the American system.[5] This pessimism ultimately leads to poor work ethics, unstable households, short-term strategies, and distrust of authority figures that is passed down with each generation.[6] In other words, Korean and Chinese Americans do well precisely because they believe in the American Dream, while African Americans fail to integrate because they have lost hope of overcoming discrimination.

In response to misguided explanations rooted in the model minority myth, a long line of scholarship has criticized that this overemphasis on culture overlooks the many structural factors that explain Asian American achievement along with underachievement. These factors include the specific context of their migration; the forms of capital that immigrants bring with them; the racial, class, and economic constraints that second-generation youth and minorities face; and the larger school and neighborhood structure within which they are raised.[7] Based on a nationwide survey of immigrants from thirty-two countries, Feliciano finds strong evidence that Asian Americans tend to do better in terms of college attendance because their immigrant parents are generally more highly educated relative to their home countries' population even if they are of lower socioeconomic status in the receiving country.[8] Disputing the primacy of culture in explaining the success of immigrants, Steinberg shows how even Jewish immigrants arrived with particular skill sets and resources associated with their urban background and social class position that made them better equipped than their Italian counterparts to adapt to the industrial society they encountered.[9] In her study on Korean American students in New York, Jamie Lew found that the parents of high-achieving students actively promoted their children's education by drawing on kinship and coethnic networks, sending their children to private afterschool programs, and hiring private tutors and counselors to compensate for their lack of familiarity with the school system. In contrast, low-achieving children had much less individual or institutional support because they came from low-income neighborhoods and families where parents had little time or money to invest in supervising and guiding their children's education.[10]

Culture nevertheless remains a persistent albeit controversial lens through which to understand the framing of educational aspirations for second-generation youth. Part of the difficulties lies in the ways cultural explanations have often been used to conflate race with "good" or "bad" moral values and pay less attention to the racial, class, and gender inequalities that stratify the American educational system. Most of these theories situate the (white) American Dream as the primary frame of reference for understanding why some students achieve while others fail. However, the assumption is that it is the triumph, not the failures, of American meritocracy that motivates the children of immigrants to do better with their lives. For example, Sanchirico argues that the children of entrepreneurs tend to be more motivated to succeed and pursue higher educational degrees because they learn from their parents the value of occupational autonomy and upward mobility based on hard work.[11] However, Kasinitz and his colleagues point out that for some second-generation Americans such as Russian Jews, the "experience of witnessing the parental drive to recapture lost status—and parental bitterness and depression when that proved impossible—may account for much of the young people's own drive to succeed."[12]

This chapter fleshes out the concept of parental sacrifice and the American Dream in conditioning the educational aspirations and career choices of American-born children of Korean and Chinese immigrant families. We

agree that parental income and education, the two components of socioeconomic status, may be central in explaining academic and career aspirations
but expand the discussion beyond quantitative indicators such as dollars and
years of schooling, in terms of their effect on second-generation Korean and
Chinese Americans. In particular, we show that the ways in which children of
Asian immigrants emotionally interpret their parents' economic situation
shape the social and cultural meanings they attach to educational success.
While the assumption is that optimism about the American Dream is what
motivates Asian Americans, we explore the ways in which both faith and dis-
illusionment rooted in their parents' specific migration struggles may drive
them to do better with their lives.

Although focused primarily on these interviews, this chapter highlights
and expands on parallel findings from an earlier study conducted between
1999 and 2001 on postcollege Chinese Americans in New York by Trivina
Kang.[13] In order to capture diverse standards of educational achievement, we
do not limit ourselves to "straight-A" and Ivy League–bound students but
offer a general overview of Asian Americans who performed respectably in
high school (overall GPA of B or A), pursued top college or postgraduate
training, and/or ended up in economically stable middle- to upper-class
occupations. It is important to note that this study intends not to provide a
causal explanation behind "Asian American success," about which much has
been already written but rather to understand how second-generation Korean
and Chinese Americans conceive of education within the context of their
family lives. Based on these interviews, this chapter then explores how this
process of sense-making informs their educational and career aspirations.
The narratives by second-generation Asian Americans highlight three different ideal-type perspectives—namely, education as a filial obligation to parents, education as the path to the American Dream, and education as a form
of self-actualization. Contrary to conventional interpretations of success, we
find that although optimistic about their own prospects, many of the interviewees are still keenly aware of how race and class inequality structure
opportunities in American society.

EDUCATION AS FILIAL DUTY

Whether or not they are able to achieve their goals, some participants in the
study viewed education primarily as a means to procure a good, stable job so
that they could provide for their parents in their old age. Their immigrant
parents may have come to the United States with high hopes and some
resources but either failed repeatedly in their businesses or struggled

considerably against poverty, abuse, and discrimination. Many of these children came from poor or working-class households or had parents who owned small family businesses—a constraint that caused youth to take on adult responsibilities. These participants tended to view education as a familial obligation, because they directly witnessed and experienced the hardships of immigration through their roles supporting their younger siblings, translating and mediating for their parents, and helping out at the family business.

The fact that immigrant family enterprise tends to strengthen filial obligation is not a complete surprise, given the greater degree of exposure that youth in such households have to their parents' work life and daily tribulations. Even if their parents' businesses collapsed or their families remained in a perpetual state of poverty, these Korean and Chinese American participants in their adulthood came to recognize the immense sacrifices their parents had made in leaving everything behind in their homeland and toiling long hours at the store in order to give their children opportunities for a better life. Instead of lowering their individual aspirations, these participants strived to preserve their family honor and compensate for their parents' lost dreams by doing something respectable with their lives. It is the perception of business failure, or the sharp contrast between their parents' lives before and after immigration, that made participants feel obligated to give back to their parents. As Lisa Park observes in her research, the children of Korean and Chinese American entrepreneurs often seek to repay their parents' sacrifices in consumptive terms, whether it be paying for cars, homes, and vacations for their parents or pursuing academic majors and high-paying careers. Those who did not have the financial means to do so. expressed some remorse and tried to show their gratitude through frequent visits and phone calls home.

For children of Asian immigrants, the cultural practice of saving face intensifies their need to redeem their family's losses. Wendy, a Taiwanese American lawyer, is keenly aware of how her parents not only sacrificed their financial standing by immigrating to the United States but also lost face among their families and friends because they were unable to keep their businesses afloat. She explained how her parents chose not to seek assistance from their affluent families back in Taiwan after both their photography and apparel businesses failed. She stated, "I don't think they felt as if they could. Everyone back there thinks you are doing well so there is pressure to stay. At least this way, you have your pride. But I also think they stayed for us, they knew that the educational opportunities were better here." Throughout the interview, Wendy expressed a strong sense of responsibility for some of her parents' tribulations because they had given up family support, financial security, and social status in order to invest in her education. Driven by regret and obligation, she conveyed a strong commitment to pursuing a career that can compensate for her parents' loss of face: "I hope my achievement can be seen as their accomplishment and make them walk a little straighter when they visit Taiwan. In a culture that values academic or financial success, at least they can say they have achieved one of the two. The most valuable thing they accomplish in United States is definitely seeing us make it through school." As with many other respondents, Wendy stated that her family's economic situation has stabilized in recent years, but the memories of the business failures remain vivid. As a result, her parents insist that she and her brother study law and medicine, not just for the purposes of achieving status but to ensure that their children do not undergo the same hardships that they endured.

For others, like Alex, the costs of hard work and sacrifice went beyond just losing social status but also affected his parents' personal health and happiness. His father worked long hours as a foreman at a garment factory while juggling a second night shift and his mother worked as a seamstress at a factory where he spent a good part of his childhood. He told me that when he was in grade school his mother developed a benign tumor in her intestines and then when he was in high school his father contracted a serious illness that ultimately led to his spleen being removed. He was not clear on the details because his parents kept most of it a secret, but he was convinced that their many years of labor had put them in very poor health and contributed to their illnesses. As a result, he said he wishes that they had been less financially conservative and more open to incurring college debt instead of wasting their lives paying for his tuition. In the following passage, Alex, who currently works as a financial analyst at a large investment management firm, explains how he felt the resulting sense of obligation to his parents played a great role in shaping his educational and career path:

> You want them to think that what they did had some meaning and you don't want to be a fuck-up. That would just be supremely insulting for them. It's been a pretty constant theme in the back of my mind. I follow the same kind of conservative path that they took, in terms of my priorities coming out of college. For a lot of people, that's a time of independence and having a good time. I was more career-oriented when I came out and I went into banking and I had stupid long hours and had no life. A lot of that was job and industry-specific but I was still very insecure about myself and about my abilities. A lot of other people took time to travel for a year and experienced different cultures and living somewhere else out of the country or viewed that postcollege period as a time to find oneself or take chances. I never got to thinking I had the freedom to do that. And to this day, I don't

think I have the ability to just put everything down and just do something out of the blue like a lot of other people that I admire, who go live in India for a couple of months, who quit venture capital and go travel with their fiancé for a year backpacking.

Alex views his financial success not as a path to freedom and personal happiness but rather as a burden he is obligated to take on in order to repay his parents for their lifetime of hardships.

For children of business owners, the costs and challenges of operating a small business are particularly great, which strengthens the emotional pull they may feel toward their families long after they leave their homes. Min argues that the decision to start a business stems a desire to make up for the huge status inconsistency immigrants experience between their premigration educational background and their lower income and occupational status in the United States.[14] Because they are disadvantaged by their lack of English proficiency and nontransferable credentials, many Korean and Chinese immigrant entrepreneurs initially experience significant downward occupational mobility from the white-collar professions they held back home so that they view self-employment as a better alternative to one of the low-paying, menial jobs available in the mainstream labor market. As the narratives of second-generation Korean and Chinese Americans suggest, their parents' constant struggle to recover the status they lost through immigration and entrepreneurship leaves an indelible mark on the memories of their American-born children. Although entrepreneurship may potentially offer the fastest road to financial success, the work entails considerable sacrifice, relies on the unpaid labor of family members including children, and can still ultimately lead to failure. Min finds that long work hours have detrimental effects on the physical and psychological well-being of both immigrant parents and their children. Because Korean businesses are often located in poor, inner-city neighborhoods, these entrepreneurs are also vulnerable to crime and rejection from their minority patrons, as well as discrimination and exploitation from their non-coethnic suppliers and landlords. Those who choose to take a gamble in the more intensively competitive ethnic enclave economy have a hard time socially and culturally assimilating into mainstream society.[15]

The hardships associated with immigrant entrepreneurship are also passed on down to their children, many of whom work in these family businesses throughout their childhood. Suzanne, a twenty-five-year-old Korean American administrative assistant, was raised in a working-class family with two older sisters and one younger brother. Her parents lived in the Asian-dominated neighborhood of Queens but owned a green grocery business in a low-income black neighborhood in Brooklyn. Because her parents worked long hours, she and her siblings raised themselves as latchkey children in their small one-bedroom apartment, and her memories of their childhood included constant worries about money and verbal and physical abuse from her father. Throughout the interview, she described some of the hardships she witnessed working as a youth in her parents' store in Brooklyn and how that shaped her future aspirations in terms of career and marriage.

Today, Suzanne works as an administrative assistant at an international nongovernmental organization but considers this a transitional stepping stone toward a more lucrative career. She is thinking of pursuing an advanced degree in law. Although her parents are no longer struggling as much financially, she explained that her sense of obligation to her parents given the hardships she witnessed during her childhood formatively shaped her life decisions: "Ideally if I were to follow my own heart, I would pursue a PhD in languages but I feel like to appease my parents, I'll go for the international law degree (ha). I think just having the pressure of knowing how hard my parents worked to raise us, we have an obligation to return the sacrifices to them by doing well in school. Even though money is not the end, seeing how my parents lived, if you wanna have children and live comfortably, you have to have a good income." Although her parents did not assist with her studies or pressure her to do well in school, she said she always felt driven not only by knowing about the sacrifices they made but also by witnessing and experiencing that sacrifice through her adult responsibilities.

The participants' deeply felt commitment to family through educational attainment may seem somewhat surprising given that most parents in these situations did not have time, money, language proficiency, or cultural knowledge to get involved in their children's education. However, in their view, the message that education is a filial obligation can be conveyed through something as simple as investments in books and school-related materials when money is scarce or by slaving away in order to make ends meet. This is the case for Mark, a twenty-seven-year-old Chinese American male who was raised by working-class parents in Jersey City. His parents worked a long line of odd jobs until they opened up their own toy store in Manhattan where he worked beginning at age six. His family was able to maintain the store for seven years until the opening of a Toys "R" Us put them out of business, but their long struggles staying afloat during the early years of immigration had a formative impact on his views on parental sacrifice, which he grew to emulate as he got older.

> My dad was the only sibling in his immediate family to drop out of college
> in order to help my grandfather's business and this actually plays a big part

in why I made a lot of decisions in my life. So I have an uncle that finished med school—neurosurgeon, quite successful, Beverly Hills, the whole deal; another uncle, successful businessman; and an aunt she's just a housewife now, but she met her husband because of college, so I guess that counts. [laughs] And because he did that, his siblings were able to succeed, and my dad has no qualms about it. He's never held it against them. And it was a big decision to move here. I feel I was very influenced by the fact that my parents were immigrants.

Because of the strong emphasis he places on family, Mark decided on his own to forfeit the opportunity to go to a good college so that he could pay for his sister's college tuition and allow her to enjoy the privileges of a private university. He said, "So when people ask me, damn I can't believe you're paid for your sister's tuition, why did you do that? But when I think about what my parents did, I think that's a bigger sacrifice. When you're not just giving up money, just paper, and they gave up their life basically to start a new one. Having experienced the sacrifices they made when we immigrated here, it taught me in a quiet way how to make sacrifices for your family in the long run—whether it's a financial need or just an emotional need." He downplays the sacrifices he made for his sister by arguing that he is merely following the footsteps of his parents who had given up even more than he did by immigrating to America for their children. Nevertheless, it is clear that he has played an instrumental role in maintaining family stability and ensuring their upward mobility through personal sacrifice. At the time of the interview, Mark was working as a creative manager for a small company but was trying to turn some of his side freelance work into a small business in the near future. He credits his parents for giving him this "entrepreneurial spirit."

Thus, people who embrace the notion of education as a form of filial obligation are more likely to have experienced or directly witnessed some of the more difficult years of their parents' settlement period. If they acculturate at the same pace as their parents, they are also more likely to understand the migration hardships even without the benefit of verbal communication. Most lower-income Korean and Chinese Americans in this category live near large working-class ethnic enclaves—in this case, Queens or Chinatown—where they are influenced by cultural values of their peers and learn their parents' native language through daily interaction with coethnics. This of course does not mean these children do not experience tremendous stress and anxiety as a result of their multiple obligations, but their values and outlook on family are oftentimes compatible with those of their parents especially as they enter adulthood because they are more closely integrated into immigrant and ethnic community life.

EDUCATION AS THE AMERICAN DREAM

In contrast to those students who are motivated to provide for their families, other participants viewed education as the passport to financial security and the American Dream. They hold more faith in the idea that they can climb their way up the socioeconomic ladder with hard work and the right educational qualifications. Success here is defined in broader ways—whether it be escaping the lifestyle and hardships associated with poverty and segregation or obtaining financial comforts and material possessions. As a result, the participants who embraced this perspective come from both the lower and higher ends of the socioeconomic spectrum. The key distinction for all these participants is that their immigrant parents were able to maintain a stable economic livelihood regardless of their class origins and immigration status, which gave them hope that education would give them the added edge and freedom to achieve even what their parents could not. Their ideologies fit well with the traditional "Asian American success story" that supports the model minority myth, but as I will explain, this dream is not without its contradictions and tensions.

Through access to different forms of social capital including ethnic networks and family support, the immigrant parents of working-class participants opened up small businesses or procured jobs in coethnic industries that allowed them to carve out a financially stable life for their families despite their humble origins. Given their parents' backgrounds, these respondents saw progress in their parents' economic stability and believed that only a lack of credentials and cultural/linguistic disadvantages prevented their parents from achieving complete wealth and prosperity. By securing financial success, they intend to provide a happy ending to the success story their parents began building for them through their hard work and sacrifice.

Lily, a twenty-five-year-old Chinese American female, lost her father at a young age, which gave her a great degree of latitude throughout her childhood; however, it also forced her and her older brother to raise themselves as latchkey kids in Chinatown with minimal supervision by her grandfather and her mother who worked at the post office. She discussed how proud her mother was to eventually move out of Chinatown into the East Village despite the burdens of raising two children on her own. As a result, Lily is optimistic that education is the key to success and that she can achieve her own dreams because she does not face the same cultural and linguistic obstacles as her mother. Inspired by her mother's upward mobility, she received her bachelor's at Hunter College and master's at Harvard, eventually working her way to becoming a dean and teacher at a public school where she works today while pursuing a second master's degree. Despite the fact that her mother cared little about her education, Lily credits her family for demonstrating the importance of education through their lived experiences and economic stability in the face of tremendous odds.

> LILY: The number one gift from my dad, my mom and my grandfather is that education is their ticket out of anything. Like public schools are great and my community college is affordable and I think that's so important: that there not be this huge division between the haves and the have-nots.
>
> ANGIE: That's interesting, so how did you know that it was important to them when you were young?
>
> LILY: I think it was one of the last things my father said to me. And then I also saw my mother struggle with English and through that, I knew she implied for me that English is important and knowing it and speaking it well was important and that was only done through school. My grandfather was a merchant marine and he was this great man, but here not speaking English, he had to work in a restaurant and it was very demeaning for him. Cause you know he was supposed to be our family provider and here in a world where he didn't have the qualifications, you weren't anything. That's kind of their American Dream: That can be something I could do that they wouldn't be able to do.

Lily views college as the so-called great equalizer despite the fact that her family did little to give encouragement or assistance with her educational and career aspirations.

At the same time, Lily says that unlike her mother, she does not view her advanced degrees as separating her from her roots in Chinatown. Despite her achievements, Lily feels she is an exceptional case among the peers she grew up with and does not believe that the American Dream applies to everyone. In fact, she uses her educational privileges to give back to her community as a teacher in a public school. Throughout the interview, she expressed how she feels "very strongly about Asian American communities, Chinatown, in a profound sense like no matter where geographically we're all connected somehow." However, as we will see, this is not necessarily the case for all participants in this study, some of whom found that these ethnic ties were a major source of conflict with their parents and an obstacle to obtaining the American Dream. Seclusion in ethnic communities was viewed as a source of ambivalence for those second-generation Americans wishing to "assimilate." On the one hand they believed their parents benefited from these coethnic associations, but on the other hand they felt that these same ties might represent an obstacle to mobility in the United States.

While Lily's story is an optimistic one about rising out of poverty and hardship, others' narratives were not as uplifting, even though in the end these different experiences led to the same desire. Raised in a poor black neighborhood in Connecticut, Jasmine struggled with racial harassment and abuse by her black peers for most of her childhood, forcing her to lead a socially isolated existence marked by depression and loneliness. Because of her past experience, she has problems interacting with blacks but also feels resentful and alienated from privileged whites who disacknowledged the continuing salience of race and class inequality in these neighborhoods. At the same time, Jasmine, who has a master's in creative writing/poetry and works as a program assistant at a university, explained how class mobility represents a way for her to escape all the reminders of poverty and race that defined her childhood.

> I lived in Park Slope for so long now, but where I work, it's been white-dominated like academia white-dominated, my neighborhood is completely white-dominated. I start doing that middle-, upper-middle-class mentality in ways so you never have to confront a black person at all. Spending so much time in a white environment for work and for living, it's kind of a Catch-22. You start becoming really used to things whether it's having all these great restaurants, having the convenience of clean streets. And then you see a black person, you just look at them kind of differently. I'm living in such a privileged setting that every time I see a black person, a part of me is like I hope they don't say something to me.

To this day, Jasmine seeks to reconcile her sense of alienation and racial identity conflict through therapy and other creative outlets. It is important to note that the racial undertones of Jasmine's perspective are rooted in the unique and traumatic circumstances under which she grew up, but the connecting theme that emerges from this passage is the heightened social meaning that class mobility takes on for those who struggle with racial conflicts and poverty throughout their childhood.

In contrast to their upper-class counterparts, many working-class participants in the study similarly described a childhood deprived of parental support and plagued by social isolation and racial harassment, pushing many of them to question some of the core assumptions about family values and racial equality central to the American Dream. As compared with those from more affluent backgrounds, they were less likely to claim that Asian American families embraced "better cultural values" than African American families, since in many cases their family experiences proved otherwise. At the same time, they were also keenly aware that as Asian Americans, they can take advantage of some of the privileges associated with the model minority myth. This does not mean however that they did not harbor animosity toward other racial minorities, especially if, like Jasmine, they had negative experiences with their black and Latino peers throughout their childhood. However, most of the participants in this category viewed assimilation as a strategic choice to avoid getting trapped in poverty and segregation, rather than an indicator of their social acceptance into middle-class white America.

In some cases, the generation gap can widen for children from working-class backgrounds who suddenly experience educational and socioeconomic mobility, because their acculturation tends to outpace that of their working-class parents, or what Portes and Rumbaut call "dissonant acculturation."[16] Without the benefit of insight from brokering for their families like the filial providers, these second-generation Asian Americans have more trouble understanding their parents' inability to acculturate and adopt less traditional values and will try to shed the more orthodox aspects of their ancestral culture that they believe may explain their inability to succeed. On the other hand, given their optimism in the American Dream, these respondents are sure to point out that their parents did not necessarily fail and that their lives in the United States are better than those they would have if they had stayed in their ancestral homelands.

The dynamics are different for middle-class participants. Like working-class interviewees, they believe that their parents benefited greatly from immigrating to the United States and were able to use their human capital to secure the future of their children. However, in their case, their parents were indeed able to achieve their goals of prosperity and wealth. As a result, education for these second-generation participants is taken for granted and is approached as a way to preserve their current lifestyle or perhaps improve it with more freedom, luxuries, and privileges. In other words, second-generation Korean and Chinese Americans from more privileged backgrounds, who are invested in the notion of meritocracy and financial success, perceive education as a means to preserve the status quo.

Chris, a thirty-one-year-old Korean American contract attorney, was raised as an only child of two physician parents who entered the country as part of a physician exchange program. Their occupational standing and financial security led to their relatively seamless settlement and adaptation in the United States. In stark contrast to the previous respondents, he grew up in a middle-class white neighborhood and witnessed few of the hardships that characterized the lives of working-class interviewees. For Chris, choosing a lucrative career was never an option since it was the only way to preserve the material comforts, social privileges, and individual flexibility he needed to live the "good life." Although limited economic opportunities during the current recession caused him to consider pursuing his secondary interest in aviation, he viewed this more as a temporary venture he could check off his bucket list, and it went without question that he would return to law once he finished. When I asked him why he wanted to go back to law school given his passion for aviation, he replied,

> CHRIS: I think it makes the most financial sense. I put a ton of money and time into my law degree. Ultimately I wouldn't be able to make a super-comfortable living as an aviator so I definitely want to use my law degree to provide for me and my future family. I think that's necessary. But I wanted to try and accomplish this other life goal while there's still a chance.
>
> ANGIE: Why is financial stability important? I mean it's important to everyone but you could've done it without being a lawyer.
>
> CHRIS: Well in terms of being a lawyer, I felt like that was the career route with a relatively high expected payout that also seems to match my personality. Maybe I could potentially make a lot more money as an I-banker or invent the next Snuggie or something like that. But yeah, it seemed to be a good match for me. In terms of why I want financial comfort, I guess I'm an only child and I've been looking back at my life and thinking about how much I cost, undergrad, grad school, law school, years in between just being a student my whole life. Although maybe I would prefer if my children were able to settle on a life quicker than I did. If they do decide to go to school until they're thirty-one, it would be nice to be able to provide that opportunity.

The last time we communicated, Chris had been applying to the army to explore his brief stint as an army aviator. Because they are not pursuing radically different career paths than those envisioned by their parents, middle- and upper-class children may receive some type of substantial financial support from their parents for their educational pursuits, as was the case for Chris. If they accumulate enough money through lucrative jobs in finance, law, and medicine, they may decide to take time off to travel or pursue other hobbies and interests before returning to their careers or even retiring and living off of their investments.

EDUCATION AS SELF-ACTUALIZATION

The remaining participants in the study view educational success as a means to discover themselves and their individual potential. Education does not have to be a means to an end; it can be an end in itself. Although the socio-economic background of their families varied somewhat, the parents of second-generation participants who adopted this worldview tended to be well educated and financially stable. They do not have to worry as much about their parents' welfare and have a safety net in case their plans fall through. This gives them more flexibility in choosing the career path that best fits their personal interests as opposed to being constrained by financial needs and parental expectations. These Korean and Chinese Americans generally regard their families' experience in the United States favorably. The main reason for this positive outlook is that relative to the parents of other second-generation Americans in this study, their parents were best able to overcome challenges related to their immigration and settlement and provide a comfortable economic foundation for their children's success. In some cases, the participants were just too young to remember many details of the earlier years when their parents struggled the most.

Given their parent's educational backgrounds, the second-generation Americans who adopted this worldview grew up feeling that forgoing college was not an option. James is a twenty-five-year-old Chinese American law student who plans to become a lawyer and financially support his aging mother, especially in light of the recent death of his father. He recalled, "In terms of strictness, my parents never really made me do chores or anything like that, but they were strict in terms of making homework a priority, wanting me to go to college and also possibly graduate school. There was the expectation that I would do well in school and not having to be rewarded for doing well. It was kind of like, yeah you have to do well as a matter of course, and if I didn't do well, then they would get worried. They would call in a tutor or something like that, make me turn my grades around." Even middle-class parents were not always actively involved in assisting with their children's studies because of language barriers or long work hours. The one difference is that they were more likely to pay for tutoring sessions if their children had trouble or needed the extra help to gain admittance to a good college, even if it meant stretching their budgets.

Most of these parents made clear to their children their expectations on college, but not all of them were adamant about having these educational achievements lead to specific careers, although they did expect them to secure economically stable jobs. Interestingly enough, the second-generation participants who embraced this philosophy were more likely to switch their majors or career goals once they found a passion that fit their personal needs and interests. James, for example, explained how his parents who owned a successful accounting business had pressured him into majoring in engineering, which plunged him into a depression, pushing him to see a therapist. Finally, he decided to go to law school, but mainly because it was an opportunity to distinguish himself from his parents' materialistic and pragmatic outlook and become more involved in political issues within the Asian American community.

> JAMES: In the end [my parents] were supportive mostly because I was able to get across to them that this would make me happy. My difficulties with grades in engineering school were probably because I was not happy there. And then once I turned around, my grades improved, my general outlook on life improved. I was just happier where I was after I switched.
>
> ANGIE: What inspired you to go into law school, like why that particular career?
>
> JAMES: Partly it was wanting to make a difference in society through the law and also partly because it was complementary to what I'd wanted to do. I thought about a political career early on. It was exciting to me, something that my parents didn't really have much experience in, you know local politics. So it was something that I thought would distinguish me from my parents. It would allow me to basically become my own person. I could be more involved in the community than they were.

Although the recent death of his father made him more concerned about supporting his mother, he claimed this life change did not alter his outlook on personal fulfillment.

Like James, many of the second-generation participants in this situation experienced personal conflicts between their immigrant parents' expectations and their need for self-actualization but were able to strategically incorporate respectable careers that achieved both objectives or begin with one money-making career that would be used to finance their desired career. This is the case for Elliott, a thirty-four-year-old Chinese American who devoted the early part of his career to banking and software firm and business school until he discovered his passion in filmmaking.

> We grew up very modest, so part of it for me was I wanted to do something that would afford me a comfortable lifestyle so I wouldn't have to struggle. So the idea of being an artist or musician or a public school teacher wasn't as attractive to me. And then you go fast-forward 2000. That's what led me to go from undergraduate, business school to the job I took after college. But after nine years in the corporate world, I realized I wasn't being very fulfilled and really wasn't happy with what I was doing. At the same time,

that was when the economy was turning down so at that point, I was like, well I'm not doing something that's really fulfilling and I'm not gonna make a whole lot of money doing it either, then I might as well do something that I always cared about. And I always liked film so that kind of led me there.

I was curious what Elliott ended up doing, especially since I knew he had recently got married and had two children. In his emailed response, he told me that he was still "leading a double life as a filmmaker and business professional." He won a prestigious award for a film he produced but returned to the corporate world in order to support his new wife and two children when the 2008 housing crisis hit. Recently, he found a job at a film studio corporation that would allow him to support his family while keeping his foot in the entertainment world. As he waits for the right opportunity to return to his creative aspirations, he muses, "There are peers in film and corporate life who have found success (and many more in film who have not), so I wonder on occasion, what if I had more intestinal fortitude or been more decisive earlier on to dedicate myself to a particular path. Regardless, I try not to dwell on that question too much and the fun/demands of a family don't provide much opportunity for that either. I feel strongly that one can never be happy if one compares himself with others. Happiness can only be found by following your heart—though that could mean taking the long route." As in Elliott's case, the financial conditions that support flexible career paths can easily change over one's life course, making it difficult to pursue one's dreams, yet the right opportunity can also lead to the realization of those lifelong desires.

In this way, class privilege and economic security certainly play a role in shaping the ways in which these Asian Americans not only perform in school but also choose their career paths given that they are afforded a greater degree of autonomy. Many of these participants recalled how difficult it was to break the news that they were dropping the careers their parents had envisioned in order to pursue a more self-fulfilling future. However, the decision was relatively easier because they knew that their parents could look after themselves financially. Sara, a twenty-six-year-old Taiwanese American who decided to pursue social work instead of going to medical school, says, "My parents have money now for retirement, they are pretty well established. If it was any other way, I'll think twice about entering a career which has little prospects for money."

As the experiences of these second-generation Asian Americans reveal, education is beneficial beyond the immediate benefits and privileges it confers. Education also translates into knowledge, symbolic status, and the broadening of perspective, all of which can represent triumph over other structural disadvantages they face because of their gender, class, and sexual orientation. Kathy, a thirty-one-year-old Korean American female lawyer, states that her father owned a small business as a broker, where her mother also helped out as a bookkeeper. They started out from humble beginnings but eventually turned the business into a successful company. Although she felt that her parents favored her younger brother, the one thing they impressed on all their children was the need to excel in school. Her parents' emphasis on education and other extracurricular activities became a personal source of empowerment for her as a woman.

> Some of the things that my parents did do is value on education and the no-dating rule so that they can concentrate on who they are and develop themselves. And so there are all these things that I think are so much more important, because girls start to think about boys at ten or eleven. My dad was always like you have to develop your mind. We had to appreciate music and also art and sports. And my parents were big on reading. They actually never read to us, but they always made us read books and so that said something. All these years, I was taught to do things by myself and for myself. Like you're going to school for *you*. You're not going to school to find a man and you're not going to school to use your education to support a household. So many people are just exhausted constantly and they do everything for everybody else. I get my woman's magazine too, and the big complaint is I do everything for everybody else and I don't do anything for me and I don't really have that problem (ha). And it's not that I'm not giving. I am. But because my needs are met and I know that they are, it allows me to be giving and actually giving instead of being resentful and giving, which is actually a very bad thing that's happening in this culture.

Kathy states that these values of autonomy and self-empowerment also laid the foundations for her career as a freelance attorney. She chose this career path because "I don't want to go into work because I feel someone's forcing me to come in at nine. I'll go in at nine if I feel like I have to be there." She also values that independence when it comes to her marriage: she told me that her husband could never walk into the house and expect her to have his dinner waiting for him.

Logan, a twenty-five-year-old Chinese American from a working-class family, also highly values the insight and self-empowerment he has gained from his schooling, which has helped him to deal with and make sense of the many conflicts he has faced over his sexual orientation, racial/ethnic identity, and financial difficulties. At the time of the interview, he was on leave from a graduate program at a prestigious university and working as an office manager at a nonprofit but expressed a strong desire to return to his schooling. Logan was disowned by his parents when he came out of the closet in college, and his worldview has been shaped by continuous struggles to earn a living, find housing, connect with other Asian Americans, and build his life apart from his family. However, he proudly explained, "A lot of people that had my story, they're out there turning tricks to make money. I never had to do that. I just kind of sat down and was like, okay let's think this out. Let's calm down and really sort it out. And luckily I was smart enough. It's not so much the education made me smart. The education made me have the kind of self-esteem where I would feel like I wanted to fight for myself, even though no one was gonna fight for me." Throughout the interview, Logan conveyed not only his extensive knowledge of historical facts about his parents' Chinese heritage but also political awareness about a range of issues related to contemporary Asian American communities. Although he said he was indifferent to his parents' rejection, he also expressed a desire to use his education to make sense of their family experiences and be prepared to engage with them in the future.

CONCLUSION

The chapter highlights some of the problems with the narrow way scholars have explained the cultural roots of Asian American school performance. No matter how Korean and Chinese immigrant parents emphasize the value of education to their children, it is apparent that second-generation Asian Americans develop different ideas on why educational success is important based on their interpretation of their parents' economic situation. Those who directly witnessed and experienced the trials, tribulations, and failures of immigrant parents by taking on adult responsibilities as youth expressed a strong sense of obligation to financially support and redeem the honor of their families by doing well in school. Others who felt a compelling need to escape poverty and discrimination or wanted to preserve their lives of privilege saw education as a means to achieve material success and upward mobility through acculturation as captured in the (white) American Dream. Still others found education in and of itself a source of personal empowerment and liberation as learned from their parents' educational values and relative economic success in America; these second-generation participants also tended to exercise more autonomy from their parents in terms of their career and life decisions than those who followed the other two paths.

This is of course not to imply that cultural values will prevail over the various racial, class, or other structural barriers second-generation Americans may encounter throughout their lives. If anything, it proves the opposite. As revealed in each of the three pathways, the different ways Korean and Chinese Americans view their individual success are very much informed by the race- and class-based struggles their parents experienced and the flexibility second-generation Asian Americans exercise in their career choices depending on their class resources. Although some Asian Americans rose above their family's struggles to achieve the American Dream, there were just as many if not more who strayed wayward from the path of upward mobility; much of this depended on how many resources their parents had and how well connected they were with the school and surrounding neighborhood communities.

In this sense, this chapter challenges some of the one-dimensional ways scholars and popular media have interpreted the social meanings of education, success, and the American Dream for children of immigrants. Some Korean and Chinese American participants do believe that hard work and educational credentials can help them overcome the hardship and inequality their immigrant parents faced as they become part of the (white) American mainstream, but many others see it as a practical way to give back to their families and ethnic communities or counter the racial and class inequities they see pervading all aspects of American society. In this way, these second-generation participants do not simply discard their ethnic ties and view education as the ultimate equalizer for all racial minorities, but understand how to strategically use education as a way to negotiate the racial, gender, and class constraints they face as Asian Americans. They also recognize that the privileges of education are not available to all.

The narratives throughout the chapter demonstrate that Korean and Chinese Americans are constantly negotiating and struggling with their life decisions within the context of their family responsibilities and experiences. As in most families, the children's obligations and commitments to family often depend not only on the broader historical context of their parents' migration experiences, but also on the specific roles and emotional relationships they build with their parents. Although most scholars have focused heavily on the educational achievements of Asian Americans, less is known about the intricate emotional dynamics that underlie familial relationships besides the stereotypes perpetuated by mainstream media. In the next few chapters, I explore how the emotional dynamics of family roles and inter-generational relationships shape the views of Korean and Chinese Americans on family, ethnicity, and culture.

CHAPTER 3

Love and Communication
across the Generation Gap

Mainstream media and academic literature tend to view Asian Americans through a binary racial lens that both extols and dehumanizes Asian parent-child relations based on stereotypical generalizations about their strict discipline, passive obedience, and hierarchical orderliness. The model minority myth claims that it is this structural stability that enables immigrant parents to promote traditional family values on filial piety and good work ethic to the next generation. Yet juxtaposed against the middle-class (white) American family, the monolithic Asian immigrant family appears as an emotionally deficient and psychologically dysfunctional space that reinforces patriarchal oppression and sacrifices humanistic values in order to breed obedient overachievers. Marriages are stoically arranged by parents or matchmakers based on practical considerations as opposed to romantic love, and the parent-child relationship is rigidly structured around discipline and subservience. The common understanding is that the physical intimacy, deep affection, and open, honest communication that are prized in the ideal American family are largely absent in the Asian family—a condition that suggests a misguided prioritization of money and success over love and affection.

The Tiger Mother is perhaps the newest reincarnation of the same myth, but this time it is racially positioned against the gendered ideal of the domesticated white American mother: Although both popularized images have been used to underscore the dangers of overparenting, the ideological construction of the Asian Tiger Mother stereotype is described more negatively as the diametric opposite of its alter ego, the Pandering White Mother. Where the white mother is conceived to be affectionate, coddling, and completely attentive to the emotional needs of the child, the Asian mother is presented as cold, authoritarian, and pragmatic in her parenting approach. In many ways, she is the maternal embodiment of the Asian Dragon Lady, the heartless, conniving man-eater of twentieth-century films—except this one raises obedient, passive, robotic children who boast outstanding academic credentials but lack leadership ability, interpersonal skills, and original thought. In other words, she is the mother figure of the model minority child.

Karen Pyke argues that second-generation Asian Americans themselves are unwittingly complicit in perpetuating this myth because of the way they internalize racial stereotypes about Asian families and idealized images of "normal American families" in the media. In her interviews with Korean and Vietnamese Americans, she finds that they invoke these stereotypes to both negatively characterize their Asian parents as "overly strict, emotionally distant, and deficient" yet express measured appreciation for cultural values such as filial piety.[1] The book *Tiger Babies Strike Back* by Kim Wong Keltner shows one common way this plays out among American-born Asian Americans. Keltner argues for the need to break some of the myths of the high-achieving Asian overachiever and encourage "Tiger Babies" to get in touch with their emotional self through affection, compassion, and gratitude. In an opinion piece titled "Tiger Moms: Don't Turn Your Kids into Robots," she writes, "As the children and grandchildren of immigrants, we may not have been starving for actual food, but we are starved for affection. In the pursuit of high achievement, our feelings got left by the side of the road, our emotions mistaken as unnecessary baggage. Maybe our parents who escaped war and poverty never expected that later in the journey, we would need emotional availability and a sense of humor as flotation devices."[2] Although this article was written as a critique of Chua's book, her assessment of parental love and communication like Chua's takes on Chinese parenting reifies and homogenizes Chinese and American culture—this time advocating the "American" philosophy on parenting—and completely misses the wide range of ways Chinese and Chinese Americans interpret and apply different parenting philosophies, as this chapter discusses.

Stereotypes like these that essentialize Asian immigrant family traits based on a cultural or generational divide between "Chinese" and "American" often conflate immigrant with native-born families, ignore ethnic and class differences, and fail to factor in the overall social and emotional environment of Asian families including those that stay together. In their study on household arrangements among Mexican families, Van Hook and Glick argue that immigrant family structures may actually reflect not cultural values carried over from the homeland but rather adaptation strategies toward the initial exigencies of the immigration experience.[3] Numerous studies on Asian immigrant families have noted how the shifting economic responsibilities of spouses and changing power dynamics between parent and child can create intense conflicts and tensions among different family members along gender, class, and cultural lines.[4] What these studies suggest is that as opposed to simply reproducing the values of the homeland, Asian families like other immigrant families will selectively preserve those cultural values and household arrangements that help them to adapt to the constraints they face in their new surroundings. Thus, the similarities and differences between immigrant parents and their American-born children may not be as clear-cut as classic assimilation studies would like to assume.

This is not to say that Asian immigrant families do not struggle with emotional disconnects and miscommunication as a result of intergenerational differences and economic hardships. Instead, I problematize the way these myths are used to construct a one-dimensional image of Asian families that reaffirms the moral superiority of middle-class white American culture. The dual image of Asian family harmony and intergenerational conflict fails to consider the complex emotional and psychological dynamics underlying parent-child relations and the way different family members including children can play an active role in negotiating these conflicts. As a result, the key to reconciliation or at least individual acceptance lies in the ability of immigrant parents and their children to recognize cultural differences in conveying love, find ways to communicate in a common emotional language, and seek mediation from extended kin and outside institutions.

Contrary to the model minority image of families as sites of discipline and order, this chapter uncovers the complex emotional dynamics of Korean and Chinese parent-child relations that emerges from economic hardship and racial marginalization and how the children of immigrants emotionally manage these painful experiences. The chapter begins by explaining how the changing context of migration and the power shift between husband and wife and between parent and child shape the daughters' and sons' emotional relationships with their mothers and fathers. In order to make sense of marital and intergenerational discord, many second-generation Asian Americans push themselves to think beyond the narrow way in which American culture defines emotions such as love and devotion, even if they choose not to adopt their parents' values in their own lives. In addition, they seek to nurture their individual emotional development, reconstruct their unsaid family histories, and create new modes of communication with their extended and immediate family without the benefit of direct verbal discourse or institutional support. In general, I show how in adapting to the time constraints and emotional availability of their parents, second-generation Korean and Chinese Americans learn to compartmentalize and channel their emotions around different networks of siblings, kin, and fictive kin throughout the life cycle—the emotional consequences of which can vary depending on their access to outside resources.[5]

LOVE AND WAR IN MARRIAGE

When individuals enter the phase in their lives when they start considering issues related to love, marriage, and children, they turn to their parents' marriage and family experiences as a model for understanding the dynamics of relationships and identifying qualities they do and do not want to emulate. For the second generation, this process of retrospective reflection and role modeling is complicated by both the difficult changes brought on by immigration as well as the different cultural ways that people cope with such situations. The shift in the power dynamics between husband and wife is perhaps one of the more dramatic changes to occur, especially for traditional East Asian immigrant families influenced by the principles of Confucian culture.

In Confucianism, an individual's roles, responsibilities, and duties within the state are informed by his or her social status, as defined by age, gender, and class. Contrary to Western misperceptions of Confucianism as emphasizing notions of superiority and inferiority, Confucianism as practiced in China and South Korea is fixated not as much on difference and dominance as on the accompanying responsibilities and behaviors associated with one's social roles that inform one's relationships with others—that is, the obligation of "subordinates" (e.g., children) to show respect and obedience to their "superiors" (e.g., parents), as well as the responsibility of superiors to protect and educate their charges. Centered on the patriarchal authority of the eldest male, the social order of the family is organized around hierarchical relationships between husband and wife, father and son, and elder and youth, with women and children expected to show piety and obedience to their male elders and the elders given the ultimate authority and responsibility for taking care of the dependents.[6]

The structural pressures and cultural subjugation associated with immigration and adaptation to U.S. society however challenge these traditional social relationships. Because of the expansion of low-paying, feminized service industries such as garment work, Asian immigrant women generally find greater employment opportunities upon migrating, which help them to compensate for the depressed wages and unemployment of traditionally Asian male breadwinners. In fact, in many Asian families, the wage-earning capacity of immigrant wives becomes central to the economic survival of the family, particularly in working-class families where women often become the family's primary financial supporters.[7]

The changing economic contributions of women and men in such families open up both opportunities and challenges that alter relationship dynamics among different members of the family. On the one hand, because of their key economic role within the family, immigrant women have more room to negotiate for greater equity in the distribution of household responsibilities, more involvement in family decision-making processes, and increased time to devote to their careers.[8] Emboldened by their new wage-earning power, women may be able to negotiate new roles within the family based on American norms of individualism and egalitarian gender ideals. Of course, the degree to which the extended economic roles will radically transform the traditional patriarchal practices of immigrant families depends in part on class background.[9]

In general, greater labor force participation has not necessarily diminished the responsibilities of immigrant women in the home or even undermined the patriarchal ideologies these families bring with them. In addition to their breadwinning role, women are still considered the primary caregivers for dependents and the elderly, especially in immigrant and poor families that cannot afford to pay for domestic care. The gendered nature of care work also explains why Asian mothers are central in both transmitting cultural traditions and facilitating the acculturation of their children into American society. Compounded by the usual hardships of immigrating and settling in a new country, the sudden transition from the traditional patriarchal household inherent in Confucian-influenced East Asian culture to more egalitarian relationships can pose a threat to their husbands' sense of masculinity.[10] Those households that are less able to negotiate and adapt to these changes can fall apart as a result of intense spousal conflicts, domestic violence, and divorce.[11] All together, these pressures create a volatile and hostile environment to which children are exposed at an early age, especially during the more difficult stages of immigration and settlement.

Within this context of conflict and change, the views of Korean and Chinese Americans on the quality of their parents' marriage ranged considerably in this study, with some reporting parents who had a warm and supportive relationship and others reporting constant infighting that in some cases resulted in separation or divorce. However, it is no surprise that many participants did recall heated confrontations and arguments between their parents, at least during the more difficult years of immigration, which in some cases escalated to excessive verbal abuse and physical violence.

Although some interviewees did have parents who ended up divorcing, it was not a common option even in the unhappiest of marriages because of cultural taboos against divorce, financial dependency among immigrant couples, difficulties in getting remarried especially for women, and, most important, the perceived negative effects it would have on their children. In their survey of 1.5- and second-generation Americans in the New York City region, Kasinitz and his colleagues found that divorce rates were relatively lower for Chinese Americans than for other ethnic groups, which they attribute to the Chinese cultural view of marriage as not an affectionate, companionate relationship but rather a pragmatic one focused on economic survival and children's well-being.[12] Indeed, many Asian parents immigrate to and remain in the United States because they want their children to have a better life and access to a quality education. In such cases, parents may delay divorce until their children are financially secure and old enough to take care of themselves.

In order to avoid the ostracism and pain of having their separation formalized, other parents opted for arrangements other than divorce, such as living separately in different countries or staying married while getting romantically or sexually involved with other people. Oftentimes, this type of arrangement led to ambiguous relationships that perplexed their children. Even if these events occurred very early on in their childhood, these family conflicts were deeply entrenched in the children's memories and in many cases shaped their general views on marriage. Some of the interviewees who had witnessed more severe or long-lasting feuds between their parents expressed some doubts about the necessity of marriage. Interestingly enough, I found that those who felt this way often did end up getting married but did not always follow the traditional path toward marriage: for example, some got pregnant before they got married, while others waited until they were older, long after they were expected to settle down.

In terms of short-term effects however, the interviewees had to devise other strategies to emotionally cope with the stress of marital friction. Henry, an outwardly tough-acting Korean American contractor and entrepreneur, claimed to have firm control over his parents, rarely giving into their numerous pressures, complaints, and arguments if they did not conform to his personal credo. He was even willing to calmly walk out in the middle of dinner with his parents at a restaurant if they insisted on pressuring him about a topic he did not want to discuss. Yet during the interview, there was one subject that seemed to elicit his emotional vulnerability in respect to his parents. When asked if he had any particular problems to deal with during his childhood, Henry responded promptly,

> HENRY: Parents fought a lot. That to me was a big problem, a big social stress. They're just two miserable people.
> ANGIE: Why do you think they're miserable?

HENRY: Cause they tell me number one. Number two they fight. Like they can't be in a room with each other for more than ten minutes before they start fighting. So you know even today as an adult, even though I know I could physically separate them and kick the shit out of both of them if I had to, it scares me. Like there's that little child that goes aaaaah, they're about to fight. I can sense it. And for me, I try to see them separately whenever possible.

ANGIE: I'm sorry, are they together?

HENRY: No my dad's in Korea, my mom's here. However when he comes here, he stays with her. Again how that works, it's beyond me. My wife's asked me a million times so I tell her, ask my mom. Personally I just don't care. I think my wife has a hard time believing that I don't care. But seriously I just don't care. I care more about this drink here, right? That it tastes kind of eh to me. I care more about this drink than I care about the problems with their relationship. Just not my problem.

Although he claimed not to care about his parents' marriage, his unveiled anger, anxiety, and disgust clearly indicate the contrary. His professed indifference may be considered a strategy for managing the painful emotions that come with dealing with conflicts among loved ones over which he has little control. Henry explained how he carried over some of the lessons he learned from these feuds into his current marriage. Because his parents fought bitterly over money, he lets his wife handle all the finances and said the only reason he would divorce her is if they fought over money.

As opposed to merely rejecting their parents' marriage because of cultural differences, other participants tried to make sense of their parents' many conflicts within the context of their hardships as immigrants. As the youngest daughter of four, Winnie blocked out a lot of the unpleasant memories of physical altercations that took place between her mother and stepfather until she was able to deal with the memories as an adult. Her seamstress mother and butcher father worked very long hours, so she was raised by her two older sisters, although she says her parents still "made their presence felt." She tried to get a handle on these difficult memories by reminding herself about the struggles of being an immigrant in a new country.

There was just a brief era of domestic violence. My brother and I shared a room next to our parents' room and there was a screen door that divided it. We would hear the fighting and we would run to my sister's room at the end of the hall cause it would scare us. And even my mom, she actually packed up her stuff one time; she was gonna leave us. I don't exactly know why, something with my father. But I would see bruises on my mom and I would see bruises on my dad. I don't even think about that stuff. You know when they say a child forgets things to protect the mind? I shut down a lot of things that I saw or experienced and when I got older, I guess I was old enough to really be able to say, yes my parents did have that experience where they did hurt each other physically. And I think it was merely because of the whole frustration of being immigrants, having the pressure of having to pay the rent, and taking care of four kids. It's just difficult. I still sometimes look at my father like okay, you hurt my mom, but I understand also where they're coming from.

From what she can remember, the fighting between her parents did not last more than a year, and she says she recalls more laughter than pain. This perhaps has helped her to get over the trauma of these memories and sympathize with her parents, especially with the help of her older siblings, who explained to her the context of these struggles.

Other second-generation participants took the more direct and assertive approach of inserting themselves into their parents' altercations, especially as they got older and found themselves in a better position to exert their authority. Oftentimes, this meant siding with one parent over the other. Because mothers were usually the main caregivers and were more vulnerable to financial manipulation and physical/verbal abuse, most children—both sons and daughters—tended to defend their mothers. Daniel, whose father emigrated as a physician from Hong Kong and sponsored his mother who was a nurse, said he lived a fairly "pampered, privileged life" as a child but described how his father held onto a patriarchal view of family and verbally abused his mother. Although he and his sister prodded their mother to get a divorce, he thought she was too traditional to follow through. So as he got older, he explained how he learned to counter his father's verbal abuse of his mother with equally small but significant acts of sarcasm and condescension:

It was really painful when they're in public and you can't yell at someone in front other people, right? But he does these really indirect put-downs. Like recently we were at my sister's husband's party and my mom is talking, having a good time and then my dad will say some fucked up shit like don't listen to her, she just talks a lot, oh she's just really drunk, and I would get so mad. And she's being great, she's being the life of the party, she's really pretty like everyone's in love with her. And so I don't know I get really petty and I start doing the same thing to my dad. I start embarrassing him in public. [short laugh] It gets me so mad so it's sort of like taste your own medicine, you asshole. So I'll join the conversation and be like oh dad, remember that time you did this? Or dad, you're joking, you never did that. Or no, you really don't know that dad. And he gets a little bothered by it. [whispering] I'm like yes! Now you know how it feels.

Daniel feels that his intervention along with his mother's new vocation singing and emceeing at organizational events have improved relations somewhat between his parents, although he continues to bristle at his father's treatment of his mother.

Several of the interviewees also believed that their father's need to exert his authority over his wife is a way of compensating for his loss in social status as an Asian male in American society. Justine, whose stepmother is not in good health but supports her and her husband with a waitressing job, felt that her father's inability to support his family both financially and emotionally had largely to do with his inability to overcome his loss of social status and privilege since immigrating from Malaysia: "I don't think he's lived up to his responsibilities especially in the later years of his life because he's stuck in this time warp of how things should be and how people should treat him."

During the hours she spent helping her father out at his machinery shop, Leah, who immigrated at the age of five, was struck by the visible contrast she saw in her father's life before and after he immigrated from Taiwan. In general, she viewed her father as a proud, confident man who lived comfortably back in Taiwan and was well respected by his colleagues. However, upon immigrating to the United States, her entire family including her three other siblings all had to live crammed into one tiny house with one of her relatives. Because neither of her parents spoke English, she watched her father toil long hours at work and deal with patronizing white clientele as she painfully reminisced during the interview:

> Growing up and seeing him interact with Caucasian clients who may not understand his English and how he struggled through that was difficult. Sitting there and knowing what a fluent American English speaker was trying to communicate to my dad but my dad just not getting it and getting frustrated and stumbling through communication was difficult. Cause he's a very assertive, confident guy but all of a sudden because of the language barrier, he wasn't able to get his point across. There were times when he was taken advantage of and when people said racially biased remarks and jokes that offended my parents. My mom probably had it worse because my dad's English became fluent very quickly because he was always at a business place and my mom was a stay-at-home mom. She always wanted to learn English but not having that outlet, she would really struggle with grocery shopping where you would have to speak English to get it done. She was pretty much dependent on me and my older sister.

Although language barriers are certainly an inevitable part of the immigration experience, the humiliation of dealing with white clientele is amplified by the racial perception of Asian men as weak, alien, and socially inept. This comes across in Leah's recollection of racist remarks and jokes made about her father at his expense. At the same time, she also mentioned that her father overcame the language barrier quickly because he was forced to interact with Americans every day at work, whereas her mother's isolation at home made it difficult to pick up the language and forced her to rely on her children for even simple daily tasks. In this way, we see how race, gender, and nativity all interact in shaping the experiences of Asian immigrant men and women and their relationship with their children in very different ways.

Logan, the oldest brother of two, has fond memories of male bonding with his father when he was young living in Hong Kong but noticed how immigrating to the United States dramatically undermined his relationship with both his wife and his children. Logan attributed this shift to his father's struggles trying to recover his status in Hong Kong amid long stints of unemployment, while his mother immediately found clerical work in Chinatown. Among other things, his father dabbled in different business ventures such as construction, real estate development, and even pearl diving in order to try to reclaim the status he enjoyed back in Hong Kong. As Logan saw it,

> When I was born and he ended up with a son, he became very happy because any young man who has a boy, he feels he has that thing where it's like, oh I'm gonna teach him all this stuff and so that's a really beautiful thing. My dad would just physically carry me everywhere like some kind of trophy, and he would take me to a lot of places back in Hong Kong. But once he came here, the relationship changed in a way where it felt very much like a single-parent family home, because it was just me and my sister with my mom all the time cause my dad would try to get jobs my mom got. And my dad couldn't find a job for various reasons. I think it's because he was not able to swallow his pride as a man of color in this country. To go into corporate, you really have to swallow your pride and be treated like a piece of crap, and as a man who in Hong Kong was kind of the shit, he could not be flexible in that way. Being an Asian guy in America is very difficult, especially in Brooklyn, in a working-class macho Italian environment. So I feel like my dad and I both had to constantly negotiate our manhood as Asian men and it's an endeavor that our backgrounds culturally leave us completely ill-prepared for. Because in Chinese culture, there's not that constant need to prove that you're a man, whereas in America, it's never-ending.

Logan still harbored resentment, although intertwined with empathy and an understanding of the broader context of Asian male powerlessness, over his father's unwillingness to start from the bottom and fight to prove his masculinity instead of taking out his anger and frustration on his mother. He said he also lost respect for his father in many ways because of his refusal to protect his mother, who was often poorly treated by his father's family members.

However, I also found that in other cases, children were able to view their parents' marriage in more positive ways, even when faced with the challenges of shifting gender roles. The main difference in these families was that both parents were willing and able to do the type of emotion work involved in accommodating to new spousal relations. In her study on transnationally split Filipino families, Rhacel Parrenas observes that even when separated geographically from their children, fathers who made an effort to incorporate nurturing acts and emotional affection into their long-distance relationships with children were better able to ameliorate some of the pain and tension of being separated.[13] In other words, both fathers and mothers must be willing to blur the gendered boundaries of masculinity and femininity by sharing maternal responsibilities of care and emotional support. The same concept applies for those whose families are forced to rethink traditional notions of men as financial providers and women as family caregivers.

This transition is smoother when there is a network of men who also validate this flexible approach to manhood. Esther, a twenty-five-year-old Korean American, explained how her mother gave up her dream as a profes- sional opera singer after she got married but then used her business acumen to start up a small but profitable dry cleaning chain in Philadelphia. The resulting shift in breadwinning roles created tensions in the marriage, espe- cially because her father's family was raised on the belief that "men should be the head of the family and they should be the main provider like my grand- father was." However, she believed that her father's sense of frustration and resentment lessened over time as he received support from his network of close male friends, who admired her mother's achievements.

> My mom has a very, very strong business sense but my dad doesn't have that sort of savvy at all. And whenever my mom went to expand the busi- ness, my dad cannot take a chance and he doesn't want to risk the money, so he'll fight her tooth and nail in every single thing—location, machinery, hiring people—and just make it very difficult for her, because I think deep down inside, he knows that in that way, he's inept. But lately that's changed because his friends who are all kind of in the same business, their wives are totally pampered and don't work and in some cases, if they do work, they create problems. They really admire my mom and so my dad is seeing that my mom is kind of special that way and unusual so that he should be thankful as opposed to making things more difficult for her.

Esther may be projecting some of her personal admiration for her mother onto her parents' relationship with one another. She herself has strong career aspirations to start her own business also in the garment industry, which developed from her mother's success in the dry cleaning business. She regularly communicates and consults with her mother about issues such as what machine to use for a garment or how to improve her business. Although she is deeply affected by her earlier years as a latchkey child and her parents' preferential treatment for her younger brother, Esther still empathizes with her mother's struggles with her in-laws and conflicts over traditional gender roles and draws strength from her mother's ability to overcome these obstacles. Her story reveals how the successful renegotiation of work and family roles among women and men can have a formative impact on the worldviews of their daughters and sons.

Participants also viewed their mothers as central in not only managing the emotions of individual family members but also brokering relations between father and child.[14] Tom, the oldest son from a well-off Chinese immigrant family, explained why he still had respect for his father even though he was never home because of his long work hours. "I have friends whose fathers work all the time and they seem to hate their dad. I think part of it is how the mother sets the tone. My mom was always like you can't make noise, your dad's sleeping. He works really hard. He does all this for you and your sister. That was the way it was always presented. We didn't flush the toilets in the morning because we couldn't afford to wake my dad up, right? Whereas some of my friends that hate their dads, I think the moms set a different tone. It's like the mom resented how hard the father was working and how he was never home to be with the kids." Tom recognized how his mother set the emotional tone for the family by managing how they viewed and ameliorated his father's stressful work life. Of course, this type of approach comes at a considerable social cost to women, who are often forced to justify the physical absence of their spouses and manage their own feelings of loneliness and stress, while juggling both household and work responsibilities. In Tom's case, both his parents worked: his mother as a teacher and his father as a restaurant owner and real estate developer. It is also possible that his younger sister may view their parents' marriage differently and have divergent ideas on what made it work. However, the fact that his mother helped to ameliorate relations with his father was clearly meaningful to Tom.

It is interesting how children—both daughters and sons—detect and interpret these subtle gender dynamics between their parents. Angela, the only child of a Chinese immigrant family, relayed to me her concern for her mother who she feared will be at a loss when her father passes away because she is completely dependent on her father, even though she handles most of the household chores and finances. However, she also considered her mother the emotional backbone of the relationship in the way she mediates and communicates her father's concerns across generational barriers. She said, "My dad is always more stable, but my dad also relies on her a lot for more than he shows. Like when he'll tell me something, he'll say well your mom's really upset, cause you didn't do this. And I know when he says it, it's him thinking of it, but he just puts it on my mom cause she's the emotional one." To Angela, this type of emotional scapegoating enables her father to convey his personal feelings to her without the awkwardness that comes with emotional expression in this cultural context. Her account reminds us of the key role women play in managing and brokering the emotional dynamics of the family in a way that has a powerful impact on the lives of their children.

Of course, not all participants viewed their parents' marriages as precarious, especially if resources and networks enabled their parents to maintain the same gender roles upon immigrating or, conversely, if they were better able to adapt to new circumstances. Espiritu argues that this transition is generally much easier to make for women in middle-class or upper-class white-collar professions, whose career ambitions and substantial paychecks give them leverage to negotiate relatively more equitable decision-making roles and male assistance with household responsibilities. In contrast, despite the fact that they tend to contribute relatively more to the family income, working-class women are less likely to challenge the patriarchal system because they are mutually dependent on the combined household income for economic survival and place stronger value on male protection and the well-being of the family as mothers and wives over their financial independence.[15] Marital conflicts also tend to have less of an impact on younger siblings, who are not witness to the kinds of conflicts that older children are privy to because they were born after their parents had overcome some of the initial hardships of adapting.

Yet whether their parents' marriage was harmonious or bitter, few participants characterized their parents as having the kind of romantic marriage that Americans idealized and they aspired for themselves. This was troubling for some because it went against the grain of everything they had learned as Americans about what a good marriage should entail—that is, one built on passion, romance, and visible verbal and physical affection. Yet at the same time, when I probed them further on whether or not their parents had a good marriage, most sons and daughters initially hesitated or wavered in their response, as in the following comments by Jinah, a Korean American from New Jersey whose father owns a lucrative dental laboratory business and whose mother who is a homemaker:

> Ideal marriage to me would be one that's based on absolute true love. And I don't think my parents have that, which is fine. I mean they love and respect each other, but I wanna have that crazy mad passionate love on top of having the good values. And to be honest, I don't think they married for love. It was just more that it was a convenience and also she liked him and I think he's always known that he was lucky to have her kind of thing so that's what makes him work really, really hard. Now that we're all older, my mother's still reflecting on her life and she says, your father is such a great man, a honest man, a respected man. He doesn't drink, he doesn't smoke, he doesn't do any womanizing, he doesn't gamble. Everything he does is for the family, everything he does is for the right reason. Okay, he's got a little bit of a bad temper, but when it comes down to it, everyone has a bad temper to some degree. Because he is thirteen years older than my mother, he's doing some estate planning. He realizes that my mother's going to outlive him at least by thirteen or more years so he's getting things in order, like he's buying some property. He says to my mother, I've amassed these properties and this house and I've got this, do you think that will be enough for you? And my mother's like [she had some tears in her eyes, the reason is that], he's realizing I've made all this and I want you to live comfortably when I die.[16]

Although they did not necessarily proclaim love as being the only foundation for a good marriage, females made a stronger distinction between romantic love and friendship than did their male counterparts, perhaps because in American culture women are socialized to be more emotionally expressive and treat the Romeo and Juliet type of romance as central to a happy marriage. Men however were more open to the possibility that love can be based on a compatible and practical—as opposed to an emotional and romantic—partnership.

Instead of immediately rejecting their parents' marriage as ill-suited, most participants tried to explain how their parents' marriage merely represented a different way of conveying sentimental attachment. They recognized the subtle ways in which their parents expressed love for each other—one that preserved the other person's dignity but showed concern for their partner's emotional state and well-being without the song and dance that comes with Western affection. Winnie, the one whose parents had gone through a brief period of domestic violence when she was younger, also recalled how her parents would fondly reminisce about how they first met and flirt with each other when they thought the children were not looking. When I asked her why her parents hid it from them, she replied simply, "My mom is very much about the face. She's like there are our kids so they can't see us doing that."

John, a twenty-eight-year-old single Taiwanese American proprietary trader and youngest son in his family, also believed his parents had a "good marriage" but struggled to come up with examples that showed they loved one another.

ANGIE: Do you think that they loved each other then would you say?

JOHN: I think they loved each other.

ANGIE: Like what made you think that?

JOHN: [long pause] The little things, the way they cared for each other. It's hard to come up with an example of those little things, but you know like my dad has trouble flying so my mom will always make him a special drink when they travel. They might yell at each other, but he always wants to be with her every year, and, it's hard to interpret exactly, but I feel like, that's a sign of something serious. Even when you have argumentative people, but you still want to spend all your time with them. It's quite nice. That seems like to me that's love.

Saving face itself represents a meaningful act of trust and devotion that signifies one of the many ways parents show their feelings for one another. Participants would pick up on subtle but meaningful cues through behaviors and sacrifices, which to them captured their parents' emotions. This is of course not something children learned over the course of a day but something that second-generation Korean and Chinese Americans begin to recognize throughout the course of their lives.

Although they admitted this was certainly not the kind of marriage they wanted for themselves, the participants in the study felt they could learn from the ways their parents provided stability and support for their family by working through difficult times and making practical decisions about the family. When asked if there was anything about his parents' marriage he would want in his own, Mike, the oldest son of Korean business owners, answered,

Perseverance is probably the strongest attribute of their marriage, or any marriage that lasts a long time, because those people have a good perspective on a long-term goal. [My parents] had really nasty fights when I was a child. Not recently, but there have been times where I was scared as a teenager. They would fight over finances, over our upbringing, but I don't think it's important what they fought about, but the fact that they fought, they dealt with it and they moved on and they're actually happy. They're staying together because they enjoy each other's company, they still love each other very much, and that's the key. I wouldn't encourage people to stay in bad situations because that does happen but it just worked out. They still laugh together, they laugh a lot. They're good partners and there's still give and take. It's not everything my father's way, it's not everything my mother's way, so flexibility to still grow with each other. If someone said to me, you can have the relationship your parents had, I might say I would take that, just because it lasted a long time. They have three kids who are fairly decent people.

At the time of the interview, Mike was still single, managing his father's liquor store. Although he admitted that he did not follow through with all the responsibilities expected of him as the oldest son, he still expressed much regard for some of the traditional family values his parents have conveyed to him such as respecting his elders and providing direction for his two younger brothers and cousins; at the same time, he believed his family's comfortable class status also afforded him the privilege to decide for himself how much of his life to devote to the family.

As one can see, the presence or absence of visible affection and romance is not a sufficient measure by which participants gauge the extent of their parents' love for one another. However, the one major reason why second-generation children may characterize their parents' marriage as "bad" and look down on them is if a parent reneged on marital obligations or practical responsibilities as a husband or wife. This may occur if a parent verbally or physically abused the other or tricked the other parent out of money through a divorce, because such acts indicated outright betrayal of loyalty and moral values that to them represented love within the cultural context of their parents' marriage.

Of course, the social contract of marriage as understood within this cultural framework often involves traditional gendered expectations and household division of labor, where the mothers are expected to be responsible for household and caregiving matters and fathers act as primary breadwinners in the family. As mentioned, this did not often align with the realities of Asian immigrant parents' lives. Yet surprisingly, only a few of the participants outwardly expressed any major disappointment with their parents if they did not fulfill traditional gender roles and responsibilities expected of mothers and fathers. As one example, Lin, who is the middle child of a Taiwanese astronaut family, informed me that her parents are married on paper but have lived almost their entire lives apart. Because her mother was busy working and taking care of three children on her own, Lynn got involved with a bad crowd and rebelled throughout her teenage years. After she graduated, her mother suggested that she go live with her father in Taiwan, who "took a lot of time out to sit and talk to me and try to figure out why I was being the way I was, whereas my mom, she didn't have the time, so she was just like, don't do this, don't do that, without really having conversations." However, looking back, she repeatedly told me that she understands that "as a single parent in that kind of environment, trying to raise three kids, putting one through college, was really difficult [for my mom]." This ability to adapt to new family arrangements does seem to conflict with what scholars such as Parrenas have found on Asian immigrant families where mothers are often blamed for neglecting their family for work as compared with fathers.[17] Given that Parrenas interviewed mostly younger children in a different cultural context, the reason for this difference may be that Asian Americans are able to feel greater empathy toward and understanding of the realities of their parents' lives as they get older. It is also possible that my participants did not want to come across as adopting a conservative "non-American" stance on gendered family roles.

Instead of preserving gender roles, participants felt it was more important that their parents be fully open and honest with one another and also with their children on all financial matters. For them, full financial disclosure not only signifies equality and trust within the relationship, but also gives every family member the means to empathize with the other and act accordingly. Several interviewees expressed concern for their mothers if their fathers did little to help them learn how to manage money since they felt this would make their mothers helpless and dependent should their fathers pass away first. Tom explained how the one major conflict he witnessed while growing up was in regard to money—not necessarily about how it was spent but the fact that his father never shared this information with his mother.

There were stresses growing up, especially related to money when money was tight and my dad never really consulted with my mom on major business decisions. I'm gonna open this restaurant, I'm gonna buy this piece of real estate. I think that hurt my mom, right? It put a lot of stress on the relationship where it's like I've gotta live with you through all the financial stresses and you don't include me in the conversation. I did have this conversation with my mom, she pointed out she was a teacher and she ran a daycare center with a staff and she gave up a career to take care of us. She helped my dad raise the money to open the restaurants. And I think part of me took it as if she was trying to justify her importance or her value and I was like I know what you sacrificed to raise me and my sister, you don't really need to tell me. But I think it was important to her that I knew.

This last observation about his mother wanting to prove her worth is a particularly poignant one. It reveals how women's work—the act of accompanying her husband to America, the work of raising children, and the sacrifice of helping run the family business without recognition—is often overlooked and devalued even in the typical immigrant tales of sacrifice and the American Dream. Tom told me that he learned from his father's mistake and makes every effort to treat his wife and three children with respect and dignity, especially when it comes to financial matters. Although he said his wife, who quit her job after the second child, usually deferred to his advice, he is always careful to consult with her on investment matters and has a financial advisor who knows all the details of their holdings so that if anything were to happen to him, she knows whom to go to for assistance.

Suzanne, one of the few whose parents' marriage was arranged, said that her parents relate to each other in a very traditional Korean way, even addressing each other by formal Korean titles like *dangshin* and *yeobo*. Nevertheless, she felt that the way her parents shared financial responsibilities and operated their green grocery businesses together day and night indicated to her the strengths of their marital partnership, as compared with her and her sisters' more American values.

> One thing I see from them is that it was really a partnership and there were no secrets. My sister's in a relationship now. She's thinking about these things like when you are married, do you have one bank account, or do you have several bank accounts. You have to think about these things when you are working separate jobs, and you separate incomes, and you have separate interests. For my parents, it was just like they make the money, they managed the money. My father says I need this much money to go buy supplies, my mom gives it to him, and there were nooo secrets. Nothing was separate; everything was together. And that's something that I really admired about them. I don't know if that's feasible, if I married and there's dual incomes and dual interests and dual retirements and all of that. And I think that they really labored together. Cause I have friends whose moms just ran the whole ship and the fathers wanna play golf or want to go drinking with their friends. My parents really stuck it out together.

Of course, the legal ambiguity that comes with merging spousal belongings can become problematic, especially if one partner, oftentimes the husband, asserts or abuses his control over the family's holdings. This is probably also why it has become a necessity for modern-day dual-wage-earning couples who are more vulnerable to divorce to legally designate their property and belongings through separate accounts, wills, and other legal mechanisms.

This is increasingly becoming the case not only in the United States but also in modernizing nations throughout Asia. Yet Suzanne appreciates the fact that her parents' definition of love and marriage is flexible and adapts to the social and economic realities of their lives.

The Language of Parental Love

Emotional communication can also be complicated between the immigrant parent and American-born child. Regardless of race, ethnicity, or nationality, second-generation children often have difficulties relating to and communicating with their immigrant parents as a result of language barriers, cultural differences between their parents' ancestral culture and their American upbringing, and conflicting pressures they face from their parents at home and their peers at school. Immigrant parents who share a common language with their children or have had greater premigration exposure to English proficiency and Western culture may have an easier time bridging some of these generational differences over time. This is not to say that cultural differences and intergenerational conflicts do not occur in many European immigrant families.[18] However, the racial marginalization of those cultural differences can magnify the shame and distress that come with family conflict. The cultural clashes that often occur in Asian immigrant families—particularly those that focus around mother-daughter relationships—have been the subject of many popular novels, autobiographies, movies such as *The Joy Luck Club* (Amy Tan) and *The Namesake* (Jhumpa Lahiri), and Asian American indie films such as *Yellow*.

In order to understand how Asian Americans communicate across this language and cultural barrier, we need to think beyond the Western frame of reference and take into account the different ways in which people communicate and express emotion across cultures. What Americans may view as viciously cold and demanding about so-called Chinese parenting reflects not a cultural inability to feel or express emotions, but rather a cultural difference in the way it is communicated. In Western cultures like the United States, communication is understood to be a linear, logical, and verbal dialogue between equally situated individuals, where each party is expected to directly articulate his or her individual feelings and desires to the other. Emotions such as love are separated into clear-cut and binary categories of sameness and difference, all of which should be openly conveyed through words and then expressed through direct individual actions. A healthy relationship between a parent and a child thus involves each party verbally expressing his or her affection for the other and sharing individual grievances in the hopes of resolving any conflicts or differences.

East Asian cultures however employ a more intuitive, relational, and contextual approach to communication in which a person's body language and actions as well as his or her history, background, and status provide important cues for understanding thoughts and feelings better than any words can articulate.[19] In collectivist cultures like Korea and China, the needs of the group supersede individual goals, and the means of communicating vary depending on one's status within the social order. One's identity is rooted not in the individual and independent self, but rather in one's position in relationship to others. From a relational perspective, emotions, just like life itself, cannot be easily dichotomized into oppositional categories of feelings such as love and hate but may encompass a complex wellspring of contradictory feelings that do not conflict but rather complement one another. Problem solving is not always the ideal objective, especially if hiding personal feelings and struggles achieves the larger goal of preserving one's dignity and sparing loved ones unnecessary pain and burden.

In one study on Chinese Americans, Chan and Leong show how parents convey their love for their children not by verbally articulating their feelings but rather tending to their physical and material needs and working hard to improve their children's future.[20] When they do want to convey emotions, they use "gestures, facial expressions, intonations, and the volume of speech" or even meaningful silence, as opposed to direct verbal communication.[21] A parent saying the words "I love you" to a child however is less meaningful, and if anything superficial and selfish, than sacrificing wordlessly for the good of the family. In day-to-day conversation, the things parents don't say are just as important as those they do, especially if they believe that revealing their feelings through the imperfect medium of another language could only aggravate intergenerational tensions. The context of immigration also requires that parents focus even more intensely on the practical matters of survival over issues of social and emotional growth. If anything, they believe that the tactic of tough love best prepares their children for the harsh realities and struggles of day-to-day survival.

Of course, some are aware of these cultural differences in parenting and love, as in the case of Leah, a twenty-nine-year-old Taiwanese American who helped out at her father's small mechanic shop, attended a Chinese church, and was raised in an Asian American–dominated neighborhood of Orange County, California. She commented, "My dad is not a very affectionate guy, very black-and-white, not very expressive. My mom was the cuddly one, very emotional and expressive verbally and physically and so naturally we were all closer to my mom. But my dad, the way he would express his love for us was through providing for us and also engaging us in activities. So it's very different ways of expressing their love."

Similarly, Cecilia, whose Taiwanese stepmother made efforts to teach her about cultural differences, observed that "Chinese people when you grow up, they don't hug you, they don't say I love you. My understanding is for the most part, Chinese people tend to show their feelings through action: making you a home-cooked meal or taking you somewhere where you wanna go, what do you need, what do you need to buy, rather than 'oh I love you,' 'have a great day at school,' hugs, kisses." But even in Cecilia's case, she needed the verbal and affectionate connection with her stepmother for her to understand all of this, which was not possible when she used to live with her abusive biological mother.

Others, like Stephanie, a Chinese American daughter of a working-class family, learned how to keep the peace in the family by internalizing these cultural norms, but also recognized how doing so created conflict in their own lives. Stephanie explained how her father had apparently struggled considerably as an undocumented immigrant laborer in Chinatown but did not learn about much of his past until she was older. She believed that it was because unlike other Chinese parents, her parents did not want their children to feel guilty and indebted because of their sacrifices. However, this notion that family members are to protect each other from emotional stress also created an immense burden on her because as the peacekeeper in the family, she could not come out to her parents and introduce them to her longtime female partner. She talks about one past incident with her mother where she learned the hard way that being honest and sharing her problems could lead to headaches for both sides.

> I admit that I'm a peacekeeper. Let's not do anything that rocks the boat too much with my family. I just want to shield them from any crap in my life. I want them to think that everything's perfectly fine and I don't want to worry them about anything. I don't believe there's such great value to the truth sometimes (ha). One example is I had an injury to my spine and I actually went to my mom. I told her, mom I want to go see your doctor. Once I did that, forget about it. The questions about my injury were nonstop. My mom would call me every day about it, bothered me every day about it, and my sister's like you never should have told her. You stressed her out. I was like oh, so there's a little bit of a guilt trip like keep my parents in this cushion. It's almost like for no good, they can't really be helpful anyway. If I was unemployed or something like that, of course my parents would open up their wallets and give me money. I wouldn't really want them to do that, you know what I mean?

Other participants who wanted to come out to their parents about their sexual orientation delayed telling them not only to protect their feelings and keep the family peace, but also to spare them the shame and isolation they would endure as part of a traditional ethnic community. This was the case for Alice, whose mother enjoys actively volunteering for the Chinatown community and, Alice fears, could face severe humiliation and ostracism if people were to find out about her gay daughter. No matter how close they were to their parents, the vast majority of Korean and Chinese Americans I interviewed reported that they never shared the intimate details of their private lives, especially their romantic relationships and struggles, for some of the same reasons. It was not just because they feared being disowned but also because of what it would do to their family and relationship with the ethnic community.

Unfortunately, those second-generation youth whose parents hide them from their hardships and who communicate less often with their parents have a hard time making sense of this way of communicating and have trouble negotiating two cultures. Although most second-generation Asian Americans sense that their parents' true intentions are often lost in translation, understanding and bridging this communication divide is an enormous task, especially when faced with the pressures of generational conflicts, cultural misinterpretation, and adaptation struggles. The process often entails a long, emotionally painful journey that can continue well into adulthood. Because of their renewed interest in cultivating relations with their family as adults, many Asian Americans in the study expressed deep remorse over making little effort to learn their parents' language as children since it offered one of the few means to better understand their family history and get in touch with their ancestral roots.

The potential emotional ramifications of intergenerational miscommunication and misunderstanding are best captured in the following anecdote by Angela. Angela, the only child born in San Francisco, said that she had heated arguments with her parents when she was younger because they pressured her heavily about her schoolwork and would not allow her to date lest it interfere with her academics. She related to me one incident as an adult in which she tried to reach out emotionally to her parents, which somehow ended in a disastrous argument: "At one point I made a big mistake and said you know I'm glad we're getting closer now. I know we're not like some other families—I don't know what it was but it was honest. And that was like too much. How could you dare say that! Even though we all know it was the truth, that we're not as close as a lot of families are, and I think they see it too but I can't speak that out loud. There's just a lot of walls up in my house." For Angela, what was an honest and heartfelt attempt to emphasize how emotionally close they had become as a family was misinterpreted by her parents as an insinuation that they had not been close all along. Angela spoke from the cultural lens of an American who believed that by honestly expressing her feelings and highlighting how their relationship had improved, she was making an emotionally difficult step to connect with her parents. Her parents however may have taken this act of airing out their family's dirty laundry as unnecessarily conjuring up negative feelings, misinterpreting their past act of concern as emotional distance, and overlooking the sacrifices they made to convey their love. Angela said she continues to value her independence from her parents since she left home for college, although she is continually pulled back home to help care for her parents in their old age. However, she believes they are less able to communicate since she speaks only very basic Mandarin while her parents' limited English proficiency has gotten steadily worse with retirement.

A Story without a Past

What is often lacking in mainstream portrayals of intergenerational conflicts is a more developed discussion on the way structural contexts that transcend individual family differences—namely, the surrounding ethnic community and the host society—can also affect the lines of intergenerational communication. This is particularly true for racial minority groups whose understanding of their own family histories and parents' ancestral cultures may be circumscribed by limited multicultural education, absence of coethnic role models, and distorted media representations. Zhou and Bankston show that in the absence of parental supervision, the presence of an ethnic community can play an instrumental role in shaping and monitoring the social behavior, internal norms, and academic achievements of the second generation.[22] The same can be said about mediating family relationships. Those who live in close proximity to ethnic communities benefit from mentors, pastors, and older peers, who may help intervene and guide second-generation youth where American society cannot. However, this type of institutional support is not available to all Asian Americans who as a result of their socioeconomic diversity live in very diverse neighborhood settings: from low-income ethnic enclaves to inner-city black/Latino ghettoes to white or Asian suburbs.

One major gap among most of the Korean and Chinese Americans I interviewed was a clear understanding of their parents' past and how this ultimately led to their migration to the United States. Unless they made deliberate and sustained efforts to learn about Asian history and culture through school or nonprofit work, second-generation Asian Americans had only a vague picture of their family histories and the homeland within which their parents' lives took shape. What little they knew was pieced together through things they overheard at home or from friends and relatives who helped convey some parts of their family history. Responses like Kathy's were common throughout most of the interviews I conducted with Korean and Chinese Americans: "I know bits and pieces, like the major events and the big stories, but I think you learn about your parents through people who knew them at that time. And we're not very close to extended family and it's very difficult for me to talk to my aunts and uncles partially because of the language barrier."

One of the interviewees, Daniel, expressed visible frustration when my research assistant pushed him to give more details about his parents' lives. Like Kathy, he claimed his parents were very vague about the details of their histories so that the little information he got was just fragments of stories from his relatives or secondhand accounts his mother passed on through his paternal kin. When asked why he thought they did not like to talk about their past, Daniel responded,

> A lot of it is maybe sheltering us from something that may have been more tragic. Maybe it's just the past and you know we're here in America, you don't have to think about it, you don't have to worry about it, you just do your thing and don't worry about my past. It might distract me from being a doctor or lawyer (ha) or being really successful and opening a business. In a lot of ways it's like protecting us from something but I always have gotten that feeling that they don't want us to think about it, because it's going to distract us from our path here in America. Like we fought to get here to America, fought so you can have a good life, so you have your good life and that's it. We went through all this stuff [but] you don't need to worry about it.

What is striking in this passage is the interviewee's sense that his parents are hiding this information not out of negligence or apathy but a deliberate attempt to help their children live a good life. It is meaningful that despite the difficulties and distance that it created, many of the people I interviewed felt this lack of communication signified to them their parents' love for their children— something that may have been more difficult to understand as children.

Those who were more in touch with these cultural differences such as Mark understood that the type of relationship they had with their parents may not be physically and verbally intimate but nevertheless was strong enough to signify to them how close they are as a family. Unlike his younger sister, Mark witnessed all the trials and tribulations his parents endured when they first immigrated to the United States, which to him was a sign of their parental love. These are complex emotions that could not be captured through simple vocabulary.

> ANGIE: How did you hear of these experiences through them? Do they talk to you about them?
>
> MARK: Well just in passing. They've never told me the story straight. I've just kind of put things together. I don't even know how my parents met yet. [laughs] Even to this day, I don't really talk to them much. Our communication is very silent. I put bits and pieces together to figure out my parents' story of coming here. So I was very independent growing up, because there's some sort of distance between us. When I say distance, I don't mean we weren't close-knit—we were definitely very close-knit—but distance in terms of communication. It's like modem versus DSL.

Mark struggled to put into words how he knew his family was close-knit but said he was certain it was because of a combination of "innate" feelings and "things my parents have done for me." Noticeably, even those who appreciated the different cultural ways of expressing affection and attachment did not frequently use the word "love" to convey this relationship and instead preferred terms such as "care for," "bond," and "close." They were keenly aware of the narrow way in which the term "love" was defined in the American context, which in many ways failed to capture the complex layers of emotion that their relationship with their parents entailed.

Not surprisingly, children were more likely to express a stronger emotional connection with their mothers because of their gendered role as the caregiver and nurturer of the family. Even if their mothers also worked long hours, they were still more likely than their fathers to spend more time with the children, cook and clean for them, drive them to school and to activities, show concern when they were sick, and just generally be more hands-on in their day-to-day lives. Given the emotionally tumultuous nature of the immigrant family experience, the role of the mother as nurturer and caregiver should not be underplayed, and those second-generation Asian Americans who have at least a minimally stable relationship with their mothers were conscious of this.

Yet interestingly, even in cases where the father was rarely present, the interviewees' narratives of their family past often highlighted the broader social significance of their father's migration, which often revolved around their paid work. This greater attention to the father's history was rooted in the belief that the migration itself was driven and made possible by their father's money and career ambitions, whereas their mothers were simply viewed as accompanying him. The American Dream itself is rooted in the assumption that immigrants (usually the breadwinner, usually male) work hard through paid labor to help their children have a better life. Of course, it was not always the case that fathers were the sole leaders behind migration, especially in cases where families migrated in order to give their children a better education, which would involve both financial and emotional sacrifices on the part of both parents. Some daughters and sons did recognize when mothers gave up their own jobs or career goals to come to the United States. However, there was a greater tendency for people to view women's role as homemaker as less interesting than men's work as wage earners unless it involved conflict with other family members. Sometimes, mothers were also complicit in downplaying their personal histories in this manner. I myself recall one time trying to interview my mother about her migration history out of personal interest, to which she responded that her life was not interesting and that I should just go talk to my father. As soon as the tape recorder started rolling, my father of course started lecturing me on what I needed to do to succeed in life. I gave up on that project very quickly.

Despite the general absence of fathers from the day-to-day lives of many second-generation Asian Americans, their presence as the abstract paternal figure was still a key aspect of their parents' immigration stories, especially for sons who sorely lacked a male role model both within and outside their families. Young is a twenty-nine-year-old Korean American investment manager who worked at a hedge firm in New York and had just moved to Chicago at the time of the interview. His father was an engineer and his mother a homemaker. Young informed me that his mother was much more involved in his life than his father, who when not working did not talk much. Yet surprisingly, Young still had more to say about his father's family history and its impact on his worldview and values. When I asked him to tell me about his father, he narrated to me the following historical account:

> YOUNG: My grandfather was the police chief in Seoul during the Korean War and he died when my father was eight years old. And so it was my father and his three older sisters, a younger brother and my grandmother. So really from a very early age, my father had to start earning money whichever way he can. He started doing that by tutoring and living a very impoverished lifestyle growing up in the 1950s. Korea as a country itself was pretty devastated after going through a civil war. So what he was able to do in terms of just earning money, tutoring, basically getting full scholarship to go to school, graduating at the top of his class, I think he very much believed in this notion that your conviction

and your sheer determination can pretty much allow you to do anything that you want. So I sort of inherited that philosophy.

ANGIE: And how did you find out all about this, about your dad, did he tell you himself?

YOUNG: Nooo, I kind of just learned it empirically from him. He never really sat down and lectured me on any particular topic. So it was always through this quiet observation that I came to realize later on in my life. He would tell me those things, but I don't think he would tell me those things in a lecturing form. He just sort of explained the facts and me kind of observing and then, absorbing certain qualities and certain traits.

Although he majored in comparative literature, Young decided that the best career path for him lie not in academia but in more moneymaking fields such as management consulting and finance. However, he told me that money was only part of the lure; he also loved the independence and the opportunity to travel around the world—desires that he partly attributes to his father.

Oftentimes, the lines of communication varied for different siblings depending on their role within the family. Because the oldest child was expected to be the authoritarian figure of the family and carrier of the family name, it was not uncommon for parents to divulge more of their family history to them while hiding the details from their younger siblings. This was not the case for every family and sometimes depended on the gender and age of the oldest sibling. But generally, oldest sons who immigrated at a later age were more likely to know the intimate details of their family history through verbal communication with their parents and direct observations as arbiter of their family problems. Winnie, the youngest daughter of four, explained to me how during her childhood, her parents and even their extended kin went out of their way to hide some of the tensions and conflicts they had with their relatives in China from her and her brother but revealed more to her oldest sister when the other siblings were not around. Only when she got older and they felt she was old enough to hear these stories did she learn with surprise about their "crappy" family history and feuds that emerged among her relatives.

To be honest, I was pretty resentful when I first found out about it cause I'm like, how come you're not telling me anything? But then I started to realize, cause I was young and they don't want me to worry. They don't want me to deal with any of the hardships that they dealt with, which is why they wanted me to do certain things or *not* do certain things. And it's too late for me to take those kind of things back, but I can try now to show them that I understand. It was just hearing about all those things and hearing about the hardships they went through in their own lives, especially my mother. She was ten, eleven when her mom died and she never even saw her father so she had to live with relatives. So I'm so lucky cause I had my family from the start. My father had to come here first to get a job and make money and send here for us [so] we never got separated. And then I guess I read more Asian American literature and it kinda made me see like, wow I'm really lucky that nothing happened to my parents during the Cultural Revolution.

In order to fill the gaps, Winnie, like many others, turned to reading about Asian and Asian American history and literature, which she said helped her to appreciate the historical context of her parents' struggles and how they affected their behavior and thinking today. Indeed, interviewees would often refer to books they had read, such as *Yellow* (Frank Wu), *The Asian Mystique* (Sheridan Prasso), *The Accidental Asian* (Eric Liu), and *The Geography of Thought* (Richard Nisbett) and usually had a strong opinion about them based on their personal experiences. In some cases, this is what drove them to participate in this research; most of them expressed interest in reading my findings as soon as they got published.

Although most other interviewees had little sense of their parents' homeland and migration histories, some Asian Americans were able to piece together fragments of their parents' past with the help of siblings and extended kin. The specific ways in which family history was conveyed and reinforced for Asian Americans through these networks—namely through extended kin—shaped the lens through which knowledge of their family past was produced and understood. Even for those who did not have strong ties with relatives, I would argue that birth order was the one common emotional ground and meaningful language through which second-generation Korean and Chinese Americans related to their parents, because it was often within that context that their own relationships, responsibilities, and expectations were defined for better or for worse.

For example, participants who were the oldest son of a father who was the oldest son in the family were keenly aware of how the expectations and privileges that were conferred onto them had to do with not only their own birth order but also the birth order of their father. The same held true for the oldest daughters in the oldest son's bloodline, such as Katherine, who told me that she received special treatment and attention from her extended kin because she was the first son's oldest child. Sometimes, a parent's lower status within the extended family hierarchy could negatively affect that parent's sons as well. Peter, a twenty-six-year-old Chinese American who has one older sister, related to me how he enjoyed the company of his father's side of the family but did not have a great relationship with his mother's side because his relationship to them was based on matrilineal descent. The mere imagined positioning of their parents within the immigrant narrative according to gender and birth order helped second-generation Asian Americans to make sense of their family histories and experiences today. It also shaped how their parents treated them knowing what position their children occupied within the larger family tree.

It should be noted that I did not find a similar focus on gender and birth order as a basis for cross-generation empathy or understanding among the second-generation Jews I interviewed. Instead, most Jewish Americans emphasized religious diversity within the Jewish community and important historical events such as the Holocaust or religious persecution in Russia in order to contextualize their parents' migration history, to understand the reasons why their parents thought the way they did about their culture, and to explain their own perspectives on the larger Jewish community. Most Korean and Chinese Americans on the other hand referred only vaguely to events like the Cultural Revolution in China or the Korean War but were quite effusive about how the family roles their parents assumed as the oldest son or youngest daughter, how their parents related to their own parents and siblings, and how their grandparents treated their parents framed their migration history and impacted their own experiences within the family. Instead of focusing on the cultural or historical dimensions of migration like the Jewish participants, second-generation Korean and Chinese Americans were better able to articulate, explain, and empathize with their parents through the vocabulary of birth order and family roles.

Second-generation Korean and Chinese Americans were also conscious of how family history and conflicts that did not directly involve them could nevertheless dramatically impact their lives and their relationship with their parents and other family members. This was the case for Kimberly, whose mother was arranged to marry her father when she was at the tender age of seventeen and became a victim to patriarchal control and physical abuse by her father and his natal family. In the following passage, Kimberly, who is very close to her mother, tried to makes sense of the way her mother physically punished Kimberly as a result of her own experience within her husband's family hierarchy. "My father's mother has six kids, so she kinda picks favorites, and my aunt would tell my mother that my grandmother wasn't treating me very well, because I'm a curious kid, so I jump around, I do this and that. I know my dad's mother used to say things to my mother about my behavior and because of that, my mom felt that she needs to spank me, just show them that oh, I'm teaching my daughter. I don't think I was ever a very quiet kid to start with but because of the pressure she got from her mother-in-law, she had to discipline me more. Where like my sister got a little bit luckier, because my grandparents are a little older so my sister didn't really get any of that." These emotional narratives represent an effort by second-generation Korean and Chinese Americans to come to terms with their parents' behaviors toward them and in some cases relate to their struggles by situating themselves in the patrilineal family hierarchy. As a result, the stories are imbued with empathy over how family roles and relationships could complicate their parents' lives.

In some cases, family conflicts could create contradictions and tensions for second-generation Asian Americans who relied on their extended kin for support they could not get from their parents but were also subject to their misdirected resentment and frustrations. Cora, a thirty-one-year-old Chinese American marketing manager, is an example of one participant who was trapped between her affection for her aunts and uncles who took care of her in her parents' absence and their resentment toward her parents for choosing to live independently from the rest of the extended household. She explained how this led to small acts of retribution directed at her and her sister, such as having them pick flint off the carpet in exchange for nickels. Although she found this cruel to do to children upon retrospect, she still felt a bond with them because they provided the kind of guidance, care, and nurturing her parents did not have time to give her and her sibling.

The one major exception where participants had more detailed knowledge of their family histories came from Korean and Chinese Americans who had been actively involved with ethnic organizations or took ethnic studies and Asian history courses on their own initiative. In the absence of a comprehensive multicultural education, ethnic institutions such as community-based organizations, student associations, and ethnic churches played a key role in helping second-generation Korean and Chinese Americans to make sense of their family's past and understand it within the broader context of historical and social forces. As a financial consultant/aspiring filmmaker, Elliott spoke to the importance of the work he did for the Museum of Chinese in America and the Organization of Chinese Americans, because "I have a mental image of my family's history from my parents and my relatives but I would like to understand how that history relates on a larger context. So doing work for [these organizations], I get to hear other people's stories and it helps fill in the gaps and gives more context to my personal stories."

Logan, who has a strong background in Asian American education and political activism, explained how this absence of a deep historical perspective, cultural awareness, and community engagement had broader implications on the political empowerment of the Asian American community. From his perspective, it made sense why immigrant parents may be more preoccupied with everyday struggles but found it troubling how these values were decontextualized and passed down to second-generation Asian Americans, who could have been in a better position to fight for their rights and give back to the community.

> What's really bad is that Asian people do not have the language but it's not about English comprehension. Within the community, I feel like there's a big lack of dialogue. People talk about it in their daily lives, but they don't bring it up to a level where it becomes activism and that's what I try to do in my life is to advance. I feel like it's about our time because our parents, they have to worry about making money so they don't die, because they're immigrants. The thing is that just because you have money, it doesn't mean the struggle's over. Because Asian culture is so family-oriented and elder respectful-oriented, a lot of kids stop thinking, stop evolving, stop taking it to the next level. You're constantly in a situation where people are trying to take things away from you. If you don't keep moving forward, you're totally being led closer and closer to the guillotine, and closer and closer to irrelevance.

In my past research on nonprofit second-generation organizations in Los Angeles, I heard similar feelings of concern among organizational leaders and activists about the reluctance of the second generation to give back to their community because of their parents, who instilled in them this drive to achieve personal financial success over everything else.

EMOTIONAL KINSCRIPTING

In the case of most Korean and Chinese Americans, very few reported having role models and mentors while growing up, whether in their schools, the local community, or the mainstream media. In order to adjust to this support gap, second-generation Asian Americans devised new strategies to deal with the emotional turmoil and bicultural world they struggled with in their day-to-day lives. One involved compartmentalizing their emotional and psychological needs by turning to different support networks other than their parents for different problems. Sunny, a Taiwanese American who took care of her younger sister in her parents' absence, explained it in this way:

> SUNNY: It's not like I don't think [my parents] don't love me. We just communicate in a very particular way. So I feel like my life is definitely compartmentalized where you have people for this, you have people for

that, you have people for other things. And our parents are there for a
particular reason and that's how we function.

ANGIE: How do they show that they love you?

SUNNY: They tell me. They do tell me that they love me, yeah. I can tell
in the way they act about work, about my sister and about my sister's
relationship with me.

It is not clear in this case whether or not she is referring to verbal communication, but it is apparent that she also understands the other ways her parents
express their love for her beyond verbal expression. At the same time, she
experiences different struggles in her life that she understands cannot be
reconciled by relying solely on her parents.

It is within this context that intergenerational interpreters and mediators
made up of older siblings, cousins, or other extended kin whenever they are
available can play a vital role in helping second-generation Asian Americans
to communicate across language and cultural barriers, gain perspective
on their family histories, and navigate the bumpy emotional terrain of
parent-child relationships. Studies have noted how in an environment of
limited resources, immigrant households will adopt nontraditional familial
arrangements that enable them to maximize and diversify their available
assets and cope with the pressures of everyday survival.[23] For example, poor
black families in the ghetto will delegate different parenting responsibilities
out to a loose and flexible multigenerational cooperative of extended kin
and friends for different caregiving needs—a process Stack and Burton call
"kinscripting."[24] They state, "As households shift, rights and responsibilities with regard to children are shared. Those women and men who temporarily assume the kinship obligation to care for a child, fostering the child
indefinitely, acquire the major cluster of rights and duties ideally associated
with 'parenthood.'"[25]

As with families that are accommodating to limited material resources,
many second-generation Asian Americans face an emotionally stunted environment that prevents them from sharing their joys and grief with family
members, from receiving verbally expressive love, concern, and guidance,
and from navigating the bicultural worlds they face at home and in school.
When available, children establish informal support channels with close relatives and friends to meet not only their economic and caregiving needs but
also their emotional needs. Moreover, I find that the process of managing
and channeling emotions can vary depending on the class resources, social
networks, and gendered dynamics within the family. For example, children
whose mothers are better able to stretch their work and family caregiving

responsibilities are more likely to keep their emotional support systems closer to their immediate family members. The same goes for families that can afford to keep at least one parent or at least a member of the extended family at home. Conversely, children whose parents are overcommitted in terms of time and availability and have little access to extended kin or ethnic networks are more likely to cast their emotional nets more widely to peers and significant others.

Older siblings and cousins—especially those who are familiar with the language and culture and have closer relations with their parents and extended kin—were the most frequent source of emotional support and intergenerational mediation. Here is an excerpt from Kimberly, who played this role for her younger sister and her mother who was struggling to raise her two daughters on her own:

> My mom and my sister can't communicate, cause my sister's Chinese isn't really that great. So when I moved up here, they were forced to talk. I think that helped them with their gap. My mom would be like, your sister did this. Talk to your sister. And then I'll talk to my sister on the phone. So it's kinda like okay so whose kid is she? Is she yours or is she mine? That's just silly. But I think my mom just couldn't tell my sister and my sister wasn't really listening. My sister's one of those persons who's like okay whatever you say is fine, but is she really gonna do it? So I would just yell at her but I'm her sister at the end of the day. It's easier for her to talk to me but it's different.

By virtue of her ability to communicate with her sister, Kimberly became the parent figure in her sister's life yet she understood the limitations of her authority at the same time. This shows us how immigrant parents can rely on other family members for parenting help, but at the end of the day, this does not always compensate for a lack of parental communication and supervision. This is also true for children who lose a major source of support during the emotionally tumultuous years of high school or college as a result of major changes in their siblings' lives.

Although the majority of those interviewed were raised within the structure of a nuclear family, it was not uncommon to find families who turned to their extended kin to help take care of the children while their parents worked long hours. Grandparents especially helped to create a stable emotional environment for children otherwise bereft of social support and preserve the continuity of the family line by conveying cultural values through their storytelling. Kathy, who lived with her maternal grandmother throughout most of her childhood, remembered her fondly, especially since her grandmother nurtured and supported her and her siblings while her parents were busy arguing with one other.

> She was such an important figure in our lives. She taught us so many things and took care of us, and actually if we got sick, she'd be the first person we'd run to. We wouldn't go to either one of our parents. We'd be like grandma I'm sick. She was our primary caregiver actually. I think what it did was it allowed my parents to be selfish; they were caught up in their own drama. Because my grandmother was there, we weren't really drawn into it that much. We were just like kids and then if anything happened, we didn't have to think about whether or not mom or dad were approachable. We just went to grandma anyway, so for so many reasons, it was a real blessing having her there.

Kathy's grandmother passed away when she was nineteen, at a time when she had a lot going on in her life and needed someone to turn to. It would have helped her considerably if another relative had been around to help through this phase.

For this reason, emotional kinscripters can have a more profound and long-term impact on the social and psychological development of children when reinforced by a more expansive network of extended kin where they can channel their emotional needs. Sunny had a particularly difficult and emotionally volatile family life as a result of a mother who struggled with a severe gambling problem throughout her high school and college years and refused to let her reach out to her biological father whom her mother described as abusive. She had a stepfather whom she intimately referred to as her "father" but who ended up remarrying after the divorce. In the face of such adversity, however, Sunny was one of the more fortunate people I interviewed in terms of having an extensive kinship network to fall back on for different emotional needs. She told me how she turned to her maternal aunts whenever she wanted to talk about boys, marriage, and having children and to her academic uncle when she needed help with school. As the third oldest child in the family, she recognized her stature as a role model for her younger cousins and doled out advice to them whenever needed.

Above all, Sunny saw her maternal grandfather as being the emotional glue that really held them all together. As a child, she lived with her grandparents in Canada for a couple of years while her mother recovered from the first divorce. She continued to maintain a strong relationship with them by calling them every month and visiting them about four times a year in Canada. She related to me how her grandfather in particular acted as her strongest advocate in all matters related to her educational and career goals by providing advice, attending all of her graduations, and buying her a computer. Beyond reinforcing to her the importance of her extended family, her grandfather offered her the gift of a historical legacy:

> I do have a role model. It's my grandfather. He told me about his life and all the things he's done. He's a very smart man. He's very, very ambitious. I really admire everything he's done with his life. He talks to me about family, he talks to me about the things I need to worry about, things to look forward to. Recently he showed me our family book and it goes back like twenty-four generations, because my grandfather was the oldest of his own siblings. So I'm looking at the book, and he's showing where his generation is—all of his brothers and sisters and then the next generation, all of my grandfather's children. And only the sons of his son are listed in line and I'm not there, my sister's not there. I got very upset about that and my grandfather had to make me feel better, saying oh it's not that big a deal, we'll make our own book. It's very sweet, you know. But it was his way of trying to get me to understand, we've got this background, we've got this history and it's very important that we make sure that it goes on.

This is of course not to argue that extended kin and even grandparents could not also be the source of extreme conflict and tension, as I will discuss. But extended kin have the potential to offer one of the few stable ways of crossing cultural barriers, learning about family history, and carrying on the family legacy when their parents are busy working. Those who did not have the benefit of older siblings or loving grandparents and relatives who lived nearby also turned to friends and significant others as an important source of emotional companionship outside their family. However, because these nonkin relationships tended to be weaker and fluctuate over the life cycle, emotional dependency on nonfamily networks entailed greater risk and instability. In addition, these relationships rarely helped to bridge the generation gap and had the potential to turn into something more problematic if their emotions were entrusted to the wrong person. For example, heavy emotional reliance on romantic partners could lead to psychological codependency or trauma if they fell apart. Some interviewees also found themselves vulnerable to the temptations of drugs, youth gangs, and abuse as a result of their psychological codependency on delinquent peers and romantic partners.

On rare occasions, some Asian Americans considered their former housekeepers/nannies as their main caregivers in their parents' absence, but the degree of emotional attachment seemed to vary considerably. One interviewee whose mother had passed away and whose father had emotionally abandoned her with an abusive stepmother recalled trying to turn to one of the many housekeepers and nannies she was left with, but said that they were so financially (and legally) dependent on her parents that they did little to support her or intervene on her behalf. Others said they had fond relationships with their paid caregiver who raised them when they were younger but their employment with the family was often too temporary to lead to a lasting relationship. This is not to say that these support systems were not invaluable for second-generation Asian Americans, especially in the complete absence of family support, but it would be problematic to assume that domestic workers, friends, and romantic partners could provide adequate parental support.

At the same time, if ethnic communities or mainstream institutions provide a stable safety net, for example in the form of positive mentors and role models, then the risks of reaching out can be considerably minimized. For those few who were fortunate enough to be connected with their local ethnic communities as youth, the one area in which nonprofit organizations filled a glaring social and emotional need was in providing role models and mentors for young Asian Americans. Suzanne was one of the lucky few to find a Korean American female mentor through an after-school program at the Flushing YWCA in Queens. Her story shows the powerful impact that such figures can have, especially for second-generation Asian Americans who lack support and guidance at home.

> SUZANNE: The youth counselor who I'm still very good friends with, she invested a lot in me too. [She starts crying a little so I turn off the recorder.] It's because of her that I really got where I am [sobbing near the end].
>
> ANGIE: You okay?
>
> SUZANNE: I'm fine. [She laughs]. I don't know why I'm crying.
>
> ANGIE: Well sometimes you feel emotional when you have a role model or someone who inspires you when everything else is pretty rough. If I were to visualize that relationship you had with her, what would she do for you?
>
> SUZANNE: Back then I don't think I really understood her. I just thought she was a very demanding person. But later on, I moved on with my life, I realized she was a feminist and she really wanted to give back to her community and really invested in youth. I remember how I was visiting colleges after I had heard from the colleges, I went to this one college in Washington, D.C., and I went for this special minority student weekend for prospectives. So students who were accepted who were minorities were invited to come and there was like seven of us. The whole school was white and I was so shocked. Coming from New York I had never

left, I thought the whole country was this immigrant country. And I called her, because I was so surprised and she really had this talk with me, saying "You can't go to these places in this country and expect it to look like Flushing cause it's not gonna look like that." She wanted me to get out of Flushing and get out of New York and do something else with my life and I saw her as being very demanding where she would push me to apply for this scholarship, apply to this school, go to this workshop on Saturday. But at the same time, she was encouraging me because she tried to get the Korean out of me. If I were saying something like "I'm sorry but can you write me a recommendation?" "If you're going to feel sorry, then don't ask me. You should be demanding these things." With a lot of Korean girls, there's a lack of self-confidence, just because you're going through adolescence, Korean boys can be very nasty, especially in their high school years and your family doesn't really help. So she was a very big advocate about being a strong Korean woman.

In a similar vein, Mia, a thirty-year-old Chinese American who lived in Chinatown until she was fourteen, related to me her feeling of social isolation all throughout high school until she came across the Committee of 100, a nonprofit, nonpartisan organization of distinguished Chinese American leaders providing a political perspective on issues in the United States and abroad. She derived great emotional satisfaction from the experience of mentoring and providing academic guidance to children who were going through the same identity crises she did when she was younger, and her activities later inspired her deeper involvement with other nonprofit organizations.

Conclusion

The narratives of second-generation Korean and Chinese American adults challenge the model minority view of Asian immigrant families as models of social order, emotional stability, and internal cohesiveness. In their memories, pressures associated with immigration and adaptation, cultural and linguistic barriers to verbal communication, and shifting power dynamics between spouses and parent and child clearly impacted their childhood experiences, relationships, and support systems. The chapter has revealed how second-generation adults attempted to emotionally navigate and connect with their parents lives even without the benefit of historical knowledge or cultural understanding. Participants devised new ways of addressing their emotional and social needs through strategies such as channeling their emotions to other support networks and establishing new modes of empathy and communication with their parents based on family roles. The chapter has shown that those who are well connected with extended kin, older sibling mediators, and ethnic organizations within the community had an easier time with this transition than others. The outcome of this emotion work depends on the different resources and networks that second-generation Korean and Chinese Americans and their families can mobilize.

This is of course not to claim that the volatile environment did not have painful effects and emotional burdens that carried over into their personal decisions on culture, marriage, and family that I discuss throughout the book. However, the assumption that such disjunctures and constraints automatically lead to a social disengagement from their family and culture obfuscates the complex, contradictory, and fluid ways second-generation Asian Americans are able to work out their emotional and social needs especially as adults. By acknowledging the different ways in which emotion work plays out in American and East Asian cultures, the chapter has shown that it is possible to create and sustain emotional parent-child relationships that involve a communal, historical, and sacrificial way of showing love—one that is difficult to articulate in terms of the Western binary approach to love and emotion. The next chapter delves further into the way that differences in household structures and children's roles within the family can refract the lens through which second-generation Asian Americans ultimately view their ethnic identities.

CHAPTER 4

Children as Family Caregivers

One of the main criticisms of the model minority myth is its failure to factor in the extra human capital and intensive labor that Asians must invest in order to match the educational attainment and incomes of native-born white Americans. Hurh and Kim show that Asian Americans may have a higher income level on average than white Americans, but the individual earnings ratio is much lower when one factors in their educational background, longer working hours, higher number of working household members, lower occupational prestige, and regional concentration in urban areas with higher living costs.[1] This chapter discusses how the path to mobility also entails significant emotional costs. The Asian immigrant family myth oftentimes masks the immense social burdens and emotional investment assumed by different family members in order to preserve this outward semblance of social integrity and order. Moreover, parents and adult kin are not the only ones responsible for helping to maintain the economic and emotional stability of Asian families. Depending on their geographic location, class resources, and access to kinship networks, some immigrant families are also forced to rely on their children to assume adult responsibilities and maintain household order in their parents' absence.

As opposed to portraying children as passive recipients or mere outcomes in the immigrant success/failure story, more studies are finding that children can also be active participants in the processes of adaptation and assimilation by facilitating their family's access to community resources and mainstream institutions.[2] In fact, children have been brokering for their families since the dawn of immigration. However, heightened economic competitiveness and inequality on both national and global scales have added more strain on working parents and caused many to separate from their families in order to seek educational and work opportunities abroad. As fewer governmental institutions provide support for immigrant families and more restrictive immigration laws are put into place, immigrants are increasingly relying on their children's labor at work and in the home. Over the past few decades, Asian American and Latino children in particular have been increasingly likely to have two working parents or live in families split across national borders, which means that they have less time to spend with their parents and have no parental supervision after school.[3]

Depending on their family situations, some children are raised as "latchkey children," who take care of their own day-to-day needs with very little adult supervision as a result of their parents working long hours or separation overseas. Other children of immigrants assume adult responsibilities in regard to family-related matters and can exercise a measured degree of power and autonomy in relation to their parents, because of their greater familiarity with the English language and American culture, educational advantages, and increased responsibilities within the household. These children are often called on to act as translators for their parents, mediators and advocates in outside disputes, surrogate nannies and tutors for their younger siblings, and financial consultants and contributors to the household and family business.[4] Depending on their family situation, they may act as cultural brokers for their parents, sibling, and extended kin, thus guiding the integration of their families into mainstream society. The peculiar strains of this burdensome migration experience can weaken the unquestioned authority of parent over child and introduce more psychological stress into their day-to-day lives.[5]

The increasing accessibility of transportation and telecommunications may help to bridge some of the physical distance, but studies by Dreby and Parrenas on transnationally split families find that such technological substitutes provide minimal emotional reassurance and social support for children facing the typical pressures of adolescence and dual identity conflicts, in addition to the demands of adult responsibilities.[6] Moreover, as I have discussed, the cultural construction of love and affection around physical intimacy and verbal communication highlights to them the stark contrast between the lives of their immigrant families from those of their American peers. This psychological disconnect in families that face time and financial constraints is expected to condition their understanding of ethnicity and family culture in distinctive ways. This chapter takes a closer look at how children negotiate the emotional context surrounding their different social roles within the family and how this frames the way they process and understand ethnicity as they enter adulthood.

Negotiating Emotion through Family Roles

The narratives elaborate on three ideal-type family roles that youth in immigrant families assume depending on class-based constraints, gendered patterns of socialization, birth order, and different household structures. These include (1) cultural brokers, those who play an active role in taking care of their families through adult responsibilities at home; (2) familial dependents, those who rely on parents for financial, emotional, and other support within traditional East Asian immigrant family structures; and (3) autonomous caretakers, those who raised themselves with minimal parental involvement because of absentee, negligent, or working parents.

Instead of reifying the diverse and complex experiences of children of immigrants as mutually exclusive categories, these different family roles are presented as ideal types that mark the varying degrees to which second-generation Asian Americans emotionally and socially engage with their parents as youth as a result of their assigned family responsibilities. Along this wide-ranging continuum, those whom I identified as cultural brokers are the most active participants in supporting their family and helping their parents to navigate mainstream society, while on the opposite end, autonomous care-takers are relatively disengaged from their parents for various reasons;[7] those I classified as cultural dependents occupy the center of this continuum because they emotionally rely on parents for most caregiving functions but are culturally distanced by this hierarchical relationship.

How children are socialized into these family roles depends on a number of factors, including their age, their birth order, the family's class status, culture, and gender norms. Working-class or dual-wage-earning families that lack the type of resources and networks to adopt alternative caregiving arrangements are more likely than other families to rely on their children for support.[8] Small labor-intensive family businesses in particular depend heavily on the unpaid labor of wives and children.[9] However, middle-class families from modern cities throughout Asia are also being forced to adapt to the exigencies of economic globalization. As ability in English and international education become important criteria for upward mobility, even middle-class families from newly industrialized countries such as Korea and Taiwan are taking advantage of their financial resources and networks to send their children to the United States under the care of relatives or minimal supervision altogether.[10] These arrangements can increase educational opportunities for youth but also strain parent-child relations and encourage delinquent behavior.

An individual's position within the family hierarchy also has bearing on the type of relationship nurtured between parent and child. Within families, daughters and the first child tend to be the ones responsible for financial management, brokering, and caregiving roles in their parents' absence in accordance with traditional gender expectations. At the same time, the chapter shows how children can also exert agency by reinterpreting and negotiating their roles and responsibilities despite the many pressures they face. This means that siblings within the same family household may assume different roles and responsibilities, which shapes their ethnic worldviews in different ways. For instance, younger familial dependents may have older sisters who brokered for their family. Moreover, the types of family responsibilities children of immigrants take may shift across the lifetime as the social circumstances surrounding these roles change or the individual begins to assert his or her own will in response to parental expectations. For example, a family may experience a significant improvement or deterioration in their socioeconomic situation or a brother who formerly assumed household responsibilities may pass on those duties once a younger sister is old enough to take over. As these children enter adulthood, they may reevaluate and reformulate their identity in relationship to their families and gain a certain degree of freedom from past obligations and expectations.

Nevertheless, I find that as they retrospectively reflected upon their childhoods, participants tended to emphasize responsibilities associated with one "master role" that laid the foundations for their relationship with their parents throughout most of their childhood. Oftentimes, this master role took shape during the most formative years of their childhood and their educational socialization between elementary school through high school. Furthermore, the way Korean and Chinese Americans perceived their assigned family roles during these formative years often carried on through adulthood perhaps in modified forms unless of course there was a major life change, such as the sudden illness of a parent that required extensive care or the introduction of a stepparent. For example, those who acted as cultural brokers for their families during their adolescent years continued to help their families with bills, mediate internal disputes, and keep in touch with parents when they got older. When participants' family roles alternated between two or more categories throughout the life cycle, I based their family role on the main family responsibilities and parent-child relationships that seemed to dominate their past and present narratives.

Cultural Brokers

Recent scholarship on Asian and Latino immigrant families has been paying more attention to how children are helping their immigrant parents support the family and navigate the host society through their roles as translators, brokers, laborers, and surrogate adults at home.[11] Those individuals I refer to as "cultural brokers" tend to be deeply involved with and well-integrated into the family structure because of their intermediary role between the family and outside institutions and their responsibility as family caregivers. In contrast to the deep sense of alienation and displacement expressed by autonomous caretakers, participants in this category are actively involved in assisting both parents and children in the family in numerous capacities—whether or not this role is assumed willingly or unwillingly as youth. As a result, they are as much dependent on their parents as their parents are on them—a relationship that may at times shift the balance of power between parent and child or even subvert traditional gender roles.

In the study, participants from working-class households were most likely to take on cultural brokering responsibilities, because financial hardship, lack of English proficiency, and limited support networks offered them fewer alternative caregiving options and forced their families to transfer adult responsibilities and burdens onto their children as soon as they came of age. However, some participants who grew up in middle- and upper-class families also reported having to broker, work, or assume caregiving duties for their families as children, because both their parents worked long hours or lived apart from their children, as in the case of "astronaut" or "wild geese" families. Children raised in astronaut families (common among the Taiwanese) are sent to the United States for schooling either on their own or under the care of relatives or paid caregivers, while their parents shuttle back and forth between the United States and Asia to manage their transnational businesses.[12] Most commonly found among affluent Koreans, wild geese families are transnationally split households where the mother migrates with the children for the purposes of education, while the father stays behind in the homeland to support the family financially.[13] In addition, families facing legal restrictions as a result of temporary visas or no documentation are also pushed to migrate in different stages and may thus depend heavily on their children to fill the role of the missing parent.

Immigrant parents also designate these responsibilities to different siblings based on cultural traditions and family constraints. Within the family, daughters and oldest siblings are expected to assume brokering responsibilities, because of Chinese and Korean cultural values that delegate caregiving roles based on gender and birth order. Daughters are the most likely to broker for their families, because these responsibilities are often consistent with traditional gender norms on care work and household labor. Because of their older age and active involvement in family affairs, firstborn children are more likely to have witnessed their parents' hardships during the early stages of immigrant settlement than their siblings, which in turn reaffirms a sense of empathy for their parents' struggles.

Suzanne, the third child of four, felt that her current life was significantly shaped by her felt obligation and empathy for her immigrant parents. As a child, she spent many hours helping out at the family business and taking care of her younger siblings when her parents were busy working. Living apart from her family later in life allowed her to reflect on how much her family meant to her in her day-to-day life and to interpret their struggles as immigrants from a new perspective.

> My father was getting violation penalties from inspectors that would come to inspect the store and he felt that they were outrageous. So then I would have to go and represent him at the Department of Consumer Affairs to either lessen the fine or fight it. I would go in front of a judge and have to kind of plead our case with the inspector there and I'm like fourteen. [short laugh] I wasn't happy to do it so I did everything grudgingly. [Now,] I don't know if they understand me, but I think I understand them a lot more. Living away made me think about how they grew up. It made me have a new kind of respect for them to see what they came from and why they live the way they do. [starts to cry]

Suzanne's desire to uncover the mysteries of her parents' lives became a stepping stone for a broader intellectual curiosity about how their experiences related to poor Koreans in other countries like Russia where she spent time on a Fulbright. The daily struggles of brokering for her family also helped her to relate better with other Korean Americans. Throughout most of her life, her romantic partners and close friendship circles have primarily consisted of other Korean Americans. She explained,

> A lot of my Korean friends, all of our parents were storeowners or worked in certain sectors like nail salons or green groceries or dry cleaning. And just sharing those experiences of having to go and work there and also having the burden of taking care of the house and being a student but at the same time, being the caretaker for your siblings and for your household, because your parents aren't available to do that. I think it also has to do with being able to talk to your friends about everyday things that perhaps a white American student won't understand, and inviting people over to your home is more comfortable if your lifestyle is similar.

In this passage, it is interesting to note that while Suzanne's struggles might parallel those of other working-class immigrant children, she herself felt that it was the similarities in lifestyle that allowed her to bond with other working-class Korean Americans who brokered for their families. She went on to say that her struggles at home inspired her to act as a cultural broker for other young girls like herself by starting up a mentoring workshop for young Asian American girls. As she stated, "I have this personal conviction that if you come from those kind of experiences and you've moved up, you should do something to give back."

Themes of sacrifice, empathy, and obligation also resonated throughout the narratives of others in similar situations. Although there were periods when she rarely saw her parents because of their long work hours, Stacey, the second child but oldest daughter of four, clearly assumed the role of cultural brokering in her family because she took on a lot of household, caregiving, and translator responsibilities and worked at her parents' restaurant throughout most of her life. She established her independence by financing part of her college education and then moving out of the house, because she felt she needed her own space to live out her curtailed adolescence and also felt "guilty not spending every moment I had helping them." Stacey has only vague memories of sneaking across the U.S.-Canada border as a child, unlike her older brother whose felt experience as an undocumented adolescent she feels clearly affected his ability to make friends out of fear of being caught. However, this distant memory was interwoven throughout her own stories about parental sacrifice and personal guilt:

> So I did have a memory of us crossing the border from Canada. I just knew we were in the mountains and we were kind of crouched down and there was a highway below and hushing. I always thought that was probably just me having daydreams and it never occurred to me that we were doing something that we weren't supposed to be doing. As a child, it was hard for me to grasp the concept of respecting your elders and appreciative of all they've given up for us. But as we grew older, it clicked with me more. I understood what it was that they did and the whole thing about them having snuck over [illegally]. My family started off undocumented, unable to take risks, less money, had to work menial jobs to get the little cash they could, and because of that, they weren't able to watch us, relate to us, understand us. I understood how hard that must've been for them to leave the whole life behind and come over and that made me want to connect with them more. And that's not necessarily an American way.

Her circle of friends and serious relationships have been mostly Chinese American, because in her words, "I could relate to them more [because they had] immigrant parents. I could vent like, oh, my parents made me do this today, or I can't believe my parents don't understand this. And I think that was important to me that I was able to talk about my background or my childhood with them." This particular interviewee feels bonded to her brokering friends, because of the unusual ethnic- and class-based stresses they all faced in dealing with their parents and holding the household together as youth.

Stacey told me that she had a hard time getting through to her parents when she was younger because they did not speak a common language, but things changed as she got older. Because her Cantonese is rudimentary, she made an extra effort to communicate with her parents by developing her language skills through Chinese language courses, making occasional visits to Hong Kong, and carrying around a Chinese-English dictionary. In general, she said she "tried harder to not have this attitude like they're completely foreign to me" and "explain to them things about my life without going into much detail." Married to another Chinese American and mother of two children, Stacey continues to act as a cultural broker in her own household by cultivating languages, traditions, and culture that will allow the family to communicate and bond across generational lines. She continuously tries to get back in touch with her parents' cultural roots by sending her kids to Chinese language school and speaking Cantonese with her family on "Chinese Mondays." When I asked why she felt this was important to maintain, she responded that she did not want her son, who was very close to his paternal grandfather, to lose that family bond she never had with her own extended family. It is clear that Stacey's approach to ethnicity centers on ideals of personal sacrifice, family bonding, and communication.

Another good example of cultural brokering comes from Mark, the Chinese American who migrated with his family from the Philippines at the age of three. Although female brokers are more common than male brokers, Mark was responsible for taking care of both household chores and parental caregiving responsibilities, because his sister was too young at the time. In this way, his responsibilities at home pushed him to cross traditional gender divides and determined his place within the family. As both the cultural broker and oldest son, Mark has noticed how his parents now turn to him for advice on major family decisions and he finds that this role encapsulates his general outlook on life—one that he considers "Chinese in the sense of saving face or basing your decision on money versus desire."

In her study on Korean and Vietnamese American children, Pyke found that eldest siblings tend to adopt a more traditional outlook on family obligations and cultural traditions, because of differences in parental expectations about each sibling's roles.[14] However, Mark also made the interesting observation that he feels more emotionally attached to his parent's culture than his younger sister because he directly witnessed the hardships of his parents during the early years of their immigration, whereas his sister grew up during a more comfortable phase in their lives.

> When she was firstborn, it was always like a running joke. People meet her for the first time, and they're like, "Oh, she's the American in the family" cause she was born here. And obviously my experience was [seeing] my whole parents' transitioning as immigrants, right? I experienced firsthand how my parents had to take different shift jobs when they first immigrated in order for us to survive. My dad would bring me to the train station and tag, you're it. My mom takes me at the train station and then my dad goes to the night job so my mom can watch me at home. My sister was too young to remember any of it, and by the time she was old enough to remember anything, we already had a decent place to live, my parents had decent jobs, so she got used to this comfortable lifestyle.

Mark also noticed that as she grew older, his sister began to follow his lead: "Recently she got a nice paycheck and volunteered to help with the family bills and she's starting to acknowledge the Chinese factor. So that's kinda neat for me to see like wow, teaching by example does help sometimes." Because they understand both cultures, participants in this category are in a powerful position to mediate family discord and help convey their parents' heritage and values to their younger siblings.

Mark is quite proficient in Hokkien, and most of his closest friends and romantic partners are Asian Americans. In fact, he does not think it is a coincidence that he has a very close friendship with six Chinese Americans, all of whom happen to be the oldest sons in the family. He explained, "We all come from similar situations where we have to look out for the family for some reason or another. All of us being the oldest sons, it definitely is a factor. It's like that comfort level I was talking to you about: you just understand certain things. They will never question why I paid my sister's tuition. Other people would, but for them, it's like okay, think nothing else of it." This sense of family-oriented cultural connectedness closely resonates with that of Suzanne, underlining how intense obligations and responsibilities to the family like those of cultural brokers can also strengthen relationships with coethnic peers who assume similar family roles.

One might assume that very negative relationships with one parent would be enough to undermine respect for the family culture, but Kimberly, a twenty-nine-year-old Chinese-Taiwanese American from Maryland, was pushed to take on a protective caregiving role for her mother and younger sister when her father's physical abuse began to escalate at home. She was the one to encourage her mother to leave, help her find government assistance, raise her younger sister, and take care of household affairs when things got tough. Although she acknowledged what she calls the "ugly side of being an Asian family," she also found that it was the strong bond that held the remaining members of the family together during the hard times that enabled them to overcome the trauma of spousal abuse. In the following passage, she related to me how she took charge in helping her mom to escape the abuse:

> What happened was they had a bad fight. So my mom and I woke up and my mom was telling me, what should we do? So I told my mom, well I'll call the cops and figure out what to do. They told me to go to this Crisis Center and then we went there until we figured out what we were going to do next. I'm sure inside [my mom] did wanna leave. But as a woman who doesn't speak English—and at the time she wasn't really working anymore—how is she gonna get through and take care of two kids? I'm sure she was just scared. She doesn't know what government help to get so I was able to help her. Again in that sense, I had to grow faster than normal kids. My mom sacrificed for both of us, my little sister and me. She told me stuff like when she was younger and I was a baby, she would want to commit suicide just because she just couldn't live like this anymore, but then she realized she had me. As a woman, I guess I can relate to my mother, the struggle that she had to go through.

As suggested, Kimberly's unstated bond to her family centers on her mother's trials and tribulations, not only as an immigrant but as a woman. She continues to hold her family together by acting as an interpreter and a mediator between her mom and her younger sister, who have trouble communicating with one another.

She believes that only other Chinese friends and boyfriends can truly understand the kind of brokering role she has taken on in her household as a result.

> KIMBERLY: When I was looking for boyfriends, having somebody that was Chinese felt important to me.
>
> ANGIE: Why is that?
>
> KIMBERLY: So they can understand where I'm coming from, like my mother, my Chinese values. I don't have to tell them why I have to call everyday or why my mom is acting this way or why do I have to take care of my sister and why do I worry about this or that. At least with somebody who's Chinese they could understand, "Okay, all right. I understand. You have to do what you have to do." Maybe they can help me too.

Interestingly, the theme of silent communication with other Asian Americans (e.g., not having to explain family obligations) is something that emerges repeatedly in the accounts of those with close family ties. Kimberly went on to say that in college she related to the values of parachute kids—or Taiwanese-born children sent off to study in the United States on their own or under the supervision of alternative caregivers—more so than more Americanized kids because of this special role she played at home.

Even if children transition out of this brokering phase, the different members of such transitioning households teach each other to cultivate a sense of family built on caregiving and sacrifice for the other siblings when the parents are away. For instance, Elliott, a thirty-four-year-old Chinese American lifetime New York resident, explained how he was raised mainly by his second oldest sister and his grandmother whenever both his parents were working long hours, but he also took on a few housekeeping and translating duties, as he reached high school age. He said that his sister became the maternal figure he and his siblings came to emulate as they grew older: "She was definitely the mother figure. I don't think she had a lot of ability to discipline us, aside from telling our mom what we did, but in many ways, she watched over us and fed us and sometimes I do say that she kinda raised me as well. And she was definitely a role model. There was always that expectation, like oh Margaret was a really good student so there's an expectation that you'll be a good student as well." As they grew older, Elliott found that his sister became the authoritative "matriarch" of the family in terms of caring for the siblings, monitoring their behavior, and doing household chores, while he became the "flag bearer" in terms of assisting with translating, paying bills, and organizing family events. In this passage, he explains how their family's lives were integrated through their complementary roles:

ANGIE: So what do you talk to them about?

ELLIOTT: Everything from idle chit-chat to some family events going on. With three siblings and parents, there's usually something. It's someone's birthday, my nephew's birthdays, Mother's Day, Father's Day, Christmas, Thanksgiving, so usually there's some sort of coordinate around that. Sometimes it's talking about the parents, like oh we need to plan for their retirement so we talk about that. Or they want to transition the title of the house to one of us.

ANGIE: And do all of the siblings pretty much do that, like they contribute?

ELLIOTT: I'd say it's mostly between [the oldest sister] and myself. So usually it's between [the oldest sister] and myself, in terms of watching out for the parents and planning things out. We call on [the younger sisters] as more of a support resource, like oh, you need to chip in for our Mother's Day present or can you make this dinner date.

This division of caregiving labor demonstrates some of the complex gendered ways cultural brokering can play out and shift over time in these types of families.

In one rare instance, Amy, a cultural broker from a middle-class Chinese immigrant family, recalled how one day she blew up at her parents for giving her brother preferential treatment because her father physically beat them throughout their childhood but rarely laid a hand on her brother. Although this did not change how they punished her brother, she noticed that afterward her parents shifted some of her brokering responsibilities such as household chores and translation work over to him. Of course, by then she and her sister had moved out of the house, so he had fewer caregiving responsibilities, but she feels that today he is expected to fulfill just as many obligations to the family as she does.

Familial Dependents

Representing the most conventional track out of the three ideal types, individuals categorized as "familial dependents" are raised in a traditional heteronormative family structure where parents assume adult roles and responsibilities both at work and in the home and can fulfill caregiving responsibilities for underage dependents within the family. I include in this category children who are raised by surrogate parents, such as relatives and much older adult siblings, who can both provide for the children's daily needs and convey to them the value of their parents' ancestral heritage. As dependents within traditional Korean or Chinese family hierarchies, these children are expected to receive care, support, and guidance from their elders in return for their piety, obedience, and obligation. Parents cultivate these relationships of dependency not only by offering regular guidance and supervision, but also by reinforcing gendered norms and expectations about the proper role of sons and daughters in the family. However, these ideals do not always play out in reality: pressuring American-born children into embracing some of the more traditional aspects of Korean or Chinese culture without the proper communication channels can often lead to bitter conflicts between parent and child.

Given the means, most immigrant parents would prefer to be physically present to care for their children, as opposed to saddling them with adult responsibilities at an early age. Thus, my interviews reveal that even working-class families try to accommodate to this type of household structure by pushing women to juggle mothering roles on top of their wage-earning responsibilities or bringing in a close relative during times of extreme financial hardship. In fact, in both traditional Korean and Chinese households, it is not unusual for children to be financially dependent on or live together with their parents until they are married. I found this to be the case for not only working-class participants in the study but also dependents from affluent families, given the relatively high cost of living in the New York–New Jersey metropolitan area,[15] the cultural acceptability of this practice, and, more recently, the economic recession. Nevertheless, it should not be surprising that households that have the financial means or extended kinship networks to provide stable caregiving arrangements are better able to sustain traditional parent-child relationships. Whether this means forgoing the wages of one parent or finding a surrogate provider, middle- or upper-income families can afford the cost of letting their children remain dependents instead of contributing to the family's productive or reproductive labor.

Given that family role is structured around one's rank within the family, dependents who appreciate their ethnic heritage tend to do so within the framework of filial piety and family hierarchy. Grace, a thirty-four-year-old Korean American attorney who grew up in a middle-class religious family in the South, described her parents as very "conservative" and "traditional" in terms of their core values on family, religion, filial piety, and education, among other things; however, she was also quick to note that her family incorporated American values and traditions into their day-to-day lives in terms of celebrating American holidays or expressing their emotions through words or hugs "in an American way." What is important however is not so much how traditional or "American" her immigrant parents were, but the way they were able to blend these cultures to create a picture of marriage, family, and tradition that she wanted to emulate in her own life.

> My parents are so great together [and] are both really strong role models. My dad was very loving but very strict. I feel like I'm my dad's favorite, not intentionally but like I'm his firstborn and I'm the most like my dad. And for that reason, I always wanted a guy like my dad and [my husband] is exactly like my dad. [short laugh] Even though [my husband] is not fluent, he understands the culture cause most of his friends are Korean. I don't have to explain things. We think alike, because of the fact that we share that culture. For example, my brother brought home this girl. She was extremely rude to my parents, and we were both like that's a deal-breaker, because how can you disrespect your boyfriend's parents. That's just not acceptable.

It was clear throughout the interview that she viewed respect, tradition, and role modeling as integral aspects of her family's culture. To this day, she regularly flies down to visit her natal family with her husband and now two young children. Although she has trouble maintaining the language regularly with her husband at home, she sends both her children to a Korean preschool in New Jersey, because she finds it important they are exposed to the language and customs of her parents' culture so they can build on these relationships in the future.

Grace values her role as the oldest sister in both her family and among her extended kin and tries to re-create these filial relationships in her own way. She explained, "I'm kind of like an older sister to my little cousins. I still check up on them, make sure they're doing well in their schools, on their SATs. I make all my cousins accountable for their little brothers and sisters, you know? I mother them too in that way." In her case, maintaining her ethnic roots means preserving aspects of her parents' cultural heritage and religious values in traditional ways, whether it be socializing primarily with Koreans, maintaining her proficiency in Korean, attending Korean church, or acting as a role model for her siblings and cousins. As a result, her role as oldest sister becomes not a marker of deficiency and inferiority with her family context, but rather a source of empowerment, even if in a gendered manner.

As I noted earlier, however, the main problem for dependents is whether or not they can reconcile the many cultural differences that separates them from their parents. Traditional family values and a two-parent family structure may lay the groundwork for improved intergenerational relations, but the interviews suggest that more important, children of immigrants raised in this type of household must be able to find a stable emotional place within the family that makes sense within their Americanized frame of reference— sometimes with the help of outside mediating groups such as extended kin, ethnic churches, or student associations.

Charles, a thirty-five-year-old resident of Fort Lee, a Korean American suburb in New Jersey, was raised the youngest and only son in a divorced household as a familial dependent but reported a relatively strong relationship with his mother and his older siblings, who played a protective role throughout his school years. He recalled that "when I was growing up, I never really had a problem with discrimination because actually my brother had a big name in the neighborhood and even my sister, she had a reputation in the neighborhood of being tough." He took pride in the fact that in contrast to most modern American families, his natal family represented to him the strong heteronormative ideal "where the father is the father, mother is the mother"—a "strong institution" that he planned to "emulate when I have my own children and my own wife." His occupation and community work involve regular contact with Korean immigrant and Korean American mentors in both New York and New Jersey, who have "helped him to become a better mentor and father for his son"—in essence, reaffirming the traditional family order. He is active in Korean American organizations, makes regular trips to Korea, speaks conversational Korean, and has had close friends and romantic partners who are mostly Korean American. At the time of the study, he had been earnestly seeking to fulfill his mother's wish for him to marry the "right" Korean woman, and I later discovered he ended up marrying such a woman and having two sons. Charles repeatedly emphasized the importance of Korean culture in reaffirming these middle-class heteronormative family values throughout the interview.

In contrast, those individuals who have difficulties adapting to such hierarchical relationships may seek ways to liberate themselves from the family roles within which they feel they have been pigeonholed, even as they convey a measured degree of respect for their parent's lives but from an emotional distance. Two such Korean Americans I interviewed, Young and Jinah, expressed an inability to connect emotionally with their parents because of the burdens associated with their different positions within the family hierarchy. As a youth, Jinah, a thirty-year-old Korean American, found it difficult to carve out a secure social role and emotional niche within a family disconnected from extended kin and heavily invested in the only boy in the family, her younger brother. Unlike Grace, the fact that she was a daughter was used not as a title of honor and respect but rather as a justification for unequal treatment by her parents who lavished most of their attention on her younger brother. As a result, she made it a point to establish her independence from her parents both emotionally and financially as soon as she left college. She was eventually able to prove her worth to her family by going to a top Ivy League college and entering a lucrative profession, but by then she had established her own identity.

Her parents, like Grace's, actively got her involved in the Korean church when she was young and were quite embedded in the local ethnic community, but Jinah greatly valued her autonomy from her parents, whose views and traditions she did not quite understand and seemed parochial to her in many ways. Her case underlines the fact that mere exposure to ethnic-based communities and institutions is not enough to cultivate a strong sense of ethnic identification among the second generation if it cannot mediate the cultural gap between parent and child. She stated simply, "I don't have anything really unpleasant [memories] other than I wanted them to be more Americanized. I always wanted them to speak English better and I didn't want them to be different. They're in their own diaspora, they were hanging out with their own crowd, they made their own world and now I realize it's fine, everyone has their own tradition. I relate more as an individual, as opposed to a community." In college, Jinah disassociated herself from other Koreans because the way they kept to their own seemed "un-American" and even wanted to be blonde-haired and blue-eyed like her white American friends. Over time, Jinah has been able to come to terms with the conflicts she had with her family by interpreting her parents' success through a cosmopolitan American lens. However, this reinterpretation does not so much create a sense of belonging for her within the family culture, but rather it helps her to emotionally reconcile this conflictual relationship by interpreting her parents' background with her own American values. She firmly stated, "My parents immigrated from Korea with nothing, they brought up this great business, they gave their kids everything. I didn't come from a lot of money, I didn't come from a castle, and I'm really proud of it. And I love saying that I'm American. My parents are the American Dream and I'm sort of perpetuating that legacy, so it's important for me." Jinah's pride in her parents centers on their ability to achieve the "American Dream," which gives her a sense of identity and importance among her peers. Her identity as a "cosmopolitan American" meshes well with this interpretation of her parents' struggles.

Young on the other hand feels a similar emotional disconnect, not for lack of attention from his parents, but rather the overbearing focus on his privileged role and the resulting expectations that come with being the only son in both the immediate and extended families. Also proclaiming to be "American" more so than "Korean American," Young explained to me how the pressures of being the only "male heir" among his female siblings and cousins made him rebel by dating non-Korean women and physically distancing himself from his overprotective parents. Although he spoke relatively fluent Korean, he said that he did not make an effort to call his parents or visit them as often as did his sisters.

> ANGIE: It's kind of ironic that even though they place more emphasis on you as the "golden child" of the family that you're still more independent than your sisters from the family. Can you explain that in any sense?
>
> YOUNG: I think to some degree it's me rebelling against that notion. So you know ideally my parents would love for me to have to marry a Korean woman and have Korean kids and so on. But I just never really subscribed to those notions that much. It's not so much I'm anti–marrying a Korean woman, but I think it's just I'll marry whoever I want to marry.

Instead, Young shows his gratitude for their sacrifices through more impersonal financial contributions. He said he purchased them a retirement house and also created a "retirement nest egg" for his parents, but concluded "that's primarily the biggest way I support them. I don't really call them. I mean I love my parents but I quickly run out of things to talk to them about."

At the same time, the one subtle yet significant emotive connection Young intimated during the interview was his admiration for his father, with whom he said he had even a more distant relationship than he did with his mother. Young expressed measured pride in his father, whose astonishing ascent from war and poverty to graduating college at the top of his class inspired Young to follow in his footsteps. He told me, "My father's very much a 'pull-yourself-up-by-the-bootstraps' kind of guy. So I sort of inherited those characteristics. So there's this intrinsic need for me to kind of earn my keep." Like Jinah's, Young's narrative focuses heavily on maintaining independence from both his family and their culture, while holding onto select values that do not infringe upon his Americanized ideals of individuality, diversity, and freedom. However, it is interesting to note that this narrative resonates with him only because it fits well with his personal belief in American ideals of meritocracy.

Of course, interest in culture and ethnicity can substantially change when the emotional environment or an individual's positioning within the family shifts. One of the most interesting and moving conversations I had about this type of identity shift was with Cecilia, a twenty-seven-year-old woman who describes her parents as second-generation Chinese from Taiwan. She had discovered my recruitment ad on Craigslist while trying to find an opportunity to volunteer with a Chinese organization as a result of her newly emerging interest in her parents' cultural heritage. She explained to me the context of her personal journey, which began with deep shame and aversion toward her Chinese background because she was racially harassed by her white peers in her small hometown in New Jersey and suffered physical abuse at the hands of her mother—a type of disciplining that she came to associate with Chinese families and culture. She explains "back then, I didn't want to have anything to do with being Chinese, I hated it" and dated only white men and socialized mostly with white friends for her entire life.

However, Cecilia's life dramatically changed after her parents got divorced during her teenage years and she made the decision to live with her father and Taiwanese stepmother. Unlike her biological parents, she views her stepmother, who is a retired university professor from Taiwan, as a very warm and emotionally affectionate figure in her life, who knows how to bridge the deep cultural gap she has long felt between her and her parents' culture. She lovingly describes the long conversations she will have with her stepmother about how Chinese people would view Cecilia's workplace experiences from their cultural perspective. In this excerpt, Cecilia gives an example of how her stepmother's mediation also helped her and her younger brother to understand and emotionally process small cultural conflicts with her father:

> My father when in disagreement with my brother about how he should take a picture said, no, no, not that, you shouldn't do that, you shouldn't put that picture there, and you should really just concentrate on this, you silly boy! And of course, my brother would be like what? Again this is where my stepmother is giving perspective but she said that my father is in the culture of a more traditional Chinese family. My dad meant that affectionately in Chinese. She said that in older Chinese families in the ancient times, a man in a house would speak down at the children not in a demeaning way but perhaps in an affectionate way, which I never knew but I could appreciate that. My brother of course was getting frustrated, because every time he would take a picture that my dad would say you silly boy! [short laugh] So we turned around and we're like you silly father! (ha) But if it wasn't for my stepmother, I think a lot of things that my dad would say would be taken out of context. My stepmother would kind of step in and explain.

Although she cognitively understands that traditional Chinese parents express their love through action, the only way she can bridge the emotional gap with her family culture is to have a cultural mediator express and communicate her love the American way. Interestingly, Cecilia also makes a clear distinction between her father's cultural values, which she associates with "ancient China," and her stepmother's more modern outlook as a Taiwanese professor. Driven by her desire to connect with her family culture, Cecilia says she is making every effort to learn more about her ethnocultural background but says she is not quite sure where this journey will lead her. One of the personal conflicts she was experiencing at the time of the interview was how to introduce her white boyfriend whom she had dated for four years to her father and stepmother, especially knowing that they strongly prefer that she marry someone Chinese. She was also concerned how bringing him to family gatherings would be very awkward and disruptive to her desire for close kinship ties since everyone at these gatherings speaks in Chinese.

Autonomous Caretakers

The children whom I refer to as "autonomous caretakers" are forced to care for not only household matters but also themselves because both parents are working long hours or are otherwise absent or negligent. These children usually have weaker emotional relationships with their parents, because their parents are rarely around to sustain a basic parent-child relationship or have some psychological/physical problem that impedes on developing a healthy relationship with their children (e.g., mental illness, physical/emotional abuse, substance abuse addictions, and gambling problems). Most research that has focused on these so-called latchkey children—that is, children who stay at home without adult supervision—often conflate or overlook the differences between autonomous caretakers and cultural brokers. However, I find that there is a subtle but highly salient difference between the two: Like cultural brokers, people in this categorical range can exercise greater power and autonomy from parents more so than those who are dependent on their parents, but unlike cultural brokers, their filial roles and responsibilities revolve less around taking care of other family members than surviving on their own.

Among the study participants, there were different ways in which children were forced to take care of themselves completely with little parental assistance. Some of the interviewees were forced into the situation because of overworked parents who did not have the means to find alternative caregivers—a structural constraint most often faced by working-class families. The struggles were compounded by the unusual hardships and isolation these children endured in adapting to their immediate neighborhood or school peers, particularly those in poor minority-dominant inner-city areas. However, autonomous caretakers were more likely to live in more unstable household structures, including those where the parents were emotionally negligent, physically abusive, or otherwise dysfunctional. Although economic hardship can certainly aggravate these problems, my interviews suggest that these types of psychological disabilities can occur across all types of household structures other than economically disadvantaged ones and can impact any member of the family, regardless of gender or birth order. Thus, it was more difficult to identify dominant patterns based on class, gender, or birth order. Inability to communicate with parents, build positive relationships with relatives, and find alternative peer support within the ethnic community intensified their sense of alienation from their parents' ancestral roots. Whereas those who were more involved with their families may have had some chance to cultivate transnational ties depending on time and money, most participants in this category were least likely to have visited their parents' homeland, regardless of whether or not they had the opportunity, because no one was available to push them in this direction.

Because of her parent's long work hours at their dry cleaning business, Esther, a twenty-five-year-old Korean American tailor, was from the age of two mostly raised by her German American neighbors whom she used to affectionately call "mommy" and "pop-pop." At the age of ten, however, she experienced a racial identity crisis as a result of her unusual upbringing and insisted on raising herself as a latchkey kid for the rest of her childhood. Because she and her sister spent so much time with her neighbors, people would ask her if they were adopted, which she felt was an insult to her parents and also made her cognizant of the fact she wasn't white. While she felt a strong emotional connection with her other family, this alternative caregiving arrangement caused her great confusion over her racial identity as she grew older.

In addition, the fact that she was not "ensconced in [her] own cultural community, whether it be [her] grandparents or Sunday school" also isolated her from her Korean American peers. Esther reported that she did attend a Korean church as a child, but she began to feel increasingly disconnected from other Korean Americans as people started to split into their own ethnic cliques in high school and she became keenly aware of the differences in their family background. As she explained, "They [her Korean American peers] were all raised by their grandparents. They all took the trip to Korea for the summer and came back totally fluent, flawlessly fluent, knowing all the right manners, knowing how to make food, knowing how to do all this stuff and I never had that experience. And also because I didn't speak Korean perfectly and wasn't raised by my grandparents, I immediately was sort of out of that set. As I went through high school, I ended up having two friends, because I sort of ostracized myself from everything." She claimed that her relationship with her parents was tumultuous throughout her childhood, partly as a result of their absence as well as their preferential treatment for her brother. Altogether, the different caregiving context within which she was raised did not allow her to create the kind of comfortable familial space within which she could cultivate respect for her parents' culture. The fact that she also had a hard time negotiating her identity with the racial cliques that began to form during her adolescence pushed her to isolate herself further from others.

These experiences instilled in her a strong awareness of her racial minority status, but because of this emotionally detached upbringing, she commented that almost all her friends and boyfriends have been non–Asian American and she jokingly calls herself a "Twinkie" (meaning yellow in terms of her physical appearance but white in terms of her inner personality). Although she does have an interest in her Asian heritage from an aesthetic perspective, she described it as a type of emotionally detached standpoint of a non-Asian outsider.

Even though I am Korean from Korean parents and from an entirely Korean family, I'm *so* Americanized and in a weird way, I've adopted this sort of colonial outlook on things. I exoticize certain things about my heritage or about other people's heritage. It's a predominantly Western European and American sort of outlook. When I would come into contact with something that I didn't know about Koreans or know about Asians in history or art history, I feel like wow. I always see myself outside of those things. I feel really amazed that I can objectify a part of myself or a part of my culture and look at it through American eyes. I guess it just has a lot to say about the separation I feel about myself and Koreans and Korean culture in general.

There is one caveat in Esther's case in that starting from the age of thirteen, she began working at her parents' dry cleaning business, which nurtured a respectful relationship with her mother and instilled in her a passion for entrepreneurship. Although they refused to raise her at the dry cleaning business when she was younger, they began to involve her with all aspects of their business and then in major household decisions as she entered her teen years. She recalled accompanying her mother when she went out to scout out a new store location and her parents starting to turn to her for advice on business deals and even the purchase of their home. I would argue that Esther's master identity still resembles those of autonomous caretakers, because the emotional context of her upbringing set the tone for her relationship with other Asian Americans. However, their mutual work interests have played a major role in cultivating her career aspirations and current relationship with her mother.

Cultural and emotional distance from family heritage does not necessarily mean that these Asian Americans simply become assimilated into a white Anglo-American mainstream. For example, Peter, a twenty-six-year-old graphic designer, identifies closely with his "Asian American" identity (a purely American-rooted construction) over his "Chinese American" identity.[16] As the "black sheep of the family," he feels he has very little in common with his parents with whom he has a difficult time communicating in Chinese, his older married sister whom he considers more "stable," and his few extended relatives whom he sees infrequently. Because of his parents' long work hours, Peter was raised as a latchkey kid with some help from his older sister, who shared in the caregiving activities but could not bridge the emotional and cultural gap that he felt from his family.

Because he feels distant from his ancestral culture, Peter repeatedly proclaimed, "I would more likely consider myself Asian American before I'd consider myself Chinese American." As evidence of this, he emphasized the importance of dating within one's race but says dating all types of Asian Americans other than Chinese Americans only is important to him in order to avoid what he perceives as the general tendency toward "ethnocentrism." He has worked mostly for Asian American organizations and once with a Chinese labor group, only because of its strong base among diverse Asian American communities. After a period of hanging out with

Chinatown gang members, Peter noted that he eventually ended up developing a close circle of Asian Americans for the kind of support his family failed to provide.

> I may not have the strongest relationship with my parents but I have a really strong relationship with a lot of my friends. In high school, I wasn't really part of any Asian organizations or anything like that, but then I started getting involved in the community. You can just get kind of influenced by the community in some ways. You meet people that are very passionate and were part of the civil rights movements in the seventies or you'll meet artists and filmmakers who talk about pushes to do things. So I mean it was just something that I felt passionate about, in terms of exposure in the public media for Asian American artists. So I kind of got involved in it and I felt like I belong.

Peter's sense of belonging is rooted not within his family and the so-called ethnocentric networks to which they belong but in the larger community of Asian American artists and filmmakers. In contrast to the broader umbrella of Asian American panethnicity, he clearly equates his parents' narrower focus on Chinese ethnicity with exclusion.

Jasmine, a twenty-seven-year-old Chinese American language program assistant, related to me how she and her older sister essentially raised themselves because their parents worked long odd hours and were not acculturated enough to provide them guidance. She had no extended relatives with whom she had close relations, was not part of any ethnic community, and was not religious enough to go to church. The two sisters took care of their own meals and household bills as they got older, but eventually Jasmine was left alone when her sister, who is four years older than her, left for college. She struggled considerably with both her racial identity and sexual orientation and felt ashamed of being Asian, because she was racially taunted and harassed by her black classmates throughout high school with virtually no support network to which to turn. She admitted, "I mean I hated the way I looked, I hated the way my parents spoke Chinese to me. Just because I hated how loud they sounded when they spoke Chinese. I hated how everyone turned their heads, as if we were like some aliens."

Although she has worked to overcome this shame, I could still sense how her outcast status continued to instill in her a deep sense of self-alienation and isolation. Jasmine did note that she worked on hanging out with Asians when she reached college but still seemed wary about becoming too attached to any type of identity, partly because her family did little to counter the hostility she experienced in school as a child.

I feel somehow more out of place now, so I think my identity has shifted to a nonidentity. I remember one situation in particular in high school as a freshman. It was a lot of racial epithets and I remember I came home crying. I was like I don't ever want to go back to high school. And I remember my mom sitting there and instead of advising me how to deal with it, she's just like well what can you do about it (ha)? So I'm very independent, meaning I cut people off really easily. And I never had big groups of friends, and I never figured how people can be normal in a group just because I've always been such an outcast. I think it was like this mentality of having to figure out how to form your own identity when you don't have a community. You want to feel special and so you craft a very individual identity that's pretty fragile because when you don't have whatever person that makes you feel special, then you realize you can't really survive that much outside of the group.

Although she has dated people from different racial backgrounds, she said she has not been able to reconcile her anxiety around blacks as a result of the childhood harassment, around whites because they make invisible her constant struggles over her racial identity, and around Asian Americans because of stereotypes she feels she may have internalized. In this sense, Jasmine's experience is defined not so much by her assimilation but rather by her isolation from any collective identity.

Most autonomous caretakers are able to avoid some of the gendered burdens that other children face, but in some cases it is the conflicts that arise over these heteronormative ideals that lead to alienation from their families. Logan, a twenty-five-year-old Chinese American, was raised as a dependent in a family torn by marital strife and divorce but was ostracized from his family as a teenager when his mother found out he was gay. When Logan was in college, he and his mother got into a dramatic confrontation after she discovered some gay newspapers he had left in the recycling bin and eventually kicked him out of the house; both his parents have since refused to acknowledge him whenever they run into him at Chinese community events or on the streets. Although he is proficient in Cantonese and familiar with his cultural background, he made it clear throughout the interview that his weak family ties as a result of conflicts over his sexual orientation make it difficult for him to relate to his more well-off Chinese American counterparts.

It's so difficult to meet Asian Americans, because I feel like I have a very special situation. I don't really fit in because of my family circumstances, in that I no longer have a connection with family. I kind of feel like that separates me a lot from other Asian Americans, although I'm probably more connected, more aware, more active than they are in the community. I went from this existence where I was totally in this world that was all family that's always gonna be there into this existence now where I'm solely on my own. So that's why I feel like I have a new perspective. I have Asian American friends. But like I said it's very difficult because they have experienced things a certain way. They never had to pay rent completely on their own, whereas I have. So I have a different take on things or maybe I see things as being more serious, and they don't really feel like it's that serious because they're more cushioned by their circumstances. They have their family as a resource, which is huge. Like you don't get a job or if the job doesn't work out, that's fine, you'll get another job but then your home is in jeopardy. You can be homeless if this job doesn't work out and you can't find one to fill in the interim. Whereas you know they kind of feel more relaxed to go to a party whereas I feel like I really need to focus in order to keep the boat afloat so to speak.

Having been disowned by his family, Logan feels a sense of disconnect from other Chinese Americans who cannot relate to the kind of financial struggles he must deal with as a self-sufficient wage earner. These differences prevent Logan from finding the kind of traditional ethnic community support that other Chinese Americans might rely on. He draws meaning from the cultural knowledge and Chinese American pride he cultivated while growing up but socializes with a racially diverse network of friends as an LGBTQ activist and identifies with his panethnic identity as an aspiring Asian American filmmaker and political advocate.

What is central in separating this category of autonomous caretakers from those of cultural brokers is the former's lack of an emotionally engaging relationship with parents and kin and their sense of ostracism and exclusion from the ethnic communities to which their family belongs. Some interviewees in fact blamed their parents' problems on their Korean or Chinese culture. For example, the heightened responsibilities one interviewee was forced to assume made him associate extended kinship and ethnic social structures with cumbersome obligations and restrictive forms of social control. If anything, he argued, the fact that they had essentially raised themselves meant that they deserved to be free of such undue family obligations and had the right to make their own life decisions.

Second-generation participants who carry on a limited range of brokering responsibilities might not feel a strong attachment to their family culture if these responsibilities did not require them to engage with their parents. In the case of Helen, a thirty-seven-year-old Korean American academic, her brokering obligations were limited to a few administrative duties that did little to mend the estranged relationship she and her sibling had with her parents, even though her parents were home throughout most of her childhood before her father decided to move back to Korea alone. Helen took care of her siblings and provided minimal translation assistance for her mother with incoming bills when her father left. It was apparent that she was close to her siblings because of this, but the translation duties did little to bridge the emotional distance she felt from her parents, who were constantly arguing with each other whenever they were together. As she described it, "Their lives are so complicated and they just spend so much time fighting, it's just not possible to help them, you know? I try to help them, but then, they come up with another problem, and then it just never gets anywhere so I just stay out of their affairs." Within this context, her friendship circles are evenly distributed among Asians, Latinos, and whites, but she does not speak Korean well, is married to a Jewish American, and seems to express only symbolic interest in Korean culture (e.g., Buddhism)—all of which prevent her from fully engaging with her parents' culture despite some interest in doing so.

CONCLUSION

The interviews clearly reveal that the varying ways children are emotionally integrated into immigrant family households formatively shape their adult views on ethnicity. As they transition into adulthood, the second-generation Americans strategically forge ethnic identities that best allow them to come to terms with the emotional context of their upbringing and the various tensions, burdens, and contradictions of living in an immigrant family. The study has shown that family roles can invoke a wide range of emotions from respect and affection to alienation and resentment in a manner that strengthens or weakens one's orientation toward one's parents ancestral heritage as well as the broader ethnic community. In particular, children of immigrants negotiate these complex sentiments by emotionally framing or emphasizing different aspects of ethnicity and culture in a way that helps them to reconcile their family roles and makes them feel a sense of belonging either within the family or outside of it.

The practice of cultural brokering strengthens children's ties with the parents' ancestral homeland either symbolically or concretely as they engage with both the nuclear and extended family matters and their immediate ethnic community vis-à-vis their adult roles and responsibilities. Their approach to ethnicity is built on reciprocated empathy. In their constant negotiation between two worlds, these so-called cultural brokers develop a sense of empathy for the vulnerable status of their parents and their racial marginalization as minorities than their American-born peers; they are more likely to learn about the traditions and tribulations of their parents, concretizing their sense of ethnic and cultural identification around themes of sacrifice, obligation, and empathy. These individuals also develop strong emotional relationships with their parents because their active engagement with the family enables them to engage with their extended kin or the local ethnic community—ties that continue on as they transition into adulthood and reaffirm their role as cultural keepers of family traditions.

Although their parents are around to fulfill their caregiving roles, the relationship of children who are dependent on their parents is based less on an empathetic understanding of their cultural values and migration experiences than a vague, unarticulated sense of obligation. Respondents who fall in this category benefit from the stabilizing presence and supervision of their immigrant parents but do not feel the kind of empathy seen among their brokering counterparts because of language barriers, lack of shared experiences, and their subordinate roles within the parent-child relationship. As the main providers and decision makers of the family, their parents represent role models or strict authority figures in the family hierarchy to be obeyed, respected, rebelled against, or feared, along with their traditions.

As a result, the way they emotionally process their childhood memories ranges from detached to deferential emulation, depending on to what degree they can carve out an emotional place within the family that fits well with their American ideals. The ethnic identities of participants in this category are much more wide-ranging than those in the other two categories—a difference that reflects the contradictory tensions that children in this intermediary category face between feeling emotional intimacy for their parents and having difficulties understanding the cultural differences because of the hierarchical nature of their relationship. As children, their undeveloped sense of ethnic identity may incite dual identity conflicts between home and school, but as adults, the socially intimate interactions they have with family leave open the possibility of finding an outside medium through which to connect with their parents' worldview and culture. How they negotiate this tension in forging their ethnic identities depends much more so on intervening factors outside the family, such as ethnic organizations or extended kin, which may provide a cultural lens through which the second-generation Americans can either better relate to their parents' cultural heritage or develop an alternative racial and ethnic identity.

Because of their weak relationship with their parents, the individuals I call autonomous caretakers develop an enhanced sense of independence and individuality and are rarely exposed to the cultural influence or pressures of an outside ethnic community. As a result, these respondents associate their parents' ancestral culture with oppressive norms and equate ethnicity with ethnocentric exclusiveness, from which they have been outcast. If left unmediated by their family members, racial harassment, stereotypes, and pressures from the outside can cause some to feel a deep sense of shame, which they may resolve emotionally but will rarely engender a strong sense of ethnic affinity. Or conversely, if other alternative racial and ethnic communities (e.g., panethnic, "white," or cosmopolitan American networks) offer a safe sanctuary to counter the conflicts and pressures felt at home, second-generation Asian Americans may choose to completely reject a Korean or Chinese identity in favor of these alternative identities. In the end, lack of understanding of their parents' cultural upbringing heightens conflict and dissonance within the family and either strengthens their sense of attachment to an Anglo American, Asian American, or inner-city minority culture or isolates them from any type of community altogether.

Certainly, the internal familial dynamics I have discussed throughout are characteristic of not only Korean and Chinese immigrant families but other Asian and Latino immigrant households where traditional caregiving functions are transferred onto children as a result of family separation and other structural constraints. A number of studies for example have noted that Mexican immigrant families also rely on alternative caregiving arrangements and cultural brokering in response to their restrictive legal status, narrow employment options, and limited resources.[17] Although it is feasible that children in white immigrant families might also share similar class-related burdens, it is unclear whether such internal family dynamics would lead to parallel ethnic outcomes, not only because of differences in the cultural acceptability of cultural brokering in some countries but also because the dynamics of racial privilege and inclusion in the social citizenry of white America offers second-generation whites other social options, emotional outlets, and support networks. As I have covered in previous chapters, the presence or absence of positive coethnic role models, multicultural education, and institutional support networks also goes a long way in bridging some of these cultural differences.

Most of the current literature has focused on racial and ethnic identities as a means to secure educational achievement, but the touching narratives of Asian Americans throughout the chapter underscore the need to explore how they can also be used to help children make sense of growing emotional disjunctures within their families. Aside from helping to explain divergent ethnic outcomes among siblings, a greater understanding of family intimacy may give us insight into why some children of immigrants connect with broader Americanized identities (e.g., panethnicity) over their parents' more narrow views on ethnicity. Depending on these internal dynamics, some are able to pull their families together by filling emotional voids as surrogate caregivers, while others opt to re-create their familial space outside their immediate family and kinship networks and still others sadly end up alone. As the next chapter explores, the renegotiation and reconstruction of gender roles and expectations are central aspects of this sense-making process.

CHAPTER 5

Daughters and Sons
Carrying Culture

Throughout the 1970s and 1980s, two Asian American female authors won public acclaim from American readers for their works on the struggles of Chinese American families with a focus on mother-daughter relations. In 1976, Maxine Hong Kingston won several awards including the National Book Critics Award for *The Woman Warrior*, a collection of fictionalized memoirs on the struggles of Chinese Americans from her perspective as the daughter of Chinese immigrants.[1] In 1989, Amy Tan made her public debut with her book *The Joy Luck Club*, the fictional narratives of four different Chinese immigrant mothers and their relations with their American-born daughters.[2] Building on its widespread popularity, the book was later readapted into a movie that grossed nearly thirty-three million dollars in the United States. Of course, Kingston and Tan were not the first Asian American authors to write in this genre; however, their works represented some of the earliest literary publications in the post-1965 period to bring Asian American female literary writers into the public American spotlight and provide validation for the emotional woes of American-born daughters of Asian immigrants in their relations with their immigrant mothers and, secondarily, their relationships with men.

At the same time, the rising popularity of these female writers also signaled a growing rift within Asian American literary circles, academics, and social activism since the 1970s over questions of racial representation, patriarchy, and ethnic authenticity in Asian immigrant families.[3] Chinese playwright Frank Chin, one of the most vocal critics of both Kingston and Tan, scathingly objected to what he called their "fake" tales of Christian "white fantasy/supremacy" and accused such writers of exoticizing traditional Chinese culture, stigmatizing

Chinese men, and perpetuating the model minority myth in order to benefit from the "racist love" of their white audience.[4] Other scholars, such as Sau-ling Wong, argued that the intergenerational relationships in these stories appealed to Americans, unlike other similar novels released around the same period, because they made the exotic and gendered Orientalization of the Asian immigrant family palatable to the predominantly middle-class white American female audience that consumed them.[5]

While acknowledging the role of the white American racial imaginary in reinforcing images of Asian male emasculation and Asian female subservience, some Asian American feminist scholars and authors have criticized the ways in which such masculinist literary figures as Chin have ironically reacted by imposing heteronormative Western patriarchal models of masculine aggression and violence in their quest to reclaim their manhood from American racism. King-Kok Cheung warns, "If Chinese American men use the Asian heroic dispensation to promote male aggression, they may risk remaking themselves in the image of their oppressions—albeit under the guise of Asian panoply. To do [so] reinforces not only patriarchy but also white supremacy."[6] As Elaine Kim states, Asian American women like Kingston who continue to value family and ethnic community often find themselves trapped between the desire to assert their individuality and undermine patriarchy in all its manifestations while affirming their ethnic heritage against a racist society that demeans Asian men.[7]

It is beyond the scope of this book to provide a comprehensive analysis of the tenets of this debate, about which much has been written. However, what the internal controversy over these literary works indicates is that a critical discussion on the Asian immigrant family as well as its mythical representation in the American racial imaginary would be incomplete and misleading without attending to the complex role of gender in shaping family dynamics. The racial construction of Asian immigrant families as emotionless, rationally calculating institutions of control has long historical and cultural roots in Western stereotypes about the cold, misogynistic Asian patriarch and the submissive, victimized China doll. Asian men are abusive, egomaniacal figures who enforce their patriarchal authority by taking on multiple wives and mistresses, controlling all areas of family decision making, and physically abusing their wives and children. This sexist family structure is said to originate from an oppressive, backward culture built on premodern ideals of domesticity and misogyny within which women are helpless victims needing outside rescue.

Although contemporary family studies have become more attuned to the growing diversity of American families today, most research on Asian immigrant families continues to overlook cultural, regional, class, and religious differences among Asian American families and generalize the way their cultural traditions reinforce patriarchal authority over women and children in the family.[8] In a similar vein, mainstream media and traditional assimilationist discourse continue to portray gender relations as a binary between traditional Asian oppression versus modern Western egalitarianism—a comparison that does more to highlight the moral superiority of (white) Western culture than to recognize gender inequality in its many forms.[9] The implication is that only in assimilating into American society can women and children in immigrant families expect to free themselves from the confines of cultural hierarchies and outmoded ancestral traditions.[10]

The problem with this overemphasis on the generational divide is that it "reifies the notion of culture . . . as something that is fixed or a given, rather than as a social process that finds meaning within social relationships and practices."[11] Ngo points out how "this focus on intergenerational conflict problematically absolves institutions of education, labor, and government of responsibility, and deflects attention from exclusionary historical practices as well as discrimination immigrants continue to face."[12] Whiteness becomes the central benchmark against which Asians as racial others are morally and culturally evaluated. As Collins argues, the problem with gauging gender equality based on white women's experiences is that it assumes that "all women enjoy the racial privilege that allows them to see themselves primarily as individuals in search of personal autonomy, instead of members of racial ethnic groups struggling for power."[13] Even though Asian families are indeed contentious sites for gender and generational conflict and inequality, these families also offer a sociopsychological sanctuary and an economic safety net for minority women and children otherwise alienated and marginalized in American society.[14]

This chapter moves beyond the oversimplified racial categorization of gender inequality as organized around a generational and cultural divide between parents and children and looks at how Asian American women find agency and voice at the intersections of racial and gender inequality. I seek to understand how Korean and Chinese American sons and daughters view their family culture and obligations relationally within the pecking order, how they renegotiate unequal gender roles and expectations, and how they selectively reconstruct ethnicity and family culture in their adult lives. Taking into account differences in individual status and family structure, I argue that the gendered manner in which these daughters and sons are emotionally integrated into the household structure lead to diverse ways of contemplating, viewing, and practicing family culture in their own lives.

GENDER AND CULTURE IN THE ASIAN PECKING ORDER

A growing field within the gender and migration literature has explored how daughters are taught to reproduce culture by managing the semblance of family purity through their public behaviors and also learning the tools to become good mothers and good wives who can maintain culture for their future families.[15] Parental control over the bodies and sexuality of daughters takes on special meaning within the broader context of American race relations. Studies on Asian and Latino immigrant families, including Vietnamese, South Asians, and Puerto Ricans, assert that the construction of female virginity and family honor and control over women's bodies are deliberate strategies to resist mainstream colonialist depictions of racial minority populations but often at the expense of reinforcing patriarchal control over girls and women in the family.[16] For example, Espiritu shows how Filipino immigrant mothers' construction of white women as selfish and sexually immoral gives them the means to "assert a morally superior public face" to outside racial marginalization and to highlight the virtuosity, chastity, and family devotedness of "good" Filipina girls and women against "bad" Filipina girls who are viewed as "too Americanized." In so doing, "Filipino immigrants claim moral distinctiveness for their community by representing 'Americans' as morally flawed, themselves as family-oriented model minorities, and their wives and daughters as paragons of morality."[17] In this sense, women are viewed as instrumental not only in transmitting culture to the next generation but also signifying and embodying the integrity and authenticity of family culture itself to the outside world.

Reaffirming current research on Asian American daughters, female participants in the study were much more likely than male participants to report that their parents were strict and overprotective about their dress, behavior, and activities especially outside the household. When there were also male siblings present, daughters angrily recalled how their parents gave their brothers preferential treatment and justified their privileges as a given because they were boys. Anna is a twenty-five-year-old Taiwanese American who depends heavily on her parents and her older brother for life guidance and support. She lived on and off with her parents when she first graduated college and started working in New York, but said at the time of the interview she was financially supporting herself. However, her parents have offered to help with the tuition and bills if she is accepted into a graduate program in art history. When asked if she was treated differently from her brother because she was a girl and the youngest child, she replied,

> ANNA: Probably. I mean he was the oldest, he was the son too, so he was
> supposed to take care of me and be responsible and be a good role

model and all that stuff. I probably had more leeway to be a brat. [laughs] He was my older brother, so everything he said was law. If he said we're going to do this, so we would do that. My brother had more leeway and going out or doing whatever he wanted, driving and I wasn't allowed as much to. Like he could go into the city if he wanted (ha) and they were more protective about me. . . .

ANGIE: So what would they say to you if you said I want to go to the city or go out?

ANNA: Well, as long as it was with a whole lot of people that they know and they trusted, it was fine, but they needed to know more about what I was doing than what he was doing.

Anna's experience is defined by her status both as a daughter but more specifically as the youngest sister in relation to the oldest brother in the family. As a result, her narrative highlights not only the way in which her parents monitor her sexuality and restrict her mobility but also the way these practices create for her a clear relationship of emotional and social dependency on her brother.

However, the question of how gender plays out in Korean and Chinese immigrant families is a more nuanced and complicated issue that reflects the position of the daughter and son in relation to other siblings within the family as well as within the overall household structure. For one, there is a subtle but meaningful difference between Anna's gendered perspective as the youngest female sibling from those of first daughters in the study who have a young male sibling, daughters who are the only child, or women in all-daughter families. Interestingly, because gendered positions are best understood in relation to others, women from all-girl or only-child families and men from all-boy or only-child families had a difficult time articulating how their parents' expectations and their responsibilities were shaped by their gender because, in their words, they had no basis for comparison.

In this respect, the narratives of first daughters provide perhaps the starkest contrast to those of youngest daughters. The experiences of many first daughters in the study were less characterized by their dependency on a male sibling but more often by their portrayal as maternal figures among their siblings. Oldest daughters were more likely to assume this matriarchal position in households where mothers were absent or too busy to oversee household affairs and less likely when parents did little to engage with their children. The following excerpt from Grace, who has one younger brother and one younger sister, demonstrates how first daughters in such households experience these gendered expectations and responsibilities in distinctive ways: "When my [younger] sister married a Caucasian guy, my dad was saying, oh it's good, it's diverse, you know it's good to have some diversity. But he always made it clear, because I'm the oldest on my dad's side, he was like you set the standard and just like I did for my generation, you set the standards for your generation. And for that reason, he always made it very clear that his expectation of me was to marry a Korean. And my brother too, cause he's the oldest boy on my dad's side and he's actually the one that carries on the name." Parents tend to give oldest daughters relatively more household responsibilities, caregiving roles, and in some cases, advisory and decision-making power on adult matters—all of which endow them with a type of maternal authority and status above their other siblings. In the case of Grace, she was more than willing to fulfill these responsibilities because her parents demonstrated and emphasized to her the honor and privileges that came with this position. Of course, as compared with the patriarchal authority of first sons, matriarchal status also entails more gendered obligations and labor than influence and privilege, causing some to reject this burdensome role altogether. Nevertheless, the narratives reveal that as compared to other female siblings, oldest daughters generally have more opportunities to assert their independence and authority as adults because of the way their roles are defined.

Even if their childhood relations was rife with sibling rivalry and conflict, younger siblings like Elliott who had older sisters willing to assume these matriarchal responsibilities retrospectively expressed their deep respect and gratitude for their sibling. Elliott and his two sisters spent most of their childhood years cared for by their oldest sister Lana, until he was old enough to assume the mantle of the oldest brother. He explained, "Lana was definitely the mother figure. From an academic standpoint, she was definitely a role model because as we went through school, everyone would say oh your sister Lana did so well. I don't think she had a lot of ability to discipline us, aside from telling our mom what we did so I think that might not have made her truly a mother figure, but she watched over us and fed us and sometimes I do say that Lana kinda raised me as well." Depending on the timing of birth, these gender roles can also shift over time. When Elliott was old enough to assume more leadership responsibilities, he stated that Lana did not lose her former obligations and authority but instead continued her role as the maternal caregiver while he became the "flag bearer" for their two younger siblings.

The narratives of sons in the study also demonstrate some of the nuances of gender roles and expectations in Korean and Chinese immigrant families. In traditional Korean and Chinese culture, the distribution of resources, authority, and privileges center on the key role of first sons as the future heads of the household in contrast to daughters who are to be given away in marriage.

In both cultures, the oldest sons are the ones who are expected to carry on the family lineage through their names and preserve their cultural traditions through endogamy. Based on this same cultural logic, both sons and daughters told me stories about how their parents and relatives gave their oldest brothers the biggest and best portions of food and the bigger bed among all siblings, granted them more leeway with late-night outings or trips with friends, and entrusted them with more decision making and advisory responsibilities within the family. Oldest sons were especially conscious of some of the special privileges they were bestowed by parents and extended kin because of their status within the family pecking order. At the same time, they pointed out how in some ways, they faced more intensive expectations and pressures as the future patriarch than did their female siblings.

Sam, a Chinese American husband and father of two children, has one older sister and one younger brother but said that his experience has been primarily defined by his status as the oldest brother in the family. In the following passage, he described some of the unsaid expectations he faced as a result of this role:

> SAM: My parents talked with us, oh you know when you get older, you have to get married and have kids and stuff like that, but I think it just became us putting the pressure on ourselves. I gotta get married so we can have kids and keep on the family name. Now that I think about it, they dropped hints about it, but they never came out and said you'd better get married and have kids and give me grandkids. They talked, they joked about it, and it just got to a point where we just pushed it on ourselves, made it a priority for ourselves.
>
> ANGIE: Why is that?
>
> SAM: I guess because we thought it was very important to our parents so I said well I should get married and have kids (ha).

In this sense, male privilege and masculinities tell only part of the story. As carriers of the family name, oldest sons are urged to marry good mothers who can convey their culture and heritage to future male heirs, to establish good careers in order to support their family, and to behave as proper role models for their siblings and cousins. At the same time, while most sons felt that the pressure was constant and suggestive, few felt that their parents were as direct, forceful, and strict in the same way parents controlled and monitored the dating behaviors of daughters in the study. Instead, it was more common that sons internalized their parental expectations in a way that led them to put pressure on themselves.

Steven, a physician and the oldest son of Korean immigrant parents, felt that these unsaid expectations affected how his otherwise liberal parents reacted to his past girlfriends, even those who were Korean American but came from the wrong background or even had the wrong name. In the excerpt to follow he refers to a former girlfriend whose birth name, "Ja," apparently held some negative connotations to his parents, because it was associated with a lower-class background and was common during the Japanese colonization of South Korea (1910–1945). "I'm the oldest of all my cousins and my parents felt that if I went away from the expectations of who they thought I should be marrying, then the rest of cousins would fall down that path is what I'm saying. I mean they were incredibly hard-lined against her. The relationship wasn't working out for completely different reasons, but that certainly was another eye-opening experience: that even within the Korean community that there were these huge differences that I had completely no awareness at all." Marriage is an important means not only to continue the family lineage, but also to create a stable union with "good mothers/wives" who can preserve and pass on both class and cultural values to the next generation of children. For this reason, children of more tradi-tional parents reported that their parents tended to show considerable con-cern in their son's marital choices, even if they were more lenient about their casual dating partners. It is important to note however that daughter-in-laws are the ones who perform the actual labor of mothering and conveying fam-ily culture. Although restrictive in many ways, male responsibilities involve less emotional and physical labor in comparison.

Nevertheless, there were a few oldest sons who expressed dissatisfaction or resentment over this type of upbringing, causing them to firmly establish boundaries as adults, distance themselves from one or both parents alto-gether, or, as in the case of Young, rebel by deliberately dating only non-Asian women. However, most first sons in the study looked back on these expecta-tions lightheartedly or expressed measured appreciation for these lessons as youth. As the following passage by Tony suggests, this may partly be because in fulfilling these gendered roles, sons also pick up the tools and mentality to succeed in other areas of life. During the interview, Tony claimed that he was disciplined much more than his sister, but went on to say,

> One of the key things that is different between myself and my sister is that I have a very deep understanding about the value of money and the work ethic that goes behind being able to provide yourself. If I wanted something when I was a kid, my parents would be like okay, well you have to work to earn it, whether it be studying hard and getting rewarded for getting straight As or you know doing extra chores or trying to incentivize me working hard to earn something that I wanted. If I wanted a bike, I had to save up for it. If later on my sister wanted a bike, my parents paid for it,

so with my sister, it was always provided versus for me, I had to earn it. And because of that my sister today doesn't really have a good sense of supporting herself [and] making her keep.

In cases where first sons felt they had to disappoint their parents by marrying outside their race, divorce their spouses, or take on careers that they feared did not meet their parents' expectations, many were surprised by the mild or even supportive reactions by their family and extended kin. This was the case for Tony who valued his role as the oldest son of the first son in the family. When he made the decision to get divorced, he decided to travel all the way to Korea to break the news of his divorce to his grandparents, who were eagerly awaiting a great-grandson, only to find that they were surprisingly understanding of the situation. The narratives reveal how patriarchal obligation and responsibility can be restrictive and burdensome for sons, but it is also important to note that with obedience and discipline come special privileges and loopholes.

As opposed to viewing cultural expectations on gender roles as homogeneous and unchanging, daughters and sons also recognize how they can be fluid, relational, and complex social categories that shift and adapt to the particular familial context within which they play out. This is especially true when distinctive personalities, sibling composition, and migration struggles make it difficult to achieve the ideal family order. For one, parents cannot expect to carry on their homeland culture through their daughters or their family name through their sons if they do not have a daughter or son. As a result, in such households, families turn to the oldest daughter or oldest son to take on responsibilities as *both* family caregiver and "male heir." This is also true when the timing of birth or parental conflicts with the oldest child make it difficult to align patrilineal expectations along strictly gender lines.

Daughters especially pointed out how their parents treat the youngest son in the family like a "sacred cow" or a "little king" whose needs are prioritized over the other siblings, but this desire to pamper the youngest brother also opened the doors for more responsible older daughters to take on some of the family decision-making roles and leadership roles usually associated with first sons. Mina, a Korean American who is seven years older than her only brother, informed me that her parents still relied on her whenever they needed guidance on any serious or important decisions involving the family—much like they would the oldest son. She said, "In Asian society, the male is usually above the female, but because of the age gap, they always entrusted me with things and even now, if my dad needs something done, he'll come to me. He still sees my brother as the baby."

Jinah is a successful investment manager and a middle child, with an older sister who has a tense relationship with the family and a younger brother who she feels was too coddled to act as the family caregiver. She told me that because of the financial burdens her parents shouldered to finance their education, she decided to take out a loan during her senior year in college and has supported herself since then, taking only the occasional pocket money from her parents. During the interview, she stated,

> In some ways, I feel as if I should've been born a guy and I should've been born the first child. I'm the most ambitious out of the three of us, I'm the [one who] has my act together. My sister doesn't have her act together as much and my brother is treated like a little king. My little brother definitely got the most amount of attention because he's the youngest, he's the only boy in the family, so they let things slide with him a little. But the funny thing is my parents have said to me, it's like you have actually surpassed all [our] expectations cause they thought that I'd just go to an Ivy League school and that's it. So they were a bit nervous but then they realized right after college, I was able to land my first job at — Consulting, which is a good respectable first job. Then when I moved to Boston, living away and being on my own, I finally decided I wanted to go to business school. They were like okay and I got in, and they're like wow, okay! But it's a little embarrassing. So for example, my mother would always be like, oh this is my daughter, she goes to Harvard or business school or this is my daughter, she just won this piano competition, and I would always cringe. I've like always been like, "mom shush! So what?" But it validates how good of a kid they've raised. So I realize that now in hindsight, but as a kid, you're just like, be quiet, be quiet, be quiet.

In this passage, Jinah, despite her status as the middle daughter, is proud of being able to demonstrate her worthiness to her parents through her educational and career achievements to the point where her parents treat her almost like the oldest son. To this day, Jinah continues to take care of her parents by making sure to spend time with them and buying them gifts, as well as providing advice and guidance for her younger brother. In this way, she performs the role of both first son as financial supporter for her aging parents and first daughter as nurturing caregiver for her entire family.

As many of these narratives suggest, one way in which cultural traditions seem to be readapting over time is parents' increasing attention to their daughters' education—a finding that is confirmed by Min's study on Korean immigrant families in New York.[18] To be sure, there were some cases where parents felt there was less of a need to encourage their daughters to get a college degree as compared with their sons and even told their daughters outright to think about getting married instead. However, in cases where parents did pressure their children to excel educationally, most participants reported that those expectations applied to both sons and daughters in the family. Zhou and Bankston argue that parental emphasis on educational achievement among daughters, although representing a significant departure from old-school patriarchal practices, actually signifies the reaffirmation of traditional patriarchal structure in nuanced ways. For fathers, well-educated daughters can better contribute to their future family's well-being, secure high-status husbands, learn the skills to become good mothers, and boost the status of their birth family. Mothers see education as a means for improving their daughters' status and bargaining leverage in respect to their husbands within the traditional family structure.[19] In the current global economy, mothers are increasingly taking on the role of managing the education of their children, a responsibility that can be cultivated only through their proper training and education.[20]

At the same time, Jinah believes that her parents' public pride in her achievements also suggests the possibility that education is not just a reaffirmation of traditional gender roles but perhaps a shift in her position within the family from a future "good daughter-in-law" to the "male heir" of her natal family. Although parents may place less priority on girls' education than boys' education if faced with financial constraints, I agree that the growing value of education in the current economy as well as the changing role of daughters in caring for their elderly parents will increasingly make education a universal expectation in many Korean and Chinese immigrant families. After all, education is considered one of the driving factors behind Korean and Chinese migration and critical for their mobility and assimilation. In families with no boys to carry on the family name, families can also project their gendered expectations on education and mobility from boys to girls.

THE GOOD DAUGHTER

As youth, second-generation Korean and Chinese Americans juggle numerous pressures and conflicts related to peer pressure, identity formation, and self-esteem and in most cases rely on their parents for emotional and financial support, making it more difficult for them to respond independently and effectively to the gendered pressures of carrying culture. For this reason, the agency of most Asian Americans is most apparent only after they transition into adulthood. It is at this stage when they achieve their independence that the second generation can forge relatively stable identities, adopt a more balanced perspective on the cultural values learned, and empathize more with their parents based on their personal lived experiences with family and career.

However, the path to independence requires that children of immigrants deal with family baggage, manage conflicting desires, and make these decisions meaningful within the context of their lives. This is especially the case for daughters whose personal aspirations often conflict with their parents' expectations of a "good daughter." In the following passage, Mike compared his worldview as the oldest son with that of a friend who is the oldest daughter of the family.

> [Her younger sister] wants to be a university professor, which might not give her a huge salary, yet she leans on her sister, who is financially independent and well-off, to provide things for her, so it's this weird relationship. The older sister does it very willingly, but it's just a weird dynamic that they have because the second child is very idealistic about the agenda she has without any regard for what she'll be doing or how she'll be doing financially down the road. She figures that will get worked out. But her sister has a very overwhelming sense of responsibility. She almost has more of a sense of duty as a firstborn female, than I do as a firstborn male. Like me, I'm sometimes very lax, and she's very gung ho about providing for her parents who maybe aren't as financially set. Every time we talk, it's always about her family and how her father is getting older and how she has to start thinking about that.

Mike acknowledged that part of the difference in their outlooks has to do with his class privilege since his parents are more financially stable than hers; however, he also believed that oldest daughters in general feel greater anxiety and personal obligation when it comes to parental expectations—a difference that I also observed among the male and female participants in the study.

It is quite apparent in the emotional tone of the interviews that daughters struggled considerably more in trying to renegotiate the terms of gender inequality in a manner that would allow them to preserve some of the positive aspects of family and culture. Expressions of guilt in particular were crucial markers that signaled formative tensions between their desire to preserve family values and family honor while extricating themselves from the more onerous aspects of parental expectations. Although these tensions often transcended class differences, feelings of guilt were particularly strong among children who had witnessed their parents struggle as immigrants, which often was the case in working-class households.

When men in the study expressed guilt, it usually revolved around decisions related to their career choice or financial dependence on their parents, as in the case of Mark:

When I was trying to figure out what I wanted to do with my life, picking majors and what school to go to, I decided to go to an art school. I had applied to one art school out of six schools. All the five were business schools. So if you're going by the numbers, most likely I would've went into a business school. I ended up saying to my parents, "can I go to an art school (ha)?" And I was very reluctant to say that to them, because here I am, the oldest boy in the family in terms of my parents' siblings, deciding to go to art school. It's like oh (ha). You're gonna screw up all the younger cousins. What are you doing? But this was already in my head and it's weird now that I think about it, why was I even thinking that at seventeen, you know? And that's where probably the culture comes in. The whole boy thing, the whole oldest thing is totally a Chinese thing. So I decided to myself I'm gonna go to an art school and how the hell am I going to tell my parents? I sprung it on them, and they're like, "okay, just get a job after you graduate. Just promise us that." And that was it! That was their only expectation.

As Mark pointed out, much of the pressure he felt was implied and to some degree self-imposed, so that when he decided to announce his career decision, he was surprised to find his parents were ultimately understanding about his decision. This was a very common experience among oldest sons who broke with family tradition, but not usually the case for daughters, who could go months or even years without hearing from their parents if they "dishonored" the family.

Although some female interviewees also noted feelings of guilt over their inability to meet expectations on career and financial independence, the focus of women's emotions encompassed a wider range of parental expectations that also intertwined with themes of saving face, emotional sacrifice, and family caregiving. Kimberly, a Chinese-Taiwanese market researcher and the oldest sister of two, reflected on how this guilt continued to carry on into adulthood: "When I go home, all I wanna do is spend time with my mom and my sister. I really don't have time for anybody else. Maybe I could see one set of friends that I have. But other than that, I feel like I just wanna spend time with them. I'd feel guilty if I didn't. And when I go home, I help my mom clean. So I always tell my work, it's not really a vacation, cause when I go back to Maryland, it's like work. I have to help my mom clean, cause she's working late hours sometimes and she works full-time so she sometimes likes to clean up.

In that sense, I feel responsible to help my mom out if I could." Guilt also surfaced in the narratives of those who made life decisions on marriage that went
against their parents' hopes and expectations. Kathy, the Korean American
oldest daughter, is married to a Jewish man. After completing the interview,
Kathy expressed to me guilt she felt over marrying a white husband primarily
because it would isolate her mother from her family life. Although she recognized this choice took shape as a result of her upbringing, she actually apolo-
gized to her mother in person for not marrying another Korean because she
understood how her mother might feel being unable to communicate with
and share these issues with her in-laws.

In more extreme cases, the angst that arises from family obligations can
manifest itself in terms of low-self-esteem and self-destructive behaviors.
Mary, a twenty-five-year-old Chinese American, works at a retail clothing
store as a sales associate but aspires to be a professional actress. Her mother
suffered from a serious mental illness throughout most of her childhood,
while her father worked long hours as a food distributor, so that she spent
most of her childhood locked up in her bedroom or being raised by her older
sister. Despite the problems at home, Mary confessed that she recently developed an eating disorder and sees a therapist regularly as the result of internal
turmoil over family obligations. When asked if her obligation to the family
was difficult for her, she responded,

> Yeah, the balance between family obligation and self-dreams to fulfill, espe-
> cially within this industry. What I feel is in order to be an actor—and a lot
> of actors do this—they separate from their family totally. And it's not that
> they have to, it just naturally happens. You pick up and go, and then you
> figure out your own income, and you figure out what *you* have to pay for
> rent and *you* have to use all of your income with headshots and resumes
> and finding the next gig. It's always about searching and trying to get your
> foot in the door. And for me, that's hard because my family is *so* important
> to me that I can't just pick up and go without feeling the sense of obligation
> especially since my mom is in that situation and especially since my parents
> are both getting older. It's just physically, financially [her father's] not able
> to. He still has a mortgage to pay off, things that start making me think
> wow, I just can't pick up and go.

At the time of the interview, Mary was taking a break from acting in order to
deal with these personal issues.

While parental control over the sexuality and behavior may promote both
conformity and rebellion among daughters against such cultural traditions,
more profound reflection and engagement with these issues can also heighten

daughters' understanding of these traditions and hence cultivate a more nuanced approach to ethnicity. Daughters tend to find indirect ways of fulfilling their parents' aspirations on family, culture, and career as opposed to simply reproducing the values and traditions their parents taught them. Reconciling these contradictions requires not simply role-modeling the traditional aspects of their culture but also role-playing the part of the good Korean/Chinese daughter while living out more independent and self-fulfilling lives. As an example, Mary expressed discomfort with the pressures she feels from other family members about her career choice but continues to role-play the "good daughter" at events even as she lives her life the way she wants. Mary told me that unlike her older sister, she is the black sheep in the family because of her decision to become an actor. I asked her if her relatives said anything to insinuate she was an outcast, to which she replied,

> MARY: It's kind of insinuated in a polite way. When I was studying, it was mentioned, "Oh it's a very hard profession" or "Oh really? You're going into acting?" So back in the day I would brush it off, but then I would be like "All right I'm ignoring you now. I don't want to talk to you." [short laugh] Not that I don't want to talk, but I just don't want to hear it. So now I'm just like, okay, I do my duty, go to the banquets and go to whatever family functions like a dutiful daughter. But a lot of times I'm just like "I don't want to go here."
>
> ANGIE: So why is it important for you to be a dutiful daughter?
>
> MARY: I think for me personally that's always how I've been raised. Family always comes first. I was very lucky in many ways because I did have a father who let me be. He was strict to a certain extent but he let me choose whatever I wanted to do, wherever I wanted to go. So in that respect, I feel like to pay back, I have to listen to him, I have to fulfill family obligations, I have a sense of "Jewish guilt" (ha), because you want to be the best for your father and you want to make your father proud, make your family proud, because they had sacrificed so much for you. You feel like that's your duty: to sacrifice for them later on.

By ignoring the negative remarks and acting like the good daughter, Mary is essentially performing little acts of "saving face" to help protect her parents' honor. This sense of duty though has not yet swayed her from her choice to become an actor, but in some ways she is trying to lessen the impact on her family by responding to people's comments with quiet dignity.

Female participants often described the very selective ways in which they practiced cultural practices and values in order to help them navigate the emotional dynamics of family relations without having to compromise their individuality or autonomy. Winnie, the youngest daughter of four from a lower- to middle-class Chinese family, related to me how she generally hated the ways people would behave in order to save face but sometimes found herself doing the same—although on her own terms. When asked what kinds of things she does to save face, she responded,

> I try to keep arguments with my significant other from my parents or my family. I don't like them to know about it, because I don't want them to see that anything's wrong and worry about it. But I try not to do the whole [saving] face thing. For example, if they're like "Give me face, because I'm your godbrother," I always hated that. I'm like, "What are you doing? Like who are you? You guys have known me for six months. How are you that close that you can tell me what to do because it's to save your face?" I just think it's a little silly. I try *really* hard not to do that whole face thing, but I do get embarrassed easily.

Winnie dislikes how Asian women feel pressured to protect their image in order to preserve the sanctity of traditional roles; however, she also sees the value of saving face when it comes to managing emotions and protecting her loved ones. Both Winnie and Mary do not want their lives to be structured by the dictates of tradition, norms, and status but recognize how saving face, or in other words doing emotion work, enables them to repay their parents for their sacrifice and preserve the positive aspects of family.

The tension between family obligation and individual liberation was most emotionally complicated for those daughters who felt a deep commitment to their family because they had witnessed the worst of their parents' immigration hardships. Leah is the second daughter of four but assumed a lot of the responsibilities of the oldest sister, because her older sister had a very contentious relationship with her parents. She recalled changing diapers and babysitting for her two younger sisters, vacuuming and cleaning the house, and folding brochures and manning the telephones for her father at work. Unlike many other child caregivers in the study though, she did not harbor deep resentment over assuming these responsibilities even as a child because she wanted to make up for her older sister's rebelliousness. Nevertheless, the strain of being the "good daughter" became an issue when she had to come to terms with her sexual orientation.

> My mom and my Asian women role models indirectly or directly said, you live for the good of the family, so there's a lot of self-sacrifice that's involved. You don't want to shake the boat. You make sure that your sisters are taken care of, that your parents are happy. So there's a sense of putting other people's happiness before yourself. And I saw that with my parents.

Their decision to come to the States was to give us a better life so just the reinforcement of family first, individuality second reinforced to me that okay, becoming gay is bad to them. That's what makes you happy but may tear up the family, you should stifle that.

Leah in fact used the "good daughter" role to cover up her budding sexual attraction to other women by pretending all the men she dated were not living up to her expectations of a good Taiwanese husband. She observed, "When I was trying to still be the good daughter, I built up a very long list of criteria so he had to be Chinese, preferably Taiwanese, he had to be Christian, he had to be all these things. But now looking back, I realize I was doing those things as a way to be in the closet and play this weird game so everyone would still think I was hetero."

RENEGOTIATING GENDER

While resenting their parents for imposing unfair and oppressive restrictions on their childhood, some female interviewees reassessed these family experiences as being formative in helping them to approach their adult lifestyles, struggles, and decisions in more self-empowering ways. These daughters perceived the travails and achievements of working mothers as a source of empowerment and in some cases a role model for their own success. For example, Esther, a Korean American daughter from a working-class family, explained how her mother's business savvy and successful management of their family dry cleaning business inspired her to start her own business as a tailor.

As a child, Kathy occasionally resented her parents' strict rules on dating and strong emphasis on educational achievement but now believes that her parents' traditional values helped her to become independent by steering her to nurture other interests aside from obsession with boys:

I didn't realize the value of the way I was raised until I became an adult. I'm so happy and I'm so grateful that I've been grounded in something, that I've spent the time thinking of myself. My parents have said, most of your friends, they're not worthwhile and that would really hurt. Or you know you can't date because whatever reason and that would be confusing and hurtful to you as a kid, because they never explained it. They would just say things like that and expect us to know. But looking back on it now, I'm like yeah! That is so stupid for some sixteen-year-old to be wrapped up in some stupid boy instead of concentrating on like sports. It's okay to have a social life but the truth is, there are only a few people in your life that you're gonna count on in your desperate hours. Those are your real friends.

Now it becomes clear what they were trying to say to me. It taught us to be self-sufficient, you know?

The lessons Kathy took from her strict upbringing may be her way of making sense of some of the gender inequality she endured as a child, but for others this did not always mean they agreed with this parenting style for their own children. Nevertheless, these narratives highlight how daughters may view their gendered upbringing as both debilitating and empowering at the same time.

To be sure, there are significant overlaps in the personal choices, goals, and aspirations of sons and daughters, but the social contexts, meanings, and processes within which these goals are understood and realized vary because of the different gender constraints they face. Take for example the matter of financial independence: many interviewees, regardless of gender, birth order, class background, or degree of assimilation, expressed a desire for financial independence often because they recognized the enormous sacrifices their parents had already invested in immigrating and raising them. However, Asian American daughters felt more poignantly the complex uses and implications of achieving financial independence and choosing a marital partner in allowing them to reconcile some of the strains of gendered obligation and expectations.

Establishing financial independence is an important turning point in the lives of most children in America, but Asian American daughters felt that "earning their own keep" enabled them to mediate the complicated emotional dynamics of parent-child relations and curb some of the negative effects of gender inequality at home. Mary, for example, has struggled to make it on her own despite her meager wages from her retail job so she can make her own decisions and live away from the constant supervision of her parents. She explained,

MARY: So during college, it would piss me off so much, because I am very proud of separating myself from my family. I know that sounds odd, but when it comes to financial means, I will not take money from my family. For college, [her father] did pay for it, but I also had major student loans which I'm paying right now. Anything luxury, anything foodwise, I'd separate. Even though I'm in the same roof with them, I totally don't want them to pay for me for anything.

ANGIE: Do you know why you felt that way?

MARY: [long pause] I don't know. So if I can afford to buy my own nice things, I will. I do not feel comfortable with him contributing in any way, because he would make certain remarks as to the certain types of food I eat, or the certain types of clothes I wear, or certain types of like "ohhhh, wow." Like "tsk tsk tsk tsk [making sound]." That's his famous thing, like the "tisk tisk tisk [her words]." So I'm very sensitive to those little things and those little things adds up to "well he doesn't approve of it so why should he pay for it?" So if he doesn't approve of it, let me separate myself. I'm like okay, well if he doesn't like that, just don't look at it. I like this and I wanna buy it so I will buy it.

Daughters are highly cognizant of how establishing their financial independence from their parents enables them to curb the amount of influence their parents have on their lives: everything from the way they dress to the career paths they choose. This awareness lies in stark contrast to the perspectives of male participants in the study, who viewed financial independence as a way to denote their entrance into manhood as opposed to providing them a means to escape gendered control.

Some daughters also described how their experiences compared with those of their female siblings who they felt enjoyed the benefits of financial support from their parents but paid the price in terms of gendered obligations. Leah, who enjoys her career as a senior manager at a financial services firm, noticed that her father treated her more like an adult and came to her for business advice than he did her sister, who is financially dependent on him and is obligated to listen to her father's opinions. She explained, "If they were providing for me, how can I go against them? So I think part of being financially independent empowered me to finally say, look dad this is my own life and I'm able to make my own decisions and I'm an adult. So it's very affirming to me, but it also sends a clear signal, because the way my dad sets my decisions versus my older sister is very different. Because he still feels like he has some control over her decisions, whereas for me he's completely hands-off." Although she gratefully accepted his support for her education, Leah has been very careful to manage how much she takes from her parents.

These daughters carry on the lessons they learn from establishing their financial independence into other parts of their lives. Amy, a Chinese American newspaper reporter from a middle-class family, was expected to take on most of the responsibilities of taking care of her two younger siblings, translating for her parents, and helping with household chores throughout her childhood. Although she had been raised to act like the oldest daughter and cultural broker for the family, her parents suddenly began to treat her like a child when her troubled sister ran away from home at the age of sixteen. When she was twenty-two, Amy decided to leave home to live with her boyfriend, which her parents fought tooth and nail, even going so far as to demand that she pay them back all the money that she owed for living at their house. Outraged, she took most of the money she had saved since she was a child from her bank account, around three thousand dollars, gave it to her parents, and stopped speaking to them for a year. Although she has since started communicating with them again, she swore that she would never depend on anyone financially again, even her boyfriend. She stated firmly, "I would never depend on anyone. I don't have to make more money than my boyfriend, but I don't want to depend on him for buying little things at the store. If I were to walk out with a really expensive handbag, I don't want anyone to tell me, oh well did your boyfriend get that for you? No, I got it with my own hard-earned money."

Having witnessed her mother suffer from domestic violence and struggle financially as a result of the divorce, Kimberly also recognizes how financial independence is an important way of achieving meaningful liberation as a woman. I asked her if it was important for her to have a job for the rest of her life, to which Kimberly answered,

> If anything should happen to my boyfriend, let's say when we get married and he's my husband, and if anything should happen to him, I should support myself and my kid. Or God forbid, him and [it didn't] work out, I don't wanna feel like I'm dependent on him. From watching my mom and my dad, I feel like I always have to have some sort of means. I don't wanna be at home because once you're home, you're away from the working world, going back it's really hard. I don't wanna get to a point where I need that. I want to be able to support myself if I had to.

As a concession to her mother, who is concerned about her safety, Kimberly has been living with her boyfriend's parents ever since she moved to New York over five years ago. However, she also agreed to the arrangement only on the condition her boyfriend find her a job; with his help, she has found full-time work as a market researcher. She says she is happy to be able to support herself instead of relying on her mother who is saddled with her own bills and her sister's expenses. She stated that she is currently putting aside money so they can eventually find their own place.

In some cases, daughters who saw themselves as less favored by their parents sought approval and recognition through their educational or financial achievements. Sue, the oldest daughter of the family, was deeply affected by her parents' preferential treatment for her younger brother. Although she did not acknowledge it at the time, she even admitted that she and her husband purchased a house next to her parents despite the fact that it was beyond her financial means in order to gain their approval. She was shocked to learn that when she later moved to the West Coast, her parents were immediately getting it ready to give to her brother, even though they had been slow to help her set it up. She felt that he "lived a charmed life" because of his ability to charm people without working as hard as she did. However, she related to me one pivotal and moving moment when she was caught off guard by a fleeting comment her mother made during a heated argument.

> Only recently did I understand [when] my mother said something to me that made me really think. She let something slip. My parents favored [my brother] so I had twenty years of suppressing all the anger. Very recently, I lost my temper and I went someplace that didn't serve any purpose other than allowing me to vent my anger, but the bottom line is I should've known better. I said a lot of things in anger, everything that I've been bottling up for years, how they treat him so much better than me and they provided him so much and I struggled every day. So I said to her that all my life, I've been number two, even though I'm the oldest. She says, what do you mean you're number two? You're more successful than your brother! And I meant, number two as in second in line in my family and she took it to mean that I was more successful than my brother. And it really blew me away that she would even acknowledge that. It's kind of like the only thing that came out of that that was . . . wow.

In this quote, Sue describes the incident as an accidental, not deliberate, comment by her mother that might otherwise be overlooked by an outside observer. To her, this seemingly minor comment was a major turning point in terms of understanding their relationship, because it was the first time her mother communicated to Sue her pride in her daughter's accomplishments. Understanding the cultural context of saving face, Sue herself regretted losing control and exposing all her feelings of resentment, instead of managing her emotions as was expected in her family.

This narrative also reminded me of a similar seemingly minor yet deeply meaningful turning point in my relationship with my mother that shed some light on the nature of intergenerational communication in Asian families. Like Sue, I had always believed that my mother favored my younger brother, but my mother would get very upset if I tried to imply that she treated us differently. When I was in graduate school, I received one of those Hallmark cards that had a preprinted message inside of it to which my parents as usual added a brief note about wishing me good health and happiness and signed the card. However, before sending me the card, my mother told me nonchalantly how appropriate she felt the card was. The preprinted message expressed how despite the fact that they did not always agree with my decisions, they have always admired my independence and courage in doing things on my own terms. Although on the surface devoid of context, this Hallmark message may seem inconsequential to someone who is unfamiliar with my parents or the way Asian immigrant families work, but it was a rare and important gesture to me, as I rarely heard my parents express those feelings verbally. To me, this was an acknowledgment that despite the arguments over how much easier my brother made their lives by accommodating to their wishes and desires, they felt a deep respect for my ability to make my own path in life. I realized then how often my mother would say how proud she was of my academic achievements; for her, pride was the same thing as love. After receiving that card, I listened more carefully to subtle comments my mother made and began to understand how sometimes she was angry with my life decisions, not because I was a disappointment or a failure, but because she was worried that those decisions would make my life more difficult and anger was the only way she knew how to express her concern—one emotion that *was* openly allowed in Korean immigrant families.

Gender, Culture, and Marital Choices

As they begin to experience similar struggles with family and career in their late twenties and early thirties, Asian American children, and daughters in particular, face the dilemma of how to negotiate more gender-equal relationships while carrying on the more positive aspects of their family's cultural heritage. Contrary to the presumption that second-generation daughters are more likely to reject their traditions altogether, Dion and Dion find evidence that the stress and tensions associated with gender role expectations in the family can in fact cause daughters in immigrant families to reflect on, negotiate, and engage more deeply with their ethnocultural backgrounds, ultimately heightening the salience of ethnic identities in their individual lives.[21] Because they are considered central figures within family traditions, the authors argue that women may actually express pride in their role in preserving certain cultural values and practices, even as they selectively do away with those aspects they consider oppressive.

Within this context, Korean and Chinese American daughters found other creative and self-empowering ways of getting in touch with their parents' culture while rejecting the terms of gender inequality. As one example, several participants who married outside their race and did not identify with their ethnic community explained how they still felt "Korean," "Chinese," or "Asian" through their deep appreciation for Asian-based arts and religion. Esther stated that although American in terms of her values and behavior, her way of viewing the world does not fit well with the Western way of thinking in that she sees beyond black-and-white dichotomies and embraces the more Asian idea that people's ideas and values can be multifaceted and contradictory. Much of this is reflected in her art. This realization later on in life helped her to overcome some of the racial anxieties she felt in negotiating her Korean heritage with her upbringing by white caregivers while her parents were working. We can see how transcending the East-West binary can help these women to reconcile some of the general tensions and contradictions of being an American-born daughter in an immigrant family.

Interestingly, several female interviewees who had had negative views or experiences with the gender inequality and ethnic exclusiveness of Korean churches during their childhood also found their self-liberation in another religion more deeply rooted in Asian culture: Buddhism. Kimberly, who first learned about Buddhism through her mother when she was younger, described to me how she reinterpreted her Buddhist faith in a way that allowed her to liberate herself from the more constraining and hierarchical aspects of Chinese culture without letting go of it altogether.

> ANGIE: Is there any aspect of Chinese culture that you practice in your everyday life?
>
> KIMBERLY: Well, my mom is a little lenient, but let's say Chinese New Year's, my boyfriend's family is very traditional. You know, not washing your hair on the day of New Year's. That drives me crazy, but I do it. Not allowing you to cut your hair for a month after Chinese New Year. Not buying shoes for a whole month. But that's because that's their tradition and I think that's more Cantonese tradition, because my mom never follows any of that. My religion is Buddhism, and I associate Buddhism with Asia more than any other culture. Sometimes when I was younger and when I was living in Maryland, I would help my mother burn incense, do the tea for my mother and things like that.
>
> ANGIE: Do you practice that now?
>
> KIMBERLY: Not, not really. But I feel like Buddhism is free. You don't have to go to temple every weekend to feel like you're part of the Buddha, as long as you live your life. But I'm sure if I go across a temple, I will definitely go in to pay my respects.

In this passage, Kimberly expresses her contempt for the more sexist aspects of traditional Chinese culture and instead, embraces the more progressive tenets of Buddhism, particularly the teachings that reaffirm freedom, including freedom from conformity, freedom from tradition, and freedom from exclusion. When she practices rituals, it is by choice only. Buddhism provides the connection she needs to Chinese culture without being constrained by the restrictive dictates of gendered expectations and religious rituals.

One important way in which the gendered perspectives of daughters and sons lead to different ways of approaching family culture is in the area of marriage. In their research on Asian American intermarriage patterns, Min and Kim found that both Chinese and Korean American men to varying degrees are more likely than their female counterparts to marry within their ethnicity and race, while women are more likely to marry white or other minority partners. They also explain that Asian parents tend to encourage their American-born sons to marry Korean immigrant partners much more so than they do their daughters.[22] In addition to recognizing that daughters may benefit less from gender inequality rooted in traditional Asian culture, parents view endogamy as central to patrilineality by reaffirming the continuation of the family bloodline. As Kibria explains, "marriage outside the group carries with it the danger of impurity or contamination, as personified by the 'mixed-race' child. ... This impurity threaten[s] family honour and perhaps even the continuity of the family line, as 'mixed-race' children [are] not acceptable carriers of the family name."[23] Furthermore, parents may also assume that regardless of where they are born, women from the same ethnic background are better equipped to pass on their language and cultural heritage to the next generation of children. Thus, although parents may encourage all their children to marry within their ethnicity, it is more important for parents that sons marry a woman from the same ethnic background.

In line with the traditional patrilineal approach to marriage, Mike described how despite his progressive Americanized outlook, one of the duties that he took seriously was his parents' expectation that he marry a Korean woman. He informed me that he has dated non-Korean women but admitted almost apologetically that he would most likely marry a Korean woman.

> MIKE: People are shocked that I only want to date Korean people, and I don't understand why. Someone recently said to me that I'm very progressive in my thinking but certain parts of me, of my core beliefs, are very old-fashioned or traditional.
>
> ANGIE: Like what?
>
> MIKE: I don't know, an idea that people have to stay married and that you do it once and forever, and certain other views they thought were kind of traditional. I think there's something inside of me—and maybe this is part being the oldest Korean son—this responsibility that I have of marrying another Korean person. But again, it's not something that my

parents beat me over the head with. It's not like they mandated it or they impressed that upon me.

One difference he does note between his standards and those of his parents is that while his parents want someone who will be a good wife and a good homemaker, he wants his wife to have her own life and, even better, her own career. Thus, while on the surface his choices resonate with some of his parents' views on ethnicity, his stated preferences and rationalization for his choices also reflect his own desire to become a more progressive male figure within his American frame of reference.

Like women who dated within their ethnicity, the men in the study who preferred coethnic partners talked extensively about the ease with which they could relate to each other's family culture and the experiences they shared because they were raised by immigrant parents. Some American-born sons like Eddie also discussed how women from the same cultural background would also be better able to cultivate ties with their natal family and nurture their parents' cultural values for their children. I asked Eddie what kinds of things he may be able to do with a Korean woman than he might not do so easily with a non-Korean women. He replied that there would probably be very few differences between being married to one or the other in most aspects except one:

> For me, it's an important thing: the relationship that my wife would have with our children, the relationship my wife would have with my parents, the relationship my parents would have with her parents. And once again, it could be race, it could be language, it could be ethnicity, it could be religious background. But for me, I wanted a woman that was Korean and shared the same culture and values and background that I had. And not only that, but my Korean is pretty bad, my spoken Korean. I want [my children] to learn Korean from my wife too. So it wasn't all about that, but it's just this is where for me the best connection was: a fellow Korean.

As with Eddie, few interviewees in the study thought that there were any major differences between marrying an Asian and a non-Asian, especially if the spouse was born or raised in the United States. However, some felt it was important to find someone who could emotionally relate to the experience of being raised by Asian immigrant parents with all its shared values and conflicts. More important, this particular passages underscores the gendered and generational expectations that may arise from women's role as mothers. In Eddie's case, he believed that his wife's strong family values and Korean language proficiency would help compensate for his own difficulties speaking Korean and help strengthen ties with his own parents. Through her role as mother, she can also help carry their cultural heritage onto the next generation.

In comparison, daughters in the study reflected more deeply on their choice of marital partners based on both their gender-based struggles with traditional cultural values and their desire to pass on positive aspects of their family culture. Some chose to do this by marrying someone of the same ethnicity or race, but others ended up marrying non-Asian partners. In the latter case, even if their choices stemmed from their experiences with sexism within their own families, it is interesting to see how some of those decisions were fraught with tension, guilt, and uncertainty. Having grown up in a predominantly Jewish town in New Jersey, Anna, who is currently single, reported that all of the men she has seriously dated throughout her life have been mostly children of immigrants and mostly white, never East Asian. Like many women who have not dated other Asian Americans, she claimed that it is not from lack of interest but that the few Asian men she has met do not see her as "docile enough." However, she conveyed considerable ambivalence and guilt about marrying outside her ethnicity because she felt that it may threaten the cultural continuity and sense of kinship that binds her family together.

> ANGIE: Do you think that when you get married that you would ever consider an Asian American husband when you got married?
>
> ANNA: I wouldn't but yeah, it would be so much easier [laughs], like dealing with my parents, understanding my parents and all the intercultural clashes. I'm the youngest of all of my cousins on my mom's side and all of my mom's side of my family is here in New Jersey. All of my cousins have gotten married to a non-Asian, and every time it's just so difficult. There's such a major transition period and misunderstanding and clashes. And when they come to our family gatherings, usually it's mostly in Taiwanese and you know they feel uncomfortable and bored and you know they don't know what's going on. It's just the food and understanding why they have to go home and not understanding those types of values I guess.
>
> ANGIE: Would your parents be pretty mad then if you brought home a non-Asian?
>
> ANNA: Oh, no [sighs]. At my cousin's wedding, my cousin married a Peruvian guy and my dad gave this wedding speech about how we're all marrying outside of the [race], none of us are marrying Asians (ha) and how you know that's great, we have all this intercultural mixing.

But there was some sort of regret in his tone that we are mixing so much. At the end, he said, "Yeah I know [Anna] is going to when it's her turn, she's going to be marrying a non-Asian too." (ha) He thinks I'm going to be marrying a white person.

Among all the choices they can make, female interviewees view marriage with a non-Asian as the means to reconstruct their families and live on more gender-equal terms but also fear that it may distance themselves from the family and cultural values they grew up with.

As a result, second-generation women, including those who do not relate to their ethnicity in a traditional sense, created alternative ways of embracing the positive features of family and culture by practicing "ethnicity by proxy"— that is, by nurturing other relationships, values, or practices they felt resonated most closely with those of their immigrant parents. For example, some women sought non-Asian partners who they feel best reinforced the more positive values of their cultural heritage, even if they were not Asian. Some found this emotional connection and cultural understanding by dating other immigrants or children of immigrants, while others felt steered toward certain ethnic groups, such as Italians or Jews, who they thought shared similar views as their parents on family and education.

Having witnessed some of the hardships their mothers endured with their own in-laws, many daughters in the study were also highly cognizant of the way their boyfriends or potential husbands related to their own parents and the importance of getting along with their in-laws. Regardless of the race of their partners, many female participants wanted to avoid men who had what they called "momma's boy syndrome." They feared that such men would end up acting like their own fathers by burdening them with more household obligations, obligating them to the traditional gendered expectations of their in-laws, and failing to defend their wives and children against their in-laws. Kimberly, who dates mostly Chinese American men, explained how her mother's relationship with her in-laws shaped her views on relationships and marriage later on in life.

KIMBERLY: My grandfather and my grandmother always felt my mom was from a poor family so they treated her really rotten. And I mean it's ridiculous.

ANGIE: Do you think it's important if you do get married, for your in-laws to be involved with your life and your extended kin in general?

KIMBERLY: Oh yeah. It would be nice if we all lived here cause family's important. I guess when I looked for a boyfriend, I didn't want my boyfriend to be one of those sons who listened to every word that their parents said. Cause I see my mom and my dad, and I don't want to be in that kind of life. I mean I'm not an unreasonable person, but I don't want whatever we decide to be because of what your parents said. So he's not like that. On the other hand, he's the opposite [laughs].

Her boyfriend's parents were generous enough to let the young couple live with them, paying only a very small token rent—a big boon in light of New York's inflated housing market. Although she considers them traditional Chinese in many ways, she says they have not saddled her with any household responsibilities or unreasonable expectations other than cleaning up after herself.

In some cases, these anxieties may also be rooted in stereotypes they internalize about Asian males in the mainstream American media as well as subconscious associations these women make between Asian American men and their fathers. Based on interviews with daughters of Korean and Vietnamese immigrants, Pyke and Johnson make a similar observation about Asian American women in their sample, whose outlooks often cast Asian families and Asian men as signifying gender oppression and white American families and white men as promoting gender equality.[24] In the following excerpt from my field notes, Kathy recalled a negative experience with an Italian ex-boyfriend who she felt was too strongly attached to his mother yet described this as a predominant feature of Korean men.

> [Kathy] said one thing she's not sure she can deal with are her in-laws because her parents alone are very controlling and want to be very involved with their kids' lives so she thinks that if she married a Korean American guy, his parents would also be like that and she doesn't feel like she could deal with the situation. She said for example, she dated an Italian guy a long time ago and he had the type of guy who hadn't cut his mother's apron strings yet and was very momma's boy and she couldn't deal with that. But she feels that with Korean American guys, that would be very true. Because she had gone through so much with her parents, she didn't want her husband's parents to be like that and try to be too overinvolved with her life.

In Kathy's case, growing up in Colorado at a time when there were very few Asians, let alone Asian American peers, meant that the only Asian male figure in her life was her immigrant father, who fought bitterly with her mother because he refused to help out with household responsibilities. Today, she is anxious to meet other Asian Americans so she can share her experience of feeling "different" but does not feel like she has the means to connect with them through her work or her social networks. Instead, she seeks that connection through Buddhism and the few books that she can find on the Asian American experience.

Those who ended up with in-laws they felt were overbearing devised other creative strategies in order to avoid potential conflicts. This was of course easier to do for those whose in-laws were in Korea. For example, Tina, a Korean American professional married to a pastor's son, told me how she would play the "good daughter-in-law" on her infrequent visits to Korea and would respectfully agree whenever her mother-in-law called to ask her if she was attending church weekly but never actually followed through with these promises, given her Buddhist roots and busy work schedule. A Korean American colleague of mine once told me that language and assimilation can be one of the easiest ways of excusing oneself out of these types of burdensome cultural obligations. In her case, she felt she was subject to more expectations and obligations from her in-laws simply because she spoke Korean, whereas her Americanized sister was excused from such responsibilities because she was seen as too American to understand. Similarly, Elliott noted how his Vietnamese wife could get out of the constant barrage of questions about having children simply because his parents didn't speak English, whereas he was constantly "under the microscope" whenever he dealt with her English-speaking parents. He remarked "so in some ways, having the language barrier is kind of beneficial in a sense."

Not all second-generation participants were involved with their extended kin, which depended on a number of factors, including where they lived, their history of family conflicts and dependency, and their immediate relationship with their parents. However, among those who did maintain or revive these relationships, most were oldest siblings—a pattern that may reflect an extension of their roles as the family patriarch or matriarch. As implied by this label, these relationships were also gendered in various ways. As the oldest of all his male cousins, Tony explains how he adopted a leadership role among not only his immediate family but also his extended kin by making crucial decisions for the family—for example, when they had to decide whether or not to put his grandmother in a nursing home. When asked what it meant to be the oldest son, Tony responded,

> TONY: Basically I have to be the keystone for the [family]. If something happens, people would look to me for an answer. So if there is a family crisis or if something happens, they're always going to look to me either to keep the peace or work things out between one side or the other.
> ANGIE: Okay, any examples of this?

TONY: Oh yeah. So my extended family on my mother's side, there's four families and after the Korean War, there was some animosity about how things went down and how the resources were shared by the four families which was one of the reasons why our family wound up coming to the U.S. because there was nothing after the war. So for almost four years, they haven't been on good terms. So last year I made it a point to go meet the four families in person to try establish keeping the peace, skipping my mother's generation and going straight for the kids that were my generation. And that was for two reasons: one, they speak English better and two, their views might be a little bit more progressive and disconnected enough from the politics. So at the end of the day, I had a meeting with them and said whatever happened in our family is in the past, was done under extreme circumstances and I want to make sure that the four families, we are family and we should keep in contact with each other. We shouldn't carry the politics and the burdens of our parents and grandparents just for carrying on the tradition of being pissed off [chuckles]. And so they agreed and we're actually on Facebook, talking which is actually kind of neat [chuckles].

The narrative offers a very poignant account of how an oldest son can become an important mediating and decision-making figure within not only the nuclear family but also the extended kinship network.

Although they could assume a principal role within their immediate families, women were much less likely to do so within their extended kin networks. Because family itself is generally the source of tension and a restrictive space for women, females are more likely to find emotional release through networks outside their relatives. The few women like Grace who did immerse themselves within their extended family network explained how other than being a role model, they also acted as a maternal figure in their cousins' lives through various acts of caregiving. In my case, despite being the oldest cousin of all my cousins and also the oldest child of the oldest son, I was reluctant to get too involved with my more traditional relatives on my father's side as a child, partly because my mother had raised me to be independent but also, because I intensely disliked the gendered burdens that I believed came with this role—for example, watching all my male cousins lounge around at family gatherings while the women were slaving away in the kitchen. I later realized this rejection did come at the cost of losing my "role model" status within the family and cultivating the type of close bonds that my male and female cousins now seem to have with one another. However, this is also the kind of emotional balancing act that women are more likely than men to find themselves forced to negotiate, because they do not have the privilege of enjoying the best of both cultural worlds.

CONCLUSION

This study complicates current understandings on cultural reproduction as they apply to the American-born children of Korean and Chinese immigrants. Given their key role in carrying on the family name, oldest sons encounter different parental pressures and privileges than do daughters and younger male siblings, all of which reinforce patrilineal expressions of ethnicity and culture as they enter adulthood. Having to learn the more involved responsibilities of motherhood, daughters face a more complicated and burdensome situation, which can lead to more nuanced forms of ethnic appreciation. Conservative views, restrictive rules, and unequal treatment may alienate them from family traditions and practices, particularly in the early years of adolescence.

Extending this argument further, one can argue that restrictive controls over their sexuality and behavior may promote greater empathy among daughters since constant reflection and engagement with gender and family issues can heighten their understanding of these traditions and encourage a more developed sense of ethnic identification. Because of their roles as family caregivers, daughters' felt commitment to culture is enhanced by deeper familial involvement and a developing sense of empathy for the mother's burdens, especially in cases where the father exercises strong control over the family. At the same time, daughters must also negotiate these emotive ties with their own desires for autonomy, personal fulfillment, and American ideals on egalitarianism. I argue that this internal tension pushes them to negotiate and create more innovative and profound ways of fulfilling their parents' aspirations on family, culture, and career.

Gender differences in socialization is most apparent among oldest siblings whose sense of duty on carrying on the family name in the case of boys or saving face in the case of girls leads to conflicting emotions. The gendered expectations and responsibilities with which sons—particularly oldest sons—are inculcated later cultivate the kind of discipline, entitlement, and skills that enable them to become family leaders and decision makers, whereas the restrictions, obligation, and emotion work that daughters experience as youth cause more internal turmoil and guilt as they try to establish their independent identities as adults. However, many of the interviews also reveal how much of this depends on where individuals stand with respect to other siblings and the constraints they face as a household. Furthermore, many

Korean and Chinese immigrant families adapt to their new surroundings and circumstances, causing the members to blur, shift, or even reverse the gender boundaries that define traditionally patriarchal cultures. Such similarities only go to show that dichotomous portrayals of Asian immigrant families as "sexist" and (white) American families as "liberated" fail to uncover the complexities of gender inequality apart from the dynamics of culture and assimilation. In the next chapter, I discuss how in this way the processes of ethnic identity formation for Asian Americans are also deeply rooted in the broader racial power structures of American society.

CHAPTER 6

The Racial Contradictions
of Being American

As the previous chapters have shown, the way in which children of immigrants negotiate their place within the family hierarchy strongly influences how they view and relate to their racial and ethnic identities. However, second-generation Americans must also find ways to manage, negotiate, and express these private identities publicly in their day-to-day relations with individuals and groups outside their home. In the case of Asian Americans, the mythical framing of Asian families and culture in American race relations makes this process tricky because, on one hand, they are viewed as the ideal family in terms of the way they raise model students and workers, but on the other hand, these same values and practices set them apart as too alien to fit in with their native-born white American peers. The strategic negotiation of these public identities is further complicated by the simultaneous desire to discard the more oppressive aspects of the family hierarchy while preserving the empowering benefits of family solidarity and sacrifice. Within this context, this chapter examines how Korean and Chinese Americans understand the relevance of these privately negotiated identities in their carefully constructed public self and translate them into actual behavior.

Given the racial contradictions of being Asian American, scholars must carefully rethink the way they conceptualize and measure ethnic identities and racial experiences. Ethnic self-identification has been traditionally used as one of the main benchmarks for determining the degree to which an ethnic group has been accepted by the host culture and assimilated into the mainstream. However, as Phinney and Ong observe in their review of ethnic identity research, there are a variety of ways in which we can evaluate the strength of ethnicity in the worldview and day-to-day lives of ethnic groups in

America beyond self-identification.[1] These include feelings of belonging, shared norms and values, feelings toward one's own group, and cultural practices that are associated with a specific ethnic group. I also build on Arlie Hochschild's observation that the presentation of the public self does not always align with the internal emotional turmoil and feelings that Asian Americans struggle with in their relations with others.

Indeed, the interview narratives throughout this book indicate only a weak and inconsistent relationship between the way Korean and Chinese Americans identify and the ideals they embrace and the actual experiences, cultural values, and social networks with which they engage in their day-to-day lives. Logan makes a similar observation in his interactions with Asian Americans: "The weird thing about it is that they would say things like, 'We get along with everybody. We don't really experience any cases of discrimination' and then in the same sentence, they'll go on and describe a totally racist situation and I'll be like 'Wait, there's no racism? Let me list all the things you just told me.' It's like we experience discrimination, experience all these things, and they can categorize it, but then somehow they stop short of calling it racism." Most participants identified themselves as both "Korean/Chinese" and "American," but how they related to other Asian and non–Asian Americans varied widely. Second-generation Asian Americans distanced themselves from "typical Koreans/Chinese" who would highlight their "foreignness" but still thought it was important to maintain their language and culture. Most expressed optimism that their parents had proven the existence of the American Dream, but many still felt they had to push and negotiate for a level playing field at work. Many participants did not see themselves as victims of "racism," but some of those very same people still felt Asian Americans were not fully accepted as racial equals by their American peers.

How do we explain these ambiguities, tensions, and contradictions? How do Asian Americans strategically negotiate these conflicts? And what does this tell us about the processes of racial identity formation and the broader context of American race relations today? From a Western perspective, one may view this seeming contradiction between what they say and what they experience as an indication of hypocrisy or self-delusion on the part of Asian Americans—hence leading some pundits to label Asian Americans as "honorary whites."[2] What is problematic with this description is the assumption that there are only two possible scenarios: either you encounter blatant Jim Crow racial discrimination that puts you in direct opposition with white Americans or you embrace and support those in power in the belief (mistaken or not) that your values and interests are the same. You are either for or against us. You cannot be both.

To disentangle some of the overlaps between racial privilege and immigrant ideology, this chapter explores the narratives of fourteen second-generation white Americans in addition to those of my Korean and Chinese American participants.[3] I begin by identifying parallel themes that emerge in the worldviews of ten Jewish Americans and those of Korean and Chinese American participants based on the immigrant family experience; I then expand my focus to include four other second-generation white Americans in order to cover the broad context of racial identity and privilege. This chapter takes as its starting point the liminal positioning of Asian Americans along the borders of racial privilege and subordination. It recognizes the ways in which Asian Americans may emotionally subscribe to the ideologies and values of white (particularly Jewish) children of immigrants around the American Dream. At the same time, Korean and Chinese Americans I interviewed were keenly aware of the way they are made to feel racially different and constantly negotiating their citizenship and belonging, unlike Americans, who have the broader option to identify as whites. The intermediary position of Asian Americans in black-white relations helps to explain the many contradictions, ambiguities, and difficulties Korean and Chinese Americans have in articulating race and racism in the post–civil rights era.

Unpacking the Immigrant Narrative

Although this does not necessarily obviate racial and class tensions, there is something to be said about the sense of empathy and mutual respect that bonds immigrants who come to the United States voluntarily. Cheng and Espiritu argue that Koreans experience less public conflict with Latino immigrants than African Americans despite class tensions partly because of parallels in migration contexts that foster an "immigrant ideology"—one in which America is viewed as the land of opportunity and a place where they can be rewarded for their hard work and past sacrifices.[4] By drawing on their family histories, the immigrant narrative helps second-generation Asian Americans not only to make sense of the conflicts they feel between their Asian upbringing and American lives but also to feel connected to their ethnic heritage and normalize their sense of racial difference by situating their family's lives within the prototypical American parable.[5]

In a similar manner, the Korean and Chinese Americans I spoke with characterized their experiences at home and school as typical for most immigrant families. Both second-generation Korean/Chinese and Jewish Americans described their parents' American Dream as involving the individual pursuit of material success, including a good home and good schools for their children, and most felt that they achieved this dream through hard work, frugality, and self-sacrifice. Like the Jewish Americans in this study, Korean and Chinese Americans thought that their parents pushed them hard to do well in school, at the same time they reinforced the value of family and importance of marrying someone of the same ethnic background. Unlike their brothers, girls in both families shouldered unequal household responsibilities and were more likely to experience strict supervision over their sexuality.

It is not surprising then that both Jews and Asian Americans regularly made cross-ethnic comparisons about the immigrant family experience. One Russian Jewish American participant joked how people liked to call his Korean American friend "Jewish" because of similarities in "how she grew up and how I grew up and those things that we have in common." Julia, a single Russian Jew from an upper-middle-class family, was attending medical school to become a doctor at the time of the interview. Her family though came from humble beginnings. She recalled when her family first came to the United States, she lived with her parents and grandmother in a tiny apartment in the Russian Jewish enclave of Brighton Beach in Brooklyn. She spoke about how Russian American children feel the same pressure to go into prestigious professions as Asian Americans do because of their felt obligation to their parents who made tremendous sacrifices in order to bring their children here:

> When I got into Columbia for undergrad my dad said, yeah, this is why we came to this country. A lot of it is internalized, that any failure of mine reflected on them. A lot of immigrant kids have that pressure to deal with. [That's why] I get along really well with Asian, Indian, African people that show their immigrant mentality. If you are an American girl and you bring your boyfriend home, American parents don't really care all that much about careers; they care about what you are really passionate about, as long as you are happy. The first thing my mother says is, does he go to law school? With immigrant parents you have much more rigid standards. You have to have a career where you are going to be able to be stable, where you always have a steady income. A lot of it is just wanting to justify to the family coming to the country. My parents wanted me to be a doctor or to be lawyer, and that's why we came to America.

As in Julia's case, not all second-generation participants—white or Asian— thought their parents had achieved the American Dream for themselves, because some had to give up careers, lost money, were swindled by other immigrants upon arrival, or succumbed to gambling and other addictions in order to deal with their pain and disappointment. Instead, they passed on the burdens of their failures and the hopes and expectations for material success to the next generation.

Jewish American interviewees recognized that discrimination was an inevitable part of this struggle and that some of that culture may even be preserved but believed that future generations would ultimately blend into New York's ethnic melting pot. Mendel is a twenty-eight-year-old Jewish American lawyer whose parents are from Israel and own a successful jewelry business in Manhattan. He made the following comparison between Jewish and Asian Americans:

> It's the same story. You come here, America's very welcoming, New York in particular. You're not made to feel like you're different that much. I grew up with Italian kids on my block who were anti-Semitic, but these were Italians that probably were as discriminated against as I was cause they were Italian. And they were just low-class, they just wanted to start fights and stuff. But that wasn't like real anti-Semitism. Asians in this country, it's the same sort of story. Yeah, there are skin color issues but more than anywhere in New York, you see white-Asian couples, you see babies that are mixed. Even in my high school, there are a lot of people of mixed Asian-Caucasian intermarrying.

Despite his extensive knowledge of Jewish traditions as a result of Hebrew school and a personal interest in Jewish literature, Mendel himself claimed he was open to marrying outside his ethno-religious and racial group and in fact believed it was a healthier approach to intermingle and marry outside one's ethnicity. Although his parents prefer their children marry another Jewish woman, they decided not to push them anymore when his older brother, who was dating a Japanese woman, tragically passed away nine years earlier. As the youngest son in the family, Mendel, who was single at the time of the interview, also said that a lot of the pressure dissipated because his older sister married someone Jewish.

The significance of the American Dream also seems to cut across class and economic situations. If they thought they were not yet able to achieve personal happiness or material success, second-generation Jewish Americans usually did not attribute this to the failures of the American Dream. For example, Tanya is a single twenty-eight-year-old working-class Russian Jew who works part-time out of the home in the technology field. She believed that children of immigrants face unique burdens to do well in school, which explained why in high school "the immigrant kids always did better than the native kids. Doing good for these kids isn't a choice, it's a requirement." She thought that her chemist mother and industrial engineer father had high expectations for her in terms of education, but she ended up feeling college was useless and was instead proud to become a self-taught computer expert with only an associate's degree.

After dropping out of medical school, Shane, a thirty-four-year-old Jewish American whose parents are both teachers, also decided to go into the teaching profession for about seven years. However, he has been financially dependent on his father for most of his life and was in between jobs at the time of the interview. Nevertheless, Shane also believed in the American Dream despite the fact that he was unable to fulfill it because of his economic situation. When asked how he defined the American Dream, he replied,

> It's really difficult. Like there's the stereotypical American Dream which is coming here and owning a house and having a family and having good jobs. That's the stereotypical American Dream, but that's not really reality for most people and that's not my version of what the American Dream is. My version is just being comfortable without big problems. I guess I'm still in the phase where I'm not where I want to be in life so that's what I'm dealing with myself right now. I'd like to be financially independent, out of debt, own a house, be married, have grown-up kids, but also have time to pursue my interest and hobbies, being able to work on that and to be successful in that regard. Financial independence I guess is the big thing. But it's not the same as just moving to the suburbs and having a nice car and a house.

Although he did not like the structure of education itself, Shane considered himself a good student when he was young and felt a lot of respect for teachers like his parents with whom he was very close. The children of immigrants are anxious that losing faith in the American Dream would be negating the importance of the sacrifices that their parents had made. As opposed to questioning the merits of the immigrant ideology, Shane redefined what it meant within the context of his life—one that does not require material goods but rather, individual financial independence.

Korean and Chinese Americans in the study also frequently referred to Jewish Americans as a reference point for understanding their parents' values. Henry, a thirty-two-year-old Korean American contractor and entrepreneur, described it as such: "My parents raised me like a typical Korean parent. Study hard, eat, get some sleep, study on the weekends, excel, really academically-oriented. You know I played three instruments as a child. Those are pretty typical Korean things like the Jewish tradition as well. Academics come first. Be literate, learn how to read and write." Similarly, Jinah stated, "It's no surprise that people say a lot of the Korean first generation are somewhat similar to the Jewish generation." Sharon, a twenty-eight-year-old

Chinese American marketing analyst, also noted how almost all of her white friends were Jewish because "some Jewish family structures are very similar to Asian's and we were the ones who always did well in school."

Like the Jewish Americans in the study, Korean and Chinese Americans acknowledged that this immigrant narrative was essential in validating the sacrifices their parents made to ensure a good life for them. Elliott, the Chinese American financial consultant and aspiring filmmaker, explained how he struggled with his career choice because of this guilt and obligation. Although he said his passion was in filmmaking, the pressure to pay his parents back for their sacrifices initially steered him toward a career in consulting. However, he believes that he has more options than his parents because "as a first-generation immigrant, you're just striving to survive, and it's that second or third-generation that has more opportunity. I'm gonna be a ballerina, or I'm gonna try to be a tennis pro." Initially labeling this as a cultural difference, Elliott later speculated on to what extent this shift in orientation may actually reflect the different socioeconomic constraints and opportunities that each generation faced.

The desire to relate to their Jewish peers also partly stemmed from a need to smooth over this underlying feeling of racial and cultural difference by following the paths of a well-integrated minority group. The ethnic positionality of Jews resonates for many second-generation Korean and Chinese Americans because they have personally observed how Jewish American peers are able to preserve their ethnicity and cultural traditions but normalize their difference in a metropolitan area that boasts a large Jewish minority. Although she was raised in Colorado, where there were almost no other Asian Americans, Kathy attended a high school that was almost a third Jewish. She explained how this experience solidified her sense of empathy and emotional connection with Jewish Americans in her school:

> Once you start getting older, you realize, oh wait, I am part of a distinct minority. And then you start noticing differences and I didn't start to really process that until I was in high school. The high school that I went to, it was about 30 percent Jewish and so if I said like oh this is the weird thing in my [family], they kinda understood even though it's not the same minority group. And they kind of understood like oh yeah, there are weird things at home that only your family does, maybe most families don't do that. So I was able to speak freely about my experiences and people would say, oh yeah in my house we do this. We had this Jewish friend in high school who was very, very strict during Passover and we'd always ask her what's Kosher and what's this, so it was pretty free-flowing about stuff like that. Because there's so few minorities so people are more curious than threatened.

Being surrounded by other immigrants, particularly those with a visible presence, allowed Kathy to fit in and also relate to others who are not as privileged as white Americans. In addition, having Jewish friends allowed her to also normalize the cultural differences that came with being part of an Asian immigrant family. Incidentally, Kathy's husband is also half Jewish.

In this sense, the choice to date someone Jewish or foreign-born black can reflect not only a desire to assimilate, but also the need to connect with someone with similar immigrant family struggles and experiences. Jasmine, whose romantic partners have been predominantly Jewish, illustrates how this sense of connection can also shape decisions on marriage and dating: "I always thought that men who were Jewish were not completely white (ha). Yeah I like Jewish men, I like the fact they had customs, I like the fact that some of them came from immigrant background as well, and they weren't always that privileged and had troubles with poverty, but mostly that they themselves not feeling that they're really white either. The Jews that I went out with, I felt like they saw themselves as another culture."

Unveiling the Racial Habitus

Based on similarities between Jewish and Asian American values, there is a tendency to predict that Asian Americans, especially Korean and Chinese Americans, are following the optimistic path toward assimilation. However, in many ways, the American Dream is a rehearsed script for Asian Americans that is intended to validate the sacrifices of immigrant parents and find commonality across ethnic boundaries but in itself does little to capture the deeper social meaning that it may take on for different racial groups within the context of their day-to-day lives. Although the immigrant parents' values and expectations may lead to similar ideals among white and Asian Americans, the reality of racial categories and experiences often creates conditions that make it difficult for Korean and Chinese Americans to achieve complete parity with their white peers. To make matters more complicated, a number of studies indicate that Asian Americans are stuck in an intermediary position between whites and blacks, making strides in areas that do not completely undermine the racial status quo but encountering barriers and hostility when they try to move beyond it.[6] Moreover, this feeling of in-betweenness on the borders of marginality and privilege cultivates a type of racial self-consciousness that permeates the narratives of Korean and Chinese Americans in the study.

Based on a comparison with Southern and Eastern European immigrants in the early twentieth century, Perlmann and Waldinger argue that the discrimination Asian Americans and other new immigrant populations encounter today is not much different from what most immigrants face when they first enter a host culture that demands cultural conformity and a docile labor force.[7] Based on the assimilationist paths of European immigrants before them, the authors predict a more optimistic future scenario for contemporary immigrant groups if they can carefully negotiate their positioning on the "right side" of the black-white racial divide. Along with other proponents of the "honorary white" theory, they argue that rapid educational progress, class heterogeneity, and intermarriage rates among Asian Americans indicate that they are well on their way toward overcoming nativist and racial barriers and achieving complete parity with native-born whites.

This interpretation of racial experiences belies the complexities of racism in the post–civil rights era particularly for groups situated at the intersections of privilege and marginalization. With the elimination of legalized racism in the post–civil rights era, overt expressions of racial bigotry such as hate violence, racial epithets, and blatant discrimination have given way to a new laissez-faire, or free-market, racial ideology that rationalizes the current racial order around ideologies about cultural inferiority and cultural superiority.[8] Premised on the notion that we now live in a color-blind American society, the argument is that some minority groups (specifically Asians and Jews) succeed, whereas others (blacks) do not, not because of racism but simply because of cultural differences in work ethic and discipline, family values, moral deficiency, and financial dependency on the welfare state.

While it may appear as if this places Asians, who supposedly possess the right cultural values, in a superior position above blacks, those very same cultural qualities—hard work, strong family values, obedience to authority, and financial thriftiness—are also used to highlight their perpetual unassimilability to U.S. culture through the stereotypical image of the academic-obsessed nerd, the desexualized male, the heartless Tiger Mom, the submissive geisha, and the racist and greedy shopkeeper. Moreover, as Claire Jean Kim proposes, these "white discursive practices" operate to triangulate Asian Americans in the current system of racial domination as both culturally inferior to whites and superior to blacks but also inherently alien and unassimilable.[9] Based on the experiences of Asian and Latinos in the United States, Glenn argues that inclusion in the social citizenry of America has been historically based on criteria of whiteness and the racialization of Asians as "noncitizens," which justifies their exclusion from the civic arena.[10] Nadia Kim observes that the racialized citizenship of Asian Americans is often obscured by studies that overlook the "specificity of racial oppression" by measuring racism through traditional indicators of black subjugation and stereotypes instead of the specific systemic exclusion they face as foreigners.[11] A comparison of the racial and ethnic experiences of second-generation white and Asian Americans reveals some of the complexities of race and racism in the post–civil rights era.

NAVIGATING DIFFERENCE AND BELONGING

Given their firm belief in the American Dream, it is not surprising that the majority of white and Asian American participants regardless of ethnicity believed that anyone can succeed if they tried hard enough, although some thought discrimination could be a barrier for African Americans and poor people. At the same time, both white and Asian American participants discussed how they felt a sense of difference and struggled with negotiating their belonging in a society that stressed cultural conformity, white Anglo-Saxon Protestant superiority, and other hierarchies of privilege. However, what became apparent in these narratives were major differences in the nature of their exclusion and isolation, as well as the ability to eventually gain control over their sense of racial and ethnic difference from the American mainstream.

When asked if they themselves had ever been treated differently because of their race or cultural heritage, most second-generation white Americans replied that they either had little trouble blending in especially in the immigrant-dominated culture of New York or experienced some type of differential treatment mostly because of their immigrant family culture and background. Emily, a thirty-one-year-old middle-class Ukrainian Jew who was raised in Fort Lee, New Jersey, but lived in New York for the last seven and a half years, stated that because New York was an immigrant city, she had never felt singled out because of her different cultural background. Even though discrimination may exist, she believed that it was "something you have to learn to deal with in the system, overcome it and just look for opportunity." Tanya, a twenty-eight-year-old working-class Russian Jew freelancer who had lived in New York for the past twenty years, suggested that although other family members who had immigrated from abroad may have had different experiences, as the first American-born in her family, she felt her childhood was just like that of any other American in New York. She stated simply "my identity to me is American. Jew is a religion, Georgia is family origins, but my culture and personality and my beliefs and core values are all American. All I have left is a name."

As suggested, the comfort that these participants feel in their surroundings can partly be attributed to the demographic and historical context of New York, which more than any other large urban area in America has had a long history of immigration, even among its white residents. This historically diverse setting helps to normalize cultural differences for second-generation white Americans, even Jewish Americans who compose a large minority in the metropolitan region. Even in other regions of the United States, however, the ability to blend in with the white population physically is also an important factor that helps second-generation white Americans to minimize the kind of ethnic tensions other racial minority groups encounter. Mendel, for instance, stated that even when he traveled to other regions in the South, he was never made to feel different in any way and recognized how some of this reflects his privilege as a white.

In some cases though, second-generation white Americans did feel that both their parents and they themselves had encountered discrimination usually when they were younger. However, most of these experiences had to do with either their parents' immigrant background or their cultural upbringing—traits that they could change as they grew older and the next generation became Americanized. Leonid, a thirty-four-year-old Ukrainian Jewish American, recalled some of the problems he had fitting in with his peers when he moved from Queens to Rockland County during his elementary school years.

> That was a bit of a shock for me, because in Queens, I wasn't the only Russian kid.[12] There were lots of Russian and Asian kids and it was kind of a mixed pot. But when I got there, I wasn't Italian or Irish or any other of the [ethnicities]; I was the Russian-Jewish kid. I was the only one that I knew of that spoke Russian, in the entire elementary school. I wasn't good at kickball or dodgeball. Even the games that we played in Queens elementary school was different from the games we played here. So I had a very tough time adjusting. My mom was shopping clothes for me at Marshall's instead of the Gap. So instead of buying me jeans and T-shirts, she'd buy me nice corduroy pants and sweatshirts with French lettering on it, cause she thought that was cute. Meanwhile, I just wanted to wear what everybody else was wearing to fit in. My mom just didn't know where to shop to make me look like the other kids. My mom also kept my hair long and floppy and my hair's curly so it ended up looking foofy. Meanwhile the other kids were getting spike haircuts and crew cuts. So they ended up calling me Wig and Wigster, which is kind of hurtful when you're nine. You don't want to be the kid with a stupid nickname. I didn't want to stand out cause standing out for me meant getting picked on. So my reaction was: okay what's different about me, let's sweep that under the rug.

Leonid believed that because his neighborhood had a large Jewish population, his Jewish background did not cause him as many issues as his Russian background. However, the influence of being raised by an immigrant family made Leonid visibly different from his peers in Rockland County.

Despite their parents' persecution back home, the advantages of associating with the Jewish community in the U.S. context may also partly explain the observation of Kasinitz and his colleagues that second-generation Russian Jews in New York tend to see their nationality and religious ties as inextricable.[13]

Despite the rough start, Leonid explained that he was able to adapt once he moved onto junior high and got the opportunity to have a fresh start with new friends from different elementary schools.

> By that time, I was more in control of the clothes I was wearing and how my hair was being cut, so I was adapting. I was figuring stuff out for my own that my parents just didn't have the context or wherewithal to figure out. In junior high, I started running track and cross-country, I started doing a sport that didn't require a lot of coordination, just a sense of mental toughness (ha). I just started making new friends cause there was a lot of new people to meet. And I always flourished academically so at that point, you start having the honors classes. In elementary school, everybody's in the same class, and from seventh grade through high school, I was purely in all the honors classes. So at that point, I was really with people who I became friends with just cause we're all in the same classes all the time. And so things got a lot easier.

Leonid felt compelled to downplay his Russian identity in order to be able to blend in with his American peers, but more important, he was able to do so by changing his appearance, engaging in sports, and mixing in with the honors crowd. Acculturation and the new friends he made in his honors classes enabled him to overcome this feeling of difference he felt as a child of a Russian immigrant. In other words, bettering himself educationally gave him access to a world where he could be accepted as an equal. Today, Leonid is a successful attorney married to a white Catholic wife of mixed-European ancestry with two young children. He proudly showed me a picture of his happy family, which he displays in his office. Because he is back in New York, he states that he is no longer ashamed of his Russian or Jewish heritage and has in fact been finding ways to integrate some of his parents' cultural heritage into his family life.

In a similar vein, Anastasia, a twenty-six-year-old Jewish American research associate who was raised in Brooklyn, talked about how people's reception to her cultural background also transformed as she got older.

> I was friends with a lot of American kids in my high school. It wasn't cool to be an immigrant and I didn't feel like it was cool to be an immigrant until I got to college. Kids are cruel and they don't really understand other people's experiences. So not necessarily because of anything that any one

person did but I definitely felt like an outsider just because I didn't have the same kind of upbringing that everybody else did. Baseball wasn't a national pastime for me, and I hadn't grown up wearing Gap so I definitely felt a little bit outside in high school but in college, everybody that I talked to was like wow, you're from Russia, that's really cool, tell me what that's like. People are more mature, and they want to hear about your background and that's when people were intrigued by my life story. So it wasn't until I got to college that I started to become a little bit more proud of my life story and then wanting to embrace it. So now I feel like I'm kind of turning back to it.

Unlike Leonid, Anastasia was not blatantly discriminated against by her peers but still felt very self-conscious about her family's cultural difference in an adolescent culture that stressed conformity as the norm. She went on to say that she struggled for many years with this inferiority complex, which she thought was more self-imposed than forced onto her by any particular group. However, once she transitioned into college, her immigrant background became a source of pride as (white) ethnic difference was seen as "cool" and "unique." Because of their ability to manage their physical appearance and behaviors, second-generation white Americans are able to exercise whatever "ethnic options" give them the most cachet in different settings.[14] As she advances in her career, Anastasia is considering ways she can use her Russian background to incorporate an international aspect to her career but regrets that she does not speak the language well enough. She stated that she would work in Moscow if she ever got the opportunity.

To be sure, not all white Americans embraced their parents' ethnic heritage as in the case of Shane, who said he continues to downplay his ethnicity in certain settings to this day. Although he had a close group of Jewish American friends throughout his childhood, he never felt completely comfortable about his ethnic background. When I asked him how he felt about his ethnic identity and family's cultural heritage, he replied,

SHANE: Mixed. I was comfortable with the people from my group but I was also a little embarrassed. Not in the full meaning of that word but I didn't always want to tell people what my group was just to fit in. I wasn't the most social person but it was important to me so a lot of my friends growing up like in elementary school, my best friend was Italian, my other best friend was maybe half black or black, and then my other best friend was Eastern European Jewish. And then in high school my friends were more Jewish. Not all of my friends were Jewish and sometimes when you're not with people of your own ethnic group, you just

don't want to call attention to it. It really just depended on who I was
with.

JOE (RESEARCH ASSISTANT): How did your views change as you grew up?

SHANE: Probably still the same in some regards. I don't call a lot of attention to my background especially when I'm meeting new people if
they're other ethnic groups. If I'm going out with somebody who's
Hispanic or black, I don't usually tell them my whole background. A lot
of people mistake me for being Irish or so I don't say anything.

Even in the racially diverse context of American cities, some white Americans
feel an unsaid pressure to blend in with the crowd—an environment that perhaps reflects some of the complexities and contradictions of American multiculturalism. Nevertheless, Shane has the option to assume different identities
depending on where he is: he is more comfortable with his Ashkenazi Jewish
identity when he is among Jewish circles but can also get away with hiding
his ethnicity by calling himself "American" among non–Jewish American
acquaintances. He does find that people in New York are more interested
in learning about someone's specific ethnic background, whereas in other
regions of America, he can easily blend in as "white" or "American." Because
he is close with his family and identifies himself as religious, Shane told
me that he would prefer to marry someone who is from the same culture
and family background—that is, Jewish and Russian. Because they have such
ethnic options, white Americans do not seem to harbor the same level of emotional intensity and self-consciousness about their identities that I will later
argue Asian Americans often struggle with in their day-to-day lives.

Some white participants I interviewed were also quite conscious of the way
their black or nonwhite immigrant friends did not have the same liberty to
hide their racial and ethnic background and experienced more discrimination and social isolation as a result. Sebastian, a thirty-three-year-old Italian
American marketing manager, said that "I do feel like I have an advantage
being white, speaking English, not having an accent, which open up doors
for me that may not for other people. It's how people interact with you on
the street, it's how you get jobs, it's who'll date you, but sometimes it's also
very subtle racism." Along the same lines, Julia, a Russian Jewish resident
physician, stated,

It's harder if you are of the ethnic group that are African or Asian or Indian.
People would look at you right away and wonder where you are from.
Whereas for Russians or my friends that are Greek, you are just like a regular
American kid, but since you are white, people don't realize that you grew
up in a different culture. My friend growing up as Indian, she has a lot of

trouble at work right now. She works for [this company] and they are really kind of white-collar Republican. It feels like people treated her differently there for being Indian. It's like *Harold & Kumar Go to White Castle* and how there was the Asian kid at the company that everyone wants to throw work at him. It feels like she is the Harold of her job. Everyone thinks that she is very academically smart, but they don't really invite her out or really hang out with her, and she feels that she's treated very differently because of her race.

This sensitivity I noticed among some white participants toward their own racial privilege may ironically stem from their own struggles with cultural belonging as children of immigrants. Or it may also be specific to the generally liberal political culture of New York City as compared with other regions throughout the United States. In addition to being children of immigrants, it is worth noting that Sebastian is a gay male and Julia is a Jewish woman, whose own experiences with ethnic, gender, and gay oppression may arguably give them insights from "overlapping approximation experiences" that may make them relatively more attuned to the dynamics of racial oppression.[15] Of course, the question of whether or not awareness translates into appropriate behavior is a different matter.

The one area where race is a relevant subject for most second-generation white participants was in the area of dating and marriage. Perspectives on the subject varied widely. Some interviewees like Mendel and Ivan were open to interracial dating at least in theory and felt eventually racial intermixing would make racial distinctions almost irrelevant in America. The same was true for Liza, a middle-class Sicilian American woman whose first husband was black and second was Puerto Rican. When she was young, her father, who was heavily involved with church and Sicilian organizations, constantly pressured her to stay rooted in her Italian heritage and interrogated her whenever she socialized with her black friends. She rebelled by taking up Spanish instead of Italian as her second language and was even disowned by her father for some time after she married her first husband. She expressed visible disdain for her father's prejudices against blacks and refuses to instill these values in her daughter. She declared, "She's free to date whoever she wants. I'm very protective over my daughter but I won't be prejudiced. I will encourage her to embrace other cultures." Liza is not sure if it is because her family took to her second husband better or because he looked white, but she said they embraced him more than her first husband. However, he passed away two years before the interview. She informed me that she has been teaching her daughter to embrace both her Italian and Puerto Rican heritages.

Others like Emily were frank about their preference for nonwhite partners but, as in the excerpt to follow, were careful to distinguish this as a cultural "preference" or "taste" rather than a racial prejudice. Emily, who was single at the time of the interview, was generally reluctant to talk about her dating history in detail. She did mention that she once dated a Colombian man for many years and even waited for him while he served in the army but eventually had problems with his sisters because of "cultural differences." In the following passage, Emily, who was interviewed by my white research assistant, discussed her current preference to date and eventually marry someone from the same background:

EMILY: Jewish would be nice but they don't even have to be Jewish, they could be Eastern European or they don't have to be . . . yeah, I would rather date a white guy. I'm being honest. My parents would prefer that and it would probably be easier for me and the kids. Not to say I haven't dated a guy of another race. It's not just white people who think like that. Other people [of other races] feel the same way. They would rather you date people of similar backgrounds and I understand that. It's just easier.

JOE: Just any race in general, or do you think there is more of a bias for someone whose black or . . .

EMILY: It's not specifically a bias it's just easier being with someone with a similar background. I wouldn't say my parents are racist. I feel other races feel the same way. When I was younger I was more willing but now I feel it's easier dating someone with a similar background.

Racial and ethnic tensions also had the potential to play a visible role in hardening color lines, particularly among second-generation whites from working-class or racially diverse neighborhoods. Second-generation whites were more willing to talk about race whenever they felt that the incursion of other racial and ethnic groups threatened territorial boundaries and job opportunities or heightened competition over valuable resources, such as education. My research assistant touched on this topic with one participant, Melina, who is a Greek American mother of a six-year-old and an infant from Queens. During the interview, she conveyed her frustration with the way her children's school focused heavily on the needs of its Asian students. She asked, "Is that discriminatory? It might be. I am going to find other ways to help her to be successful in school if the teachers don't want to spend as much time with her or cater to her needs because she is not Asian."

Although not as common, there were also two instances in which second-generation white Americans were bullied by black Americans, especially in neighborhood settings where they were seen as the numerical minority. The first interviewee, Mendel, said he was generally open to intermingling with people from different races having attended a competitive and racially diverse high school in Manhattan but admitted that two racially motivated attacks while walking in the "wrong neighborhood" altered his views on black Americans outside the school setting.

> Everybody's biased. I'm racist, I can tell you that for sure. I've been the victim of two racial attacks where I was intentionally attacked because I was white and everybody else is black and it's like let's get the white guy and I happen to be white. That really pissed me off and I'm racist in some ways cause of stuff like that. I went to live in Philadelphia for awhile which is actually where I had that first racial attack where I was walking in the wrong neighborhood and I knew I wasn't supposed to be there. I basically got chased by a bunch of black kids. Before that chase happened, people were looking at me in the street and looking at me like you're in the wrong neighborhood, why are you here and I just kept on walking. Eventually I got punched by a bunch of dudes and luckily was smart enough to just not try and fight back. I looked around and realized these guys were about to really severely beat me and just ran away really fast (ha).

Mendel recounted other incidents that made him aware of his whiteness, including one time when he visited a coffee shop in a segregated black neighborhood in Philly and heard people talking about how they hated white people. Some people may call this an example of "reverse racism" perpetuated by blacks against whites. However, such a simplistic interpretation glides over the broader structural context of racial segregation, poverty, and discrimination that feeds the frustration of black urban youth and socially confines them to economically declining neighborhoods to which many white Americans are only briefly exposed. Although certainly traumatizing in its own right, this is also one of the few rare moments when Mendel was forced to think about his racial difference and feel what it was like being a minority. As a result of these racial encounters, it is telling how quickly American-born children of immigrants learn the rules of U.S. race relations, which leads to a vicious cycle that further separates blacks from whites with each generation.

Compared with native-born white Americans who live in their own neighborhoods, children of immigrants are more likely to face these unpleasant racial confrontations as youth since many immigrant parents begin their early years in urban ghettoes where they must compete with racial minorities for scarce resources. In the following passage, Ivan, a twenty-seven-year-old Russian Jewish male, described his experience as a racial minority in a

Westchester school that became predominantly black after a race riot spurred white American flight. Although he initially labeled his experiences as partly "reverse racism" because of the different players involved, he qualified this statement by pointing out that all of those who stood out in terms of their dress or their behavior were also targets of bullying. He stated, "So that was weird being the minority within the majority in a way. I mean it went towards Asians, and it went towards gay people, and it went towards anyone who wasn't the same. They even had a different style of dressing, they would be bullied. I don't think that was necessarily because I was white but because I was not black or Hispanic [short laugh]."

In Ivan's case, he decided that these difficult experiences made him want to choose a college where he would not have to run into many blacks:

> Other than [Monmouth] being the school that I really wanted to go to because of its reputation and being in New York, I was looking at the racial breakdown of the school when I was looking through their stuff. And I remember being like, oh it's the complete opposite of my high school and I'm really excited to have that experience. African Americans make up like 4 percent of the population [or] something really low. And then the second highest were Asians, and then whites and then black and Hispanics were somewhere but very little. I was really excited by it and I was talking to my friends and it was like, sorry what are you talking about? [laughs] Why are you so excited about it? I was like it's going to be the complete opposite. That's kind of cool. So when I got to [Monmouth], I had mostly white friends. I had maybe one black friend and that was it.

What is telling in this narrative is how Ivan eventually had the choice to move onto a predominantly white college where he could avoid such racial confrontations and even African Americans altogether. Thus, despite their bicultural struggles, second-generation whites generally have both the ethnic option of crafting a desirable ethnic identity with which to gain social acceptance as well as the racial option of moving into more homogeneous neighborhoods and school systems where they do not have to witness the effects of racial discrimination.

WHEN RACE MATTERS

Whereas most second-generation whites experienced ethnic discrimination because of cultural differences, Asian Americans were more likely to recount instances of unequal treatment because of their phenotypical differences from white Americans and their racialization as noncitizens and model minorities. Not all Korean and Chinese Americans in the study explicitly reported experiencing "racial discrimination" and in fact, when asked directly about racism and discrimination, differential treatment, or even social belonging, many simply replied that they did not feel that they had personally encountered anything they would consider racially motivated as adults. At the same time, as their life stories unraveled, some of the very same participants still gave examples of situations where they were treated differently because of their race. Some reported experiencing blatant racial taunting or discrimination by both their peers and adults as youth, reported unequal treatment as they transitioned into school and later the workplace, and believed that in general, Asian Americans were not in equal standing with white Americans.

Because of the subtle ways in which racism operates, the manifestation of racism itself is not always apparent even to those who perpetuate racist acts or hold onto racist views. Bonilla-Silva asserts that racism is not rooted in "individual character or morality" but in the "deep cultural conditioning that reproduces and legitimates social formations."[16] In what he calls the "white habitus," whites are socialized both overtly and subconsciously around a cultural belief system that perpetuates these racial stereotypes, preferences, and values and is reinforced by other like-minded whites under an overarching rhetoric of color blindness.

One of the ways in which this racial habitus operates is through the cumulative acts of daily racial "microaggressions." As defined by Sue, racial microaggressions refer to "the brief and commonplace daily verbal, behavioral, and environmental indignities, whether intentional or unintentional, that communicate hostile, derogatory, or negative racial, gender, sexual-orientation, and religious slights and insults to the target person or group."[17] Whether or not these types of remarks and acts are intentional, Sue points out the ways in which these daily racial microaggressions serve to remind Asian Americans about their racial inferiority, perpetual alienness, and rightful exclusion from the white norm but because of their indirect and muted character, these acts are difficult to identify and explain. Moreover, some scholars argue that because of the powerful yet ambiguous nature of racism in the post–civil rights era, Asian Americans like other racial minorities may also "collude in the white racist system by adopting not only many white ways of doing and speaking, but also numerous stereotyped views and notions from the white racial frame."[18]

In the face of daily racial microaggressions, many of the incongruities in the narratives of Korean and Chinese Americans have to do with the difficulties they face in finding an appropriate vocabulary to articulate the subtleties and complexities of their experiences in the post–civil rights era. Even though many studies on African Americans have pointed out the ways in which perceived black cultural inferiority and asserted white privilege persist in different forms today, the frame of reference within which racism continues to be described in the mainstream public discourse is oftentimes a binary and oppositional one: black versus white, the Jim Crow past versus the color-blind present, the liberal North versus the racist South, the backwardness of Asia versus the modern multiculturalism of America. Limited by this narrow American view of race and racism, we see a similar ambiguity and confusion playing out in the languages of Korean and Chinese American interviewees, as in the case of Anna:

> ANGIE: Do you think your parents went through any hardships?
>
> ANNA: Yeah. Going to a foreign country, starting a new life is hard. Not as hard as in Taiwan where at certain points you're actually starving. They weren't starving here I don't think. But it's hard learning English, all of that. My dad still has a chip on his shoulder about discrimination that he encountered when he first moved here and he's always telling me, how much white people discriminate against you and he's very bitter about that. I don't think it's as bad as when he came here. Obviously it still exists, but I haven't really dealt with it in any very profound way. I mean in passing comments and little things but I don't think I've encountered that in a way that would make me as bitter as my father.

Anna acknowledged that both she and her father had experienced "passing comments and little things" that stayed with both of them to different degrees, but *compared* to Taiwan and compared to racism in early immigration years, she felt that it was not worth discussing. These two locations become extreme reference points for assessing her current situation.

Sometimes, the effects of racial microaggressions are blurred by other forms of disparagement, as was evident in the personal narrative of Daniel, a twenty-three-year-old gay social activist. In the following passage, Daniel began by explaining that racially derogatory comments did not bother him as much as his sense of marginalization as a gay man when he was young. Although he had heard the occasional "chink" remark throughout elementary school, it did not bother him as much as when people started to belittle and harass him for being gay and flamboyant throughout middle school and later on. However, as he got older, he also started to recognize how his experiences as a gay man were intertwined with the feminization of Asian males and the persistence of white privilege in American race relations.

> Growing up, it was more of a queer thing that I felt oppressed by than the Asian. And not to put a hierarchy on it cause I know in a lot of ways that they perceived me as queer because I was Asian, like being viewed as very

feminine so that may be where they intersect. But at the time, I thought people were picking on me because I am gay. I think to be Asian is to be invisible, to be gay is to be invisible too. So I feel doubly invisible in this community and you have to put yourself out there more than maybe another person to get your voice heard. College and postcollege, I did come out in a very white atmosphere. The queer community at [my college] was very diverse but the queer community was very white, at least the out and proud queer community. And since it was pretty small in general, I didn't feel like there was racism, but clearly they didn't have a race analysis. All the stuff that they did was very white. And looking back at it, it's sort of like these people thought that because they were queer, that meant that they weren't privileged in other ways. Do you know what I mean? It's sort of how white queer people think that they can't be racist and they could say whatever they want, because oh I'm already oppressed so I can say all this shit. Like because they're queer, that gives them an automatic in into these oppressed communities. They don't recognize their privilege as males, as upper-middle-class people, as white people, as able-bodied people. And I still see that now in queer communities across the board.

Daniel was hesitant to label white privilege within the queer community as racism, not only because of the way racism is differently imagined by most Americans, but possibly also because he is in the delicate situation of having to negotiate different layers of oppression within an already oppressed community. One of the dangers of speaking about racism so loosely is that the intersectionality of racial experiences can easily lose its nuance within the binary Western framing of privilege and oppression. This strategy of avoiding the term "racism," then discussing racism, then distancing oneself again, is an underlying pattern throughout most of the interviews I conducted.

Today, Daniel is working more closely with Asian LGBTQ advocacy groups and says that while this involvement has instilled in him a greater sense of identity and empowerment, it has also made him feel increasingly more distant from his gay white friends from college. When asked how he identifies personally, he called himself a "gaysian American" or simply "a young queer Asian American living in New York City." His friendship circles and romantic partners are mostly Asian American with a few exceptions. An underlying theme in each of these accounts is a pervasive feeling of racial self-consciousness and cultural difference from their white counterparts. Even Daniel, who said that he has never felt "completely white-washed" and expressed pride in his heritage, admitted that he went through cycles throughout his adolescence when he wanted to flaunt his ethnocultural background in order to get attention but then felt burdened by the stereotypes and expectations that came with being Asian American. He explained that "there were some instances where I resent it and some instances where I was really proud of it so there was a balance between those two extremes."

Another factor that differentiates the experiences of Asian Americans from those of second-generation whites is the way they are defined by their seemingly positive image as a hardworking model minority, which is ironically used to justify their unequal treatment especially in the arena of education and work. The ambiguity and uncertainty of being in-between play out most clearly in the model minority stereotype. I found Korean and Chinese Americans felt conflicted about being treated as a model minority, as captured in the opposing perspectives of Mike, a Korean business owner, and Kimberly, a market researcher for a media corporation:

> MIKE: I have arguments with a friend of mine who just did her PhD and she doesn't like the term model minority. But for me, to have a badge like that is more of a benefit than a negative, especially compared to other minorities that have a lot of negative baggage like Afro-Americans or Latin Americans. I don't have as much issue with it, but she seems to hate that term.

> ANGIE: In New York, do you feel that anyone can succeed if they really try hard enough or do you feel like there are other obstacles?
> KIMBERLY: I think there are other obstacles cause the corporate world is still very male-dominated and still very white-dominated. In a sense, you just have to learn to play the game. If you know who to kiss up to, you probably could move up. I mean there's a lot of these people who are Asian males who are like presidents or CEOs, but they're kind of stereotyped to me, cause they're always in the same industry, you know computers or things like that. I'm female and I think a female in the workforce isn't as equal as people want us to believe. I think we still have a long ways to go.
> ANGIE: How about as an Asian American?
> KIMBERLY: Asian Americans too. I mean we're a little bit better than other minorities cause we're always viewed as the smart people. But then I also think we're being used, because they know we work hard and some Asians don't say anything. So there's a negative in that sense. They'll hire us, they'll let us do a lot of work, but are they gonna promote us?

The model minority stereotype shows the murkiness of Asian American positionality in U.S. race relations in that the positive stereotypes can often hide the pervasiveness of informal and subtle discrimination. However, one can also argue that the ability to take advantage of the model minority stereotype depends on the context in which it is employed. For example, Mike's occupation as a self-employed male entrepreneur gives him more maneuverability to use the model minority myth to attract clients, whereas Kimberly faces more obstacles to a management position as an Asian American female working in a white-male-dominated corporation. This in turn can make a difference in how they perceive the benefits and disadvantages of the model minority myth.

In general, Korean and Chinese American participants varied greatly in terms of the ethnic composition of their friendship and dating preferences and in many cases, these preferences evolved as they transitioned from their early twenties to their thirties. Regardless of which groups they chose to fraternize with, only a few participants claimed that they were blatantly excluded from socializing with white Americans. If anything, those who did observe the formation of racial and ethnic cliques were more likely to argue that it was either because people felt more comfortable with those who shared the same cultural values and family upbringing or because coethnic peers chose to voluntary segregate themselves away from others.

Similar to the discourse on Asian American stereotypes, however, the discussion often seemed to belie the sense of racial difference and exclusion some of them felt when in the presence of their white counterparts. In the following passage, Sam, a thirty-four-year-old Chinese American male raised in Queens, tried to explain why he tended to socialize mostly with other Asians since high school but had trouble articulating the source of his discomfort.

SAM: I don't think I was ever really comfortable hanging out with Caucasian people in high school. I just never felt like I fit in with them with whatever it was that they did. I didn't feel comfortable around Caucasian people that weren't of my- . . . . not even just that. Just Caucasian people in general.

ANGIE: Anything they do or say that makes you feel uncomfortable?

SAM: No, no. Maybe I just didn't like the feeling of being the Chinese guy in a group of Caucasian people. Maybe I didn't want to put myself in a position for them to say, oh why is he here? He shouldn't be hanging out with us.

ANGIE: Is there something different about them, like anything you relate to Asians that you don't think Caucasians would understand?

SAM: No, not really. You know what, now that I think of it, I think it's all coincidence that I'm more comfortable around Asian people, maybe because most of the people I know are Asian. I'm sure if I meet somebody who's a Caucasian person who's nice, then I'll be able to connect with them and talk with them. But I don't know if I would be able to get to the point where I would be able to call them up and say, hey let's hang out.

ANGIE: So do you think it wouldn't have been strange if you ended up
    marrying like a Caucasian woman or- . . .
SAM: No. I don't think so. I think it would still be the same way.
ANGIE: But you could've imagined a scenario like that?
SAM: Yeah. Well I think it was just a coincidence. I could definitely say I
    was never really comfortable around Caucasian girls. I don't know why.
    Maybe because [long pause] . . . you know, I just thought that that's
    how things were, it's like Caucasian girls hung out with Caucasian
    guys (ha).

Judging by the way he pauses, retracts, and contradicts himself in this passage,
Sam is clearly struggling to articulate and clarify the source of his discomfort.
In general, he seems very self-conscious about how he is perceived by his
Caucasian peers both male and female, which makes him uncomfortable
socializing with them on a regular basis, yet he claims this is all a coincidence.
One could make the argument that his white peers are not to blame for his
discomfort, but the question is why some Asian Americans feel this way and
why none of the second-generation whites in the study reported similar
discomfort in their relations with Americans.

Throughout their lives, the one area in which many Korean and Chinese
Americans did find visible evidence of racial stereotyping at work was in
dating and romantic relationships. Men, particularly heterosexual men, were
keenly aware of how the racial devaluation and demasculinization of Asian
American males in the American media and culture played a key role in shaping their dating prospects and experiences. Because much has been written on
this topic, I will discuss only a few examples.[19]

Near the end of our interview, Peter, a heterosexual Chinese American
actor, raised the issue of interracial dating among Asian American women
and men. Although he has not yet had a serious relationship, he himself has
dated women regularly but finds that his prospects outside Asian Americans
are quite limited by racial stereotypes about Asian men. During the interview,
Peter stated firmly that Asian Americans should date outside their ethnic
group, but not with white Americans because he believed the relationships
were often built on stereotypes about the hyperfemininity of Asian women,
which gave them a "stereotypical advantage." He asked why else the majority
of Asian-white marriages would be between Asian females and white males.
When I asked if he ever felt personally marginalized as an Asian American
male, he responded,

> I don't but I do. It's funny because I don't really see myself racially but
> I identify as being Asian American. I feel like because of how Asian

Americans are perceived and especially Asian American males are perceived in this country, I don't see myself as that, because I'm totally different than everything that an "Asian American male" is in this country. I am not quiet and I'm not into certain things that they say, that my interests are very varied. So in that sense, I don't identify with it, but at the end of the day, I know that when I walk down the street, I think the first thing they're gonna see is not the fact that there's this man walking down this street, but there's an Asian man walking down the street. And it's always in the back of my mind. You cannot have the luxury of not thinking of yourself as a person of color, because especially in this country, you're always reminded of that.

In this excerpt, Peter attests to the racial and gender politics of interracial dating but also says pointedly that he does not identify with Asian American males. On the one hand, he recognizes that he is viewed differently because of his racial phenotype, but on the other hand, he wants to distance himself from the racial typecasting that comes with identifying as an "Asian American male." It is almost as if racial identification is inseparable from racial stereotypes in his mind.

Daniel made a similar observation about racial hierarchies in dating among gay males in New York. During the interview, he explained how there is an "attractiveness scale" among gay males where white Caucasian physical features are valued more highly than those of other people of color. As a result, he argued that "average-looking white guys will hit on people of color that are out of their league, because they think that those people of color think that all white guys are really attractive, whereas they would not hit on a white guy who was out of their league." He talked about one incident where one white man's interest in him at a club quickly turned sour because of this racial presumptuousness:

DANIEL: I was at the Ritz one time with a friend and this guy was buying me a drink and I wasn't drinking then so I was like no, that's okay but thank you.

FRANK (RESEARCH ASSISTANT): He was white?

DANIEL: Yeah he was white. He got really upset at me and he actually started yelling at me at the club.

FRANK: What did he say?

DANIEL: Oh just some racial stuff like oh you stupid chink. You know oh come on, you know you want to get with this. God what's your problem, come on. What are you like a virgin or something? Why don't you just go out with me? Why are you being so uppity? And I was off, I was going crazy, I was yelling back and I was like you mother-fucking piece of shit (ha). We got him kicked out because he was really being inappropriate.

Daniel went on to say that there were probably similar parallels in the experiences of Asian American women from what he had heard so believed that racial stereotyping about Asian femininity crossed barriers of sexual orientation. Because of his growing awareness about these racial dynamics, he said that he prefers to date other people of color, especially Asian Americans, and usually frequents gay clubs where minorities tend to socialize.

The deal breaker for most of the heterosexual Korean and Chinese American women I interviewed, regardless of their dating preferences, were attitudes, remarks, or behaviors that made them stand out as racially different. Mia, who was raised in a large working-class family in Chinatown, has had a long history of dating mostly Chinese American men along with a few African American and Latino men. She recalled though the one time she dated a native-born white American from Long Island who went around telling people that he had an "Asian girlfriend," which offended her tremendously. She reacted in disgust, "I think with him, it's more than a cultural boundary. I mean it was a cultural boundary in terms of he'd like to say stuff like 'I have an Asian girlfriend.' I'm like why would you say that? I don't go around saying 'I have a white boyfriend.' What the hell is that? He was just totally oblivious to what it's like to be a New Yorker." Whether or not she sees it as such, it is interesting how Mia does not explicitly frame his remarks as "racist" but rather as a cultural difference that comes from his lack of exposure to diverse ethnic groups in New York.

Some of them confided that they also tried to avoid men who they suspected had "Asian fetishes." These participants did not clearly articulate what differentiates Asian fetishizers from non-Asian fetishizers, other than the fact that these men were "too interested" in all things Asian. However, the participants explained that you could sense when someone was interested more in your race than you as a person, which was a turnoff for many of them. Esther, a heterosexual Korean American, has dated only white boyfriends throughout her life because, according to her, she prefers "big manly dudes," which she feels is hard to find among Asian American males she has encountered. Her current boyfriend, whom she said she thought she may end up marrying, is mostly native-born white American with an eighth Native American blood. When I asked her if her boyfriend took an interest in her culture too, she responded carefully,

Yeah like he's really interested in the food, but not too interested to the point that it's creepy. Because there's kind of like this label that I stick on these guys. . . . I don't know maybe you've had this sort of experience too where you meet a guy and he's not Asian. He's white or Hispanic or black and after so many words, you know that their sole interest in you is because you're an Asian because you're a woman. It's not because there's something about your personality that sparks his interest. It's because they basically have an Asian fetish. And that's something that I've been really, really weary of since I came to New York and since I started dating and being in relationships.

Even for those who date white men, the dangers of dating Asian fetishizers is the way their indiscriminate preferences blatantly highlight their partner's racial foreignness as Asian Americans based on preconceived stereotypes. Again, we see an instance in which a stereotype that makes Asian Americans seem more appealing actually disguises hegemonic understandings of heterosexual women and gay men's bodies as the racial properties of white men.

Other than dating, Asian Americans in the study were most vocal about the unequal treatment they received at school and in the workplace, probably because those were one of the few settings in which racial stereotypes about model minority achievement clearly led to tangible differences in the distribution of labor, resources, and opportunities for mobility. For white-collar professionals in particular, these incidents highlighted to them how race and racism was still salient despite their elevated class status. Steven, a Korean American physician, explained the ways in which Asian American stereotypes justified unequal workloads and promotions when he was working at a consulting firm as an intern and even later on as a physician at a hospital.

To give you one example: I was put on a project that was extremely labor-intensive but incredibly dull, and my project manager asked me to pick people that I felt would be good for this kind of project. It's more of a quantitative project as well. I put together a list of people that I thought would be good, and then, he kinda said, you know this person's not so good, well let me kind of tweak it a little bit. And so we called a meeting together of all the people that were picked. It was every single Asian American research assistant in our firm. There was one woman there who is very much more of a letters person as opposed to a numbers person. And I just felt like this is a project where they just want to staff it with people that have some perceived qualities for quantitative skills and will be just quiet and not complain about it, you know? I really took offense to that because I think there's this common perception that Asians are poor communicators, are ill-suited for leadership roles, and here at this hospital, you look around you, and you look at the number of people in training that are of Asian descent—30, 40 percent. And you look at division chiefs and there's not a single Asian. So the glass ceiling is everywhere.

Although disadvantaged in this sense, white-collar professionals are usually in a better position to avoid these experiences than their working-class counterparts, for example by moving to another company where their skills are more valued. In Steven's case, he chose to leave his current position at his hospital in New York to work at another hospital where he viewed racial minorities were better represented in top management.

Despite the fact that many professionals were familiar with the term "glass or bamboo ceiling," most of them still had trouble articulating how race shaped their day-to-day experiences.[20] I asked Tony to give me an example of something that makes him different from white Americans, to which he answered:

> TONY: I don't look the same [laughs].
>
> ANGIE: Do you think that is important too?
>
> TONY: Yes and no. The biggest problem with me is my face. I look very young for my age and the business world, it's always been a challenge for people to take me seriously, because I look so young. That's always been a challenge for as long as I remember and the only way to get around that is to prove myself versus I know if this Caucasian counterpart that would never be the case.
>
> ANGIE: It's kind of interesting because you're talking about age but then you're saying other Caucasians wouldn't have to go through that necessarily. . . .
>
> TONY: Right. So I mean you know even a Caucasian who's younger than me who still looks young, that wouldn't necessarily be an issue. In the workplace, I've definitely seen that but there's no real way to prove it.

When asked if he felt he was treated differently from other white Americans, Tony began by describing how his youthful appearance had become an obstacle for him in the business world, in a way that may mislead one into believing he was actually talking about ageism. In order to clarify what he meant, I asked him whether or not he was still talking about racism, and he responded by comparing his experience with other young-looking Caucasians but saying it was difficult for him to prove it. This passage is telling in that it shows how racism can operate in coordination with ageism so that youthful appearance reinforces racial stereotypes about Asian male passivity and weakness. This makes it more difficult to explain how race operates given that racism in the Western imaginary is often described in the categorical language of "either-or."

Tony believed that it was the combination of his youthful appearance and racial stereotypes about leadership ability that played a huge part in affecting his promotion chances at a pharmaceutical and medical care company he used to work for. Whenever he worked on a team project, he found that he rarely got credit for his leadership and involvement. "We worked both equally on it, both of us would get accolades over it. However that one guy would get a promotion just happened to be Caucasian versus I wouldn't. So even though it was the same exact project, same workload, same perception of the job being done. So it's a little interesting (ha)." In another leadership development program he was involved in, he found that "I would be passed over or not taken seriously, even to the point where it's actually garnered some comments like who hired the summer intern in here? I'm like dude, I'm on a second-year rotation so it's not like I'm new to this! Yeah it's a little interesting in that sense." Throughout many of these interviews, the term "interesting" was a commonly used marker that Asian Americans used to signify something they suspected to be discriminatory or unfair but were uncertain or unwilling to label as racism.

Even in the workplace, racial discriminatory practices are often cloaked under the guise of "culture" and what's "practical." Thus, if the management decides not to select a qualified Asian American for a leadership position, they justify their decision by arguing that Asian Americans are socialized to be passive and obedient because of weak communication skills or different cultural upbringing. In the same breath, an Asian American candidate who is aggressive and demonstrates those same desirable leadership qualities can also be dismissed as being overly competitive and incapable of teamwork. Given the ambiguous, contradictory, and informal way in which racial politics plays out, it is not always evident to Asian Americans themselves if they are being singled out because of their race, occasionally causing them to resort to the more easily understood vocabulary of culture and pragmatism as a means of explanation. Drawing on a passage from *Yellow* by Frank Wu, Peter talks about the common question that nags people of color who go into an interview and don't get a job: "There's always in the back of your mind, did I not get the job because I'm Asian or because . . .?"

Take for example the following passage by Anna, who aspires to be a museum curator but struggles over what area of art to pursue based on the guidance she received:

ANNA: I think I am more credible as an Asian art scholar or expert than I am as a European art expert.

ANGIE: What do you mean credible?

ANNA: Because I'm Asian and that counts for something subconsciously for people. I found it a little bit harder than it should be to be accepted as a European art person.

ANGIE: Can you think of an example of something that showed you this?

ANNA: [pause] You know what? It was the suggestions of people, my professors and my recommenders. I always had this split interest between
French and Asian art and I didn't even mention that I was interested in
Asian art, but they said, why don't you do Asian art? [we laugh] To
them, maybe it was just a practical thing because the field is more open
but I don't have any language [proficiency] at all and so it doesn't work
for me in a way. I'm pretty fluent in French and Italian but having that
suggested to me and just understanding that it's not like I can go to
France and teach French because that's their own art. I'm not gonna be
accepted anywhere except in the U.S. so I don't have any possibilities
outside of that. If I went into Asian art, I do have possibilities outside of
the country if need be.

Anna initially began by stating that she was interested in both French and
Asian art. She then retracted her statement when she remembered that Asian
art was not really her idea, and she was actually steered in this direction by her
professors because it was more practical and would open up more doors of
opportunity, despite the fact that she did not speak any Asian language. One
is compelled to ask: if the person was a second-generation Russian Jew, would
he or she also been steered to study Russian art instead of say Asian art if that
person was also fluent in Chinese?

The ways in which white male standards become the marker of good leadership and the uneven way in which this criterion is applied creates an atmosphere of self-doubt and uncertainty for Korean and Chinese Americans.
In the following narrative, Sunny, a thirty-eight-year-old Korean American
attorney, vacillates back and forth between characterizing her workplace
experience as an example of differential treatment then blaming it on her
cultural upbringing and then once again remarking on the unfairness and
lack of clarity in workplace standards.

ANGIE: Have you ever been treated differently because you're Asian
American?

SUNNY: Have I ever been *treated* differently? Other than the general
stereotype that come along with being Asian American? It's like my last
work interview, they say you need to be more aggressive and you need
to speak up more. And frankly, that just cuts against my general
upbringing to speak up more and to be more aggressive. I don't even
know what that means. I tried to explore it with the people who give me
the reviews, but I don't think they really know. I think it's more of a
"I'll-know-it-when-I-see-it kind of thing." But I was concerned that my

not being aggressive or not speaking up more meant that my work progress was not as good, which I don't think is necessarily the case. I think they wanted to see a particular level of input, but I don't think they were telling me my work is bad. So that's the kind of thing that I find to be really interesting.

ANGIE: And you say that came from your upbringing, that's cause your parents raised you that way?

SUNNY: Right. I'm not gonna just speak out if I've got nothing productive to say. Half the time I'm just listening, because I want to be able to gauge what it is that has to be done. I'm here to listen and process and that's how I am. My point being the suggestion in the review was you're not acting in a certain way, or you're acting in a certain way, that was problematic.

It is not always easy to assess to what extent the inequalities they face have to do with the cultural values Asian Americans learn at home or the racial and gendered stereotyping of those cultural values. Nevertheless, the tendency to blame Asian cultural values for discriminatory practices regardless of the individual's personality, background, or skills is a self-fulfilling prophecy that can cause Asian Americans to doubt their own judgment and qualifications. This passage also attests to the difficulties of challenging these promotional decisions since they are often based on subjective evaluations and closed-door decision-making processes.

Perhaps feeling as if this was not the most obvious example of racism, Sunny moved on to another incident from law school. She had lived most of her life in the Asian immigrant enclave of Queens but then temporarily moved to a more racially homogeneous area in upstate New York for law school. There, her feeling of racialized foreignness was highlighted by the presence of foreign-born Asian students with whom she felt she was often lumped together. She recalled one time when her instructor went around the room to field questions and hit a group of foreign-born Asians who had trouble articulating their thoughts clearly. She was shocked when he then skipped over her, which she assumed was his way of avoiding having to deal with another foreign-born Asian. She mused, "maybe I was being paranoid about it, but that's what it felt like." Sunny implies that racial discrimination is not always easy to articulate in words but is something that is sensed and felt.

Suzanne, the twenty-five-year-old Korean American who works as an administrative assistant at an international nongovernmental organization, expressed similar doubt and uncertainty about the source of unequal treatment at her workplace. When I asked her if she ever experienced any type of differential treatment or discrimination, she began by describing the way people racially stereotype her as a "young Asian girl" but then ended up blaming it on her parents' culture.

> SUZANNE: I think people in New York are really just racist in general. Even in this job, they see me as the young Asian girl who will do whatever you ask her to do.
>
> ANGIE: Can you give me a specific example?
>
> SUZANNE: You know, because by nature I can't confront people and if someone asks me to do something, I'll do it even if I'm overwhelmed. People ask me to do it anyway, and when I make a mistake, they get very angry about it and [sighs] you know it's not fair.
>
> ANGIE: And you don't respond?
>
> SUZANNE: I do respond, but it takes me a long time. I have to let it build and then I just let it out in a very negative way.
>
> ANGIE: Is that something you learned from your parents or is that just how you are in general?
>
> SUZANNE: I think that's just something I learned from my parents that's in my culture. That's something I need to learn how to change but it's hard.

Both Asian American men and women across different industries feel the brunt of racial stereotypes, but as these interviews reveal, the ways they shape work opportunities vary depending on other factors such as class and gender. Many Korean and Chinese American males are keenly aware of the ways in which they are demasculinized in the mainstream media and treated as foreigners in casual and romantic social interactions. At the same time, the preference for Asian American women within the arts and entertainment industries because of their racialized femininity can also act as a double-edged sword that is used to question their leadership ability in white-male-dominated work settings, such as law and finance.

COSMOPOLITANISM AND RACIAL OTHERING

Given their liminal status between their immigrant parents' ethnic roots and their white American phenotypical features, second-generation white Americans have the opportunity to selectively identify with those parts of their ethnicity that do not highlight their difference from the mainstream. The social meaning of whiteness within the urban context however adds a different twist to the contemporary narratives of white Americans. Whiteness is a deliberately ambiguous category that is based not on any real genetic or cultural differences but a socially imagined construction that is defined in juxtaposition against the racialized Other embodied by racial minorities.[21] In other words, whiteness is not characterized by any specific value, culture, or behavior that is universal to all whites but is instead important in defining what whites are not (e.g., not as lazy as blacks or not as passively obedient as Asians or not as hypersexual as black women). In urban contexts where they are fast becoming a racial minority, Horton points out that white Americans "now reluctantly face the loss of their unhyphenated American identity in exchange for no identity (the 'other') or some unacceptable, reconstructed racial ('white') or ethnic identity ('Anglo' or 'European American'), a sign that they are an odd piece in the ethnic mosaic that has replaced the melting pot."[22] By exoticizing and reifying ethnicity, this construction of whiteness represents a lack of understanding of how such hegemonic identities can constrain and marginalize the lives of racial minorities.

Within the socially progressive culture of New York City, whiteness is especially tainted by its association with privilege and oppression, antithetical to the melting pot ideal on which New Yorkers of all races pride themselves. Part of this has to do with the region's distinctive demographic profile and historical roots. As the longtime gateway for immigration since Europeans first arrived in masses during the early twentieth century, New York City stands out for being home to not only immigrants of color but also many white immigrants and their descendents. The dominating presence of immigrants thus permeates the culture of New York, more so than even Los Angeles, where most whites are many generations removed from their immigrant roots.[23] As Ivan puts it, "There's no New Yorker really. Everyone's from somewhere else." As opposed to identifying themselves as an American, many second-generation whites (as well as a few Asian Americans) chose to emphasize their regional roots in the multicultural New York metropolitan region. As a lifetime resident of New York City, Mendel is one example of someone who expresses considerable pride in identifying as a secular Jewish New Yorker.

> I couldn't identify as being American even though I was born here and raised here because it's not part of my roots. Sometimes I say I'm New Yorker, because I don't particularly feel American. I've been out West once but that was when I was young. I actually did a very American thing after college and I hiked the Appalachian Trail. Yeah, it's like a very American type of experience, or at least neo-American experience. It's one of these things that a lot of Americans do. And not surprisingly when I went, there's Germans, there's an Israelite there, people all over the world that like to hike this trail. And I got to see a lot of America. But I don't identify with being a deep southern individual.

By associating America with the South and the South with Jim Crow racism, white participants from New York are essentially distancing themselves from the parochialism and racial offenses of white America. Instead, they view themselves as part of a more enlightened, cosmopolitan world city whose exposure to a diverse, immigrant-dominated population makes them more sensitive to the plight of minorities and more politically aware of issues beyond the nation's borders. Recognition of racial privileges and inequalities is certainly one step toward rectifying America's race problem. The problem arises however when this professed awareness of racial privilege is used to overlook one's own racial predilections or promote the idea that we now live in a color-blind society.

Even those working-class whites who witnessed rising ethnic tensions with new immigrant groups were careful to differentiate race relations in their neighborhoods from those in the South. Born in Ireland, Colin immigrated to the United States at the age of four and was raised in a transitional working-class white immigrant neighborhood in Queens that included a diverse mix of Italian, Greek, Russian, and Arab residents, a small population of Asians, and very few African Americans. Throughout the interview, he spoke nostalgically about the friendships and associations he cultivated in his neighborhood block and how that shaped his identity as a youth. In the following passage, he reflects on the dynamics of race relations in his neighborhood and, like others, argues that even ethnic conflicts he observed were nothing like what one would see in the South. As he described it, "So I did think there was some tension between groups here and there but nothing too big. It's not like what you have in the South, Alabama and Georgia. People here would live with each other. You would see that Arabs would have some problems with Asians or maybe the Greeks had some problems with the Arabs here and there, the blacks . . . there weren't that many blacks so I think you didn't have that much racial tension." Of course, the dynamics that Colin describes among the different white ethnic groups may play out differently if other racial minority groups were to become a more visible presence in his neighborhood. Nevertheless, it is worth noting how "the South" becomes a comparative frame of reference for describing race and ethnic relations in New York in this narrative.

In the case of second-generation white Americans, invoking their parents' ethnic heritage allows them to assume a more inclusive, classy, and less burdensome identity than the restrictive and racially loaded label of being called white. Given the cultural, political, and demographic context of New York City, most of the participants in the study expressed either ambivalence or aversion toward the white identity label, opting instead to emphasize their parents' immigrant heritage, as shown in this quote from Sebastian:

> ANGIE: Do you consider yourself a white American first of all?
>
> SEBASTIAN: Yes.
>
> ANGIE: Is that part of your identity? What does that mean to you?
>
> SEBASTIAN: It's kind of like what I'm not. I don't consider myself Asian, I don't consider myself Latino or black, so I'm in that other bucket which is just white. I mean people ask me sometimes what I am and I say I'm Italian American.
>
> ANGIE: Why do you say that?
>
> SEBASTIAN: Well it's interesting cause I'm really not. I really should say I'm an American Italian because predominantly I'm American. As opposed to a fourth generation Italian American, I'm first generation, so I feel closer to it as someone whose great grandparents came here.[24]

As discussed earlier, some white interviewees like Sebastian acknowledged the privileges that come with being white but did not embrace this identity as having any personal meaning in their day-to-day lives beyond the benefits it conferred. Sebastian understood whiteness as representing what he is not, thus imposing a label devoid of any meaning as compared with the cultural richness he derives from identifying as the child of Italian immigrants.

For other participants, race—whether it be in terms of identifying as white American or acknowledging white privilege—seemed irrelevant to their understanding of their day-to-day experiences. Ivan has struggled to make sense of his place in U.S. black-white race relations, having immigrated at the age of eight from Russia where he saw almost no blacks to an urban neighborhood where he became the white minority and then transitioning to a college where he no longer has to interact with many nonwhites. In the following excerpt, Ivan, who identifies simply as Russian, explained his problems with the term "white":

> ANGIE: One of the things that people might identify you as is white. So how does that play a part? Do you think that's part of your identity?
>
> IVAN: You know it's funny because I always really get kind of offended by that. The first time I noticed it was when we were filling out college applications, you have to put your [race] and I was like well I'm not really white. And they're like what do you mean you're not white. You're the whitest person ever. And I was like yeah but I'm not white America cause I identify more with whatever the other is. So I always find it's kind of weird and every time on a job application or tax work, I'm always weirded out by that.

ANGIE: So you don't identify but do you think other people identify
   you . . .

IVAN: Yeah of course.

ANGIE: Like if someone else were you to see you, would they treat you
   differently?

IVAN: Oh yeah of course. I mean they would label me white. And I mean
   I am white. It just seems like that's a limiting thing, you know?

ANGIE: So do you think on any level like outside of the school . . .

IVAN: People treated me differently? Not that I know of. I mean not that
   I can see where I was like if I was up for a job against a black person.
   No I've never had. I never saw it.

ANGIE: So do you think that racial part of that identity affected you in any
   way then whether it's privilege or advantage outside of the school?

IVAN: I mean yeah I don't know. Probably in a certain way it's an
   advantage. But maybe not. I guess it also depends on the situation you
   are [in].

Like Sebastian, Ivan finds the label "white" as burdensome and limiting, but
in his case he also seems ambivalent about whether or not it has given him
any sort of advantage over nonwhites. He told me that he does not believe
that America is a color-blind society but feels that because of increasing
intermarriage, it will eventually be difficult for people to discriminate based
on race alone.

As the narratives suggest, cosmopolitanism becomes an important
framing reference for the identities of second-generation whites, who can
draw on their proximate ethnic roots to distinguish themselves from what
they perceive as more narrow-minded and less enlightened white Americans
outside of New York. Of course, these findings should be interpreted with
some caution since the sample included more participants from middle-class
backgrounds. Vertovec and Cohen argue that the idealistic notion of cosmopolitanism reflects the class privilege of people who have the luxury to
travel, learn other languages, and educate themselves on other cultures.[25]
Either way, the idea that New Yorkers are bounded not by parochial ethnic,
local, or national ties but rather by a shared and inclusive morality as "citizens
of the world" was most poignantly felt among the middle-class participants.
Of course, further research with a larger sample would need to be done to
flesh out the class dynamics, but what is clear is that middle-class white interviewees felt that direct ties with the cultural heritage, transnational ties, and
immigration struggles of their parents gave them a worldly and modish
perspective that separated them from their fellow native-born white peers.

For second-generation whites, it was thus easy to draw on their ethnicity as a source of pride, especially within the cosmopolitan culture of New York City.

Sebastian, the oldest son of Italian immigrant restaurant owners, grew up in a wealthy white neighborhood in Long Island and expressed considerable pride in his parents' Italian heritage. Because of his parents, he went on regular trips to Europe with his family throughout his childhood, explored a variety of foods from other cultures, and met people from diverse backgrounds. In the following passage, he explained how this early exposure to other cultures played an important role in shaping his identity.

> SEBASTIAN: I'm an American but the Italian part matters too. I'm very proud of my Italian heritage. It's really neat growing up and having an attachment to a certain type of food or tradition. Even though [my parents] landed in a suburban area and they really loved that, they were also very worldly. My mother speaks French. They travel all the time with and without us. Growing up in Europe gives you a different sort of sensibility. So I think at least it taught us not to be afraid of people that were different. I didn't really grow up with a lot of people that were black or even Asian or anything that was sort of different than white. But my parents always had friends from Europe that would come and that's the way I first learned about a kiwi. I didn't know what a kiwi was but my parents friends had brought it with them from somewhere and it was just all this exposure to different things.
>
> ANGIE: Do you think that experience makes you different from other nonimmigrant white Americans?
>
> SEBASTIAN: I think I'm pretty open-minded. Like I still desire to see the world. I don't want to be isolated and I love Europe because of my parents, the exposure I got with them. I remember going to school my first year in Cornell and I remember thinking that I was stuck on this very white campus that was a lot of Long Islanders and I just remember thinking that everyone was so unaware. I have a strong interest in international politics, and I don't think a lot of Americans do.

In this narrative, Sebastian uses his parents' ethnic heritage to differentiate himself from the parochial racial and cultural outlook of his white American peers from Long Island. This strategy of racial distancing was most apparent when he remarked on his greater openness toward racial minorities such as blacks and Asians because of his global outlook.

Interviewees with parents from other countries also used their ethnic heritage as a means to distinguish themselves from native-born white Americans as in the case of Julia, who stated simply "I still think Russian people are a

little more worldly and more able to connect with other people." Another
respondent, Emily, whose mother worked as a clerical worker and father was
employed as a cab driver, also identified herself as "not totally American"
because of her immigrant background. She expressed a desire to bring that
worldly perspective to her children in the future and teach them to "look a
little bit outside your surroundings and what's in the world." In the following
excerpt, Anastasia, who immigrated to the United States when she was six
years old, argues that even though she does not remember much about her
experience in Russia, the fact that her parents were immigrants engrained in
her a more cosmopolitan outlook on the world.

> ANGIE: And you used the word "immigrant" to describe yourself even
> though you came at a pretty young age. Do you feel that's an important
> part of your identity for any reason?
>
> ANASTASIA: I do, because it gives you a different perspective on life, and
> not necessarily through my own experiences, because I was so young
> when I came here. I don't really remember what growing up in Russia
> was like, but the fact that my parents made that decision to move at such
> a young age. I was completely uprooted from everything that I knew and
> brought somewhere new and had to adapt. I used to date a Republican
> who just had a very limited worldview and he always said to me that he
> thought my view was very cosmopolitan and that it had to do specifi-
> cally with my experience. I didn't really think about it that way until he
> said so. I think that has more to do with my parents, that they're the
> ones who have seen the world. So those are the values that they instilled
> in me. I haven't been back to Russia since I left, but my dad goes back
> and I hear from him how the country has changed and what's going on
> in the economy so I think that that gives me a different perspective
> where I can look at you know what's going on in America and realize so
> many people have it so much worse. I don't think I'd have that outlook
> if I was just an American kid.

When asked how she identifies, Anastasia responded "Russian" because of
"where I was born, my name, my ability to speak the language other than
English." She adds, "It's unique. It's cool. It's a lot cooler than being American,
especially nowadays." By emphasizing their cosmopolitanism, second-
generation white Americans are able to project a more positive, self-affirming,
and privileged image of their parents' culture that helps them to differentiate
themselves from racists but blend in with the urban progressiveness of
New York with a relatively muted sense of conflict. As Anastasia observes
though, this outlook does not have to be cultivated through socialization in

another country but can be simply passed on through their linkages with their immigrant parents.

As compared with their white American peers, Korean and Chinese American participants regardless of class background very rarely made references to cosmopolitanism as a means to highlight the trendiness of their parents' culture. I argue that this is because the American racial imaginary associates Asianness not with "coolness" and "multiculturalism" but rather with "racial deviance" and "alienness" even with the context of New York's immigrant culture. At best, participants explained how the racial diversity of New York made this cultural difference either acceptable or invisible but did not necessarily believe that it nurtured a sense of belonging with their American peers. Here, it is not what is said, but what is not said that is meaningful. For example, Henry acknowledged that there may be racial barriers that make it difficult for Asian Americans to achieve their goals, but said that living in New York, he doesn't "feel so estranged by the fact that someone's trying to oppress me. I love the fact that when I get off the subway, I'm not the minority and I'm not the majority. It's not a function of whether or not I'm an Asian American or Korean American." Having traveled to other parts of the country, Henry found New York to be a stark contrast to places in Kentucky and Ohio, where he felt less "comfortable as the only colored person in miles." The difference with white American narratives is subtle but his narrative reveals how New York is a great place to live for Asian Americans not because it makes being Korean or Chinese seem hip and unique in a positive way, but rather, because it erases the feeling of being the racial Other.

Young recalled feeling a similar sense of wonderment and relief when he started traveling frequently to other countries during his first year out of college. In the following passage, he speaks to how he was moved by the experience of not being labeled and treated as Asian but rather as an American or a member of a "global community." He said thoughtfully, "When you travel internationally the whole notion of the Asian American experience becomes a bit diluted because you take into consideration a global community, as opposed to just what it means to be Asian in America. That changed my views on things a lot as well. When I went to countries, it wasn't really an issue where it's like oh he's Asian or he's Asian American. At that point, he's just an American." Thus, it is not that ethnicity gives Asian Americans a ticket to cosmopolitanism as it did with second-generation whites, but rather, it is the sense of belonging to a global culture that enables them to downplay their sense of racial difference. The narratives by both working-class and professionals parallel the findings of studies on middle-class black Americans that show how class may allow racial minorities to shield themselves from blatant racism or respond to it more effectively, but racial formations still pervade the lives of racial minorities across class barriers.[26]

In the rare instances that participants did refer to their cosmopolitan identities, it was intended not to call attention to their cultural heritage but rather the opposite: as a way to transcend racial and ethnic boundaries and prevent people from typecasting them as either culturally insular as Asians or ignorant as Americans. This was the case for Jinah, who identifies with a cosmopolitan American identity and expresses disdain for people who try to typecast her as the "typical Korean" or the "typical American." Since her college years, she has developed closer friendships and romantic relationships with internationals from around the world but has maintained her distance from other Asian Americans whom she considers too ethnocentric.

> I wanna change the concept of Americans, cause I meet people who are like "ugh, American's are so whatever" and I feel as if I'm really saying "well I'm American." Friends of mine would say, "you're not really a typical American" in that I speak different languages, I'm well-travelled and well-educated, I'm not fat, I'm not ignorant, I read books, pretty well-cultured. So [in college] I had a group of American friends, international friends, Korean friends—I don't like being typecasted into one. So when I went to Dartmouth, I actually pooh-poohed the Koreans, cause they made it like either you hang out with us or you don't. And I was like, you know then fine, if you're gonna be like that. So I hung out with just all Americans.

The excerpt is intertwined with references to a cosmopolitan identity based on her higher class and educational background that enable her to transcend her sense of social displacement within the ethnic community and mainstream American society. Indeed, most Korean and Chinese Americans I interviewed were more likely to associate their ethnicity and culture with ethnocentrism and cultural insularity—which to them threatened only to reaffirm their sense of racial difference. Even if they themselves embraced their parents' ancestral culture and socialized mostly with other coethnic peers, they were always careful to distinguish their parents and their friends from "typical Asians" by the mere fact that they valued things other than academics or drinking and hanging out with other non-Asians.

A few middle- and upper-class participants also drew on their New York cosmopolitan roots as a strategic means to respond to racist reactions and comments they occasionally encountered with other native-born white Americans. For example, Min, who was born and raised in a white-dominated neighborhood of New Jersey that eventually attracted a large Asian population, remembered how on a visit to Florida, white Americans blatantly stared at them and asked them what country they came from. Although their reactions made her self-conscious, she said she simply thought to herself how "I was almost embarrassed for them, because they had so little knowledge of what was out there. They were so ignorant of other cultures." Several Korean and Chinese Americans recounted incidents where they had to educate their less well-informed white colleagues and peers when they made racially derogatory or stereotypical comments about Asians—an approach that enabled them to assert a sense of moral and class superiority over such parochial and ignorant worldviews without accentuating their foreignness. In other words, they could be more American by showing how open-minded and knowledgeable they were about other cultures.

As opposed to perceiving their ethnic identity as something that connected them to the outer world, most participants viewed their ethnicity and cultural values as something more personal and family-oriented. Even as adults, Korean and Chinese Americans reported how they valued visits to their parents' homeland or enjoyed learning their parents' language not for its ability to connect them with other New Yorkers but rather to nurture their family relationships. For example, Bryan expressed interest in teaching his children Chinese because "if they can speak the language automatically there's a bond with your family, and I think it's a beautiful thing to have that sense of history, that sense of culture and that tie to your family." A few participants also believed that Korean or Chinese language skills and cultural knowledge could help them to compete in a globalizing economy. For example, Tony who is proficient in Spanish and Japanese expressed regret that he did not try to learn Korean at an earlier age given the country's rapid economic rise in recent decades.

Conclusion

On some levels, the narratives of second-generation Korean and Chinese Americans resonate with those of second-generation white Americans, in terms of how they emotionally negotiate the pressures, obligations, and gratitude that come with being a child of an immigrant. It is at the crossroads of immigrant dreams and second-generation struggles that both white and Asian Americans can subjectively nurture an emotional connection with one another and seek both hope and guidance by trying to follow in the footsteps of their European predecessors. Just as Korean and Chinese immigrant parents looked wistfully to the success of Jewish immigrants, their American-born children find solace and empathy in the experiences of young Jewish Americans who also struggle to negotiate their bicultural worlds.

However, the chapter has also shown how similar aspirations and ideologies do not always lead to the same life experiences. Second-generation individuals viewed as "white Americans" are more readily able to select aspects of their ethnic heritage that allow them to blend into the cosmopolitan culture of New York City with a relatively muted sense of conflict. Korean and Chinese Americans are more conscious of the negative stereotypes associated with their race and how invoking such ethnic options would simply highlight their racial otherness. In contrast to the experiences of second-generation white counterparts, racial transgressions framed against mythical understandings of Asian family and culture are a pervasive part of the everyday experiences of Asian Americans. On the surface, Korean and Chinese Americans may deny having encountered race and racism in their lives yet provide descriptive accounts of incidents and attitudes that highlight their exclusion from social citizenship. Because of the ambiguities, tensions, and contradictions of being Asian American, participants must on the one hand rely on mainstream themes of the American Dream, family values, and the model minority myth to highlight their alignment with mainstream values; at the same time, the narratives clearly reveal that middle-class Asian Americans recognize and respond to daily racial microaggressions in their own ways.

Of course, no one racial label can adequately describe the range of Asian American experiences, especially because the participants come from all walks of life, family structures, and neighborhood contexts. However, the one theme that resonates across most of these narratives is the desire not to let their racial phenotype define and limit them (typical Asian) or let it negate the American Dream for which their parents sacrificed. Nadia Kim describes this Asian American strategy as "mainstreaming their ethnic differences"—that is, moving away from the ethnic niches toward middle-class white jobs and neighborhoods while maintaining a strong sense of their ethnonationalistic identity in a way that minimizes their foreignness.[27] Kim argues that Asian Americans are in fact aware of racial discrimination and inequality but need to articulate their pride in their ethnic differences by emphasizing values that separate them from the stigma of being black in America.

The chapter has also shown how this disjuncture between external presentation of self and internal feelings of racial discrimination can be partly attributed to the ambiguous, contradictory, and uneven ways in which racism applies to Asian American that is difficult to articulate in the Western vocabulary and framework of binary oppositionality. In this sense, the Asian immigrant family myth provides a covert way to legitimize social ostracism, discriminatory college admissions processes, and unequal work

and promotion opportunities against Asian Americans, while simultane-
ously highlighting the cultural inferiority of other racial minority groups
(namely, African Americans). By appearing as positive stereotypes, these
various myths not only make invisible the actual racial experiences of Asian
Americans through a twisted interpretation of their cultural superiority but
also make it difficult for Asian Americans themselves to articulate the
source of their racial marginalization. The outcome of this struggle depends
on the relationships they cultivate in the broader ethnic community as well
as their racial experiences as Asian Americans at school, at work, and in
other public spaces.

CHAPTER 7

Behind the Family Portrait

Feminist scholars and activists have made great strides in contesting the middle-class white ideal of the heteronormative nuclear family that dominated the public imagination during the greater part of the nineteenth and twentieth centuries. Although expectations on women's maternal and household obligations persist in other ways, research studies on white American families show that the idealized separation between work as a male sphere and home as the female domain has been significantly blurred with the increasing incorporation of women into the workforce and the diversification of family structures in recent decades. Rather than unconditionally glorifying motherhood and caregiving as a female-only domain, feminists are now debating where maternal/familial nurturing ends and individual autonomy begins, how the economic structure hinders the formation of egalitarian gender relations, and what the role of societal institutions should be in assisting with women's work at home.[1] We are also broadening the definition of what constitutes a "family" and giving increasing recognition to the growing number of people embracing new types of relationships, including gay couples, blended families, single-female-headed households, childless couples, adoptee parents, and even interracial families.

However, as feminists of color have pointed out, what is a new phenomenon of blurred home-work boundaries for white America is in fact nothing new for women of color who have historically straddled the dual burdens of wage work and domestic responsibilities as a result of the depressed wages of minority men and the growth of low-paying female-dominated industries. A long line of scholars, including Evelyn Nakano Glenn, Pierrette Hondagneu-Sotelo, and Patricia Hill Collins have repeatedly called for greater attention to the way minority families both past and present have adopted alternative household structures and family values in order to accommodate the multiple constraints imposed by racial isolation and economic hardships. Women and girls face unique struggles within this stratified order—on one hand shouldering the gendered burdens of caregiving and preserving honor for the family while financially contributing to the economic well-being of the household. The priorities of middle-class white women, such as family leave policies, mean less to Asian immigrants, particularly wage laborers whose economic survival depends on the relatively lower wages both parents bring to the table.[2] Housing, inheritance, social security, and medical leave policies that focus on the middle-class white nuclear family structure neglect to see how new familial arrangements composed of extended kin and fictive kin provide a crucial source of social and emotional support for minority children who otherwise would be bereft of adult supervision and caregiving.[3]

Even as American society is slowly reopening the discourse on family, the cultural myth of the Asian immigrant family juxtaposed against the myth of the black family continues to maintain a tenacious hold on the racial imaginary of public officials, media, and academics. Despite repeatedly questioning the notion of a monolithic family type, family studies and white feminists continue to treat Asian immigrant families as static, homogeneous bastions of culture and tradition that can withstand the forces of social inequality and change occurring on the local, national, and global scales. As Ishii-Kuntz points out, as compared with research on black and Latino families, most research on Asian American families continues to fixate on cultural explanations, to the complete neglect of historical, economic, and political contexts.[4] These studies ignore how culture itself can adapt to broader structural constraints and vulnerabilities in the environment from the family to the neighborhood to the global economy. They also fail to recognize the way race, class, and gender intersect in shaping both inequality and empowerment within immigrant families in such a manner that culture becomes both a source of oppression as well as a tool of empowerment against societal marginalization. And more central to this study, scholarly preoccupation with assimilation and the generation gap does so to the complete neglect of the intricate emotional dynamics with which second-generation Asian Americans engage with their parents, siblings, and extended kin and revisit their ethnicity and culture as they enter adulthood. Without this understanding, what we are left with is the empty shell of a one-dimensional Asian family portrait, devoid of all human feelings and individual agency and destined to be forever objectified as the racial Other.

As a corrective to this approach, this book has revealed how the broader structure of race relations and growing class inequality sets the backdrop within which all immigrant families, including Asian immigrant families, must readapt their cultural value systems. While some Korean and Chinese families are able to achieve the ideal of the traditional nuclear family (for better or for worse), others must stretch their limited resources, redistribute responsibilities, and adopt new worldviews in order to maintain the semblance of personal dignity and family honor. This can mean devising alternative means of love and communication, delegating new roles and responsibilities to mothers, children, and extended kin, or advocating those cultural values and racial myths that enable them to make sense of discrimination and hardships. When immigrant parents fail to make an emotional connection with their children as a result of long work hours or personal challenges, these children do not necessarily succumb to emotional neglect and victimization but actively seek solace and support through other means. However, such psychological disconnects with their parents can leave an indelible mark on the identities and lives of second-generation Asian Americans in ways that are made invisible by the model minority myth. Whatever the path, the book shows how this process of making sense out of these convoluted family histories has enormous bearing on their views on ethnicity and culture as adults and not always in the direction of assimilation.

BARRIERS TO MAKING FAMILY

Although recognizing the way Confucian culture informs relations in Korean and Chinese immigrant families, the book problematizes the way the model minority myth reifies these sociocultural attributes in a way that is meant to accentuate the racial alienness of Asian American families. Instead, the study highlights how structural vulnerabilities outside the family heighten the psychological alienation and burdens of children in Korean and Chinese immigrant families. As the study has shown, changing family structures in a new globalizing economy open up new sets of responsibilities and burdens for younger members of the family. For one, the dual-wage-earning family structure may evolve at the expense of children, who have less time to spend with their parents and must assume greater domestic responsibilities in their absence. Today, it is not uncommon to see immigrant households split in two or more countries, with one or both parents working and living in one country and the child raised and educated in another—a situation that adds more emotional complexity to childhood experiences. Aside from juggling their growing work and household responsibilities, more disadvantaged immigrant parents lack the human capital, English skills, and familiarity with the workings of American institutions to assist their children to their fullest capacity. As the narratives have shown, such hardships not only increase the likelihood of social problems among immigrant parents (e.g., substance abuse, gambling, mental illness, abuse) but also can contribute to increased depression and low self-esteem among second-generation youth.

In response to the changing environment, immigrant families today are reconstructing traditional roles and value systems to make the most out of limited opportunities that have opened up in the postindustrial economy. Immigrant families both disadvantaged and advantaged, can show considerable resilience and resourcefulness in adapting to social and economic constraints—in this case, delegating children to fulfill adult responsibilities, relying on intergenerational kinscripters to help with child care, emotional nurturing, and mediation, saddling family members especially women with extra work and home responsibilities, and holding onto antiquated cultural traditions on gender and family in their quest for racial validation. The book has revealed how, contrary to their outward appearance of rank order and social stability, the children of Korean and Chinese immigrant families view their lives as being formatively shaped by their obligation to broker, translate, restrain, and care for themselves and their family members in ways that subvert traditional Confucian hierarchies on age and gender. When immigrant parents are physically or emotionally absent, children are pushed to take on adult responsibilities and, if they are fortunate, turn to extended and fictive kin who can act as cultural mediators and surrogate caregivers. When there are no viable first sons to carry on the family name, oldest daughters can fulfill some of their parents' unrealized dreams by assuming more key decision-making roles and preserving family honor through their educational and occupational achievements. Both daughters and sons learn both painful and self-empowering lessons about love and independence by observing the shifting marital relations between their mothers and fathers.

Of course, this transformation has not occurred without some degree of doubt and resistance, nor has it been felt equally across the board since some families are better equipped to either maintain the status quo or adapt to these pressures than others. Asian and Latino immigrant families today, unlike European immigrants in the early twentieth century, have come from diverse backgrounds and economic situations and are entering at a time when opportunities for stable jobs and upward mobility are increasingly sparse, setting the context for multiple assimilation paths among the next generation of American-born children.[5] Their ability to adapt and assimilate depends heavily on the resources and networks these families can access, the specific context of their homeland and settlement experiences, and the reception they encounter within the host society.[6]

Among the Korean and Chinese Americans I interviewed, the hardships of immigrant adaptation generally created all kinds of social stress and problems for their families, but those that have the financial wherewithal, kinship support, and community networks were better able to provide nurturing caregivers, mediate cultural differences, and establish a healthy emotional environment for their children. Not surprisingly, working-class children of Korean and Chinese immigrant families tend to shoulder more adult responsibilities that help some to feel greater empathy with their immigrant parents' experiences while traumatizing others into pursuing a path away from their difficult home environment. In contrast, most middle-class Korean and Chinese Americans are better able to sustain the semblance of family stability and order but without the proper cultural channels, may pay an emotional price by losing their family ties.

It is within this shifting social and economic terrain that both immigrant parents and their American-born children must emotionally negotiate their family obligations and expectations in order to make sense of their ethnic identities and ties with their family culture as they transition into adulthood. In so doing, Asian Americans hope to be able to give meaning to their parents' sacrifices and hardships as immigrant minorities. In some ways, the emotional, identity-seeking process that second-generation Korean and Chinese Americans undergo, as this study has illustrated, is not much different from the process confronting other immigrant groups that face the same external pressures in respect to intergenerational tensions and family obligations, although to varying degrees depending on their class standing and their country's positioning within the global economy. In terms of their hopes and aspirations, we see some parallels in the ways Korean and Chinese Americans evoke immigrant ideologies about the costs and rewards of the American Dream that parallel those of second-generation white Americans in the study as a result of the immigrant family experience.

For Korean and Chinese Americans, however, I find that the specific nature of their cultural, gender, and racial positionality also limits the paths they can choose in order to realize their educational and career goals and find happiness in their life decisions. The narratives throughout this book reveal that despite the hope and motivation it inspires, Asian Americans come to believe that the promises of the American Dream are not available to all depending on where they stand in the racial and class order. These children first learn this by observing and experiencing their parents' past successes and failures during the early immigration years, which lay the foundations for their cultural beliefs on education and upward mobility. However, as they enter their twenties, Asian Americans realize that rejecting the American Dream would only seal the nail on the coffin of their parents' struggles and failures so they achieve the semblance of "success" in whatever way possible, whether by obtaining a college or GED degree, paying for their parents' mortgage, or acting the part of the "good daughter/son." However, as they get older, second-generation Asian Americans are forced to negotiate some of the resulting contradictions that emerge between the pressures of family values and gendered expectations, between class privilege and racial marginalization, and between immigrant parents' American Dream and their individual life goals.

The book has shown how second-generation Korean and Chinese American adults reconstruct the social meaning of their personal educational achievements, their ethnic identities, and their gendered obligations in order to make sense out of their family's lives before and after immigration. Because these histories are often untold, the participants in the study struggled to assemble the fragments of childhood memories and kin-scripted narratives with the help of family brokers in a way that helps them to reconcile the pain and burdens of parent-child relationships. In the face of language and cultural barriers, they find other means of expressing their love and empathy and in the process re-create new modes of communication and caregiving across the generational divide. Some of the participants in the study are able to pull their families together by filling roles as surrogate caregivers, while others opt to re-create their familial space outside their immediate family and kinship networks. The ways in which participants compartmentalize and channel their emotional commitments and the risks associated with doing so vary widely depending on their access to networks and resources. Asian Americans are better able to minimize and manage those risks when they have greater access to positive mentors and community-based organizations within the neighborhood, yet compared to those that cater to white Americans, they are usually few and far between for most Asian Americans.

Even as the American government and its institutions continue to ignore the plight of Asian families, their family-based problems are only growing in the current global economy. Increasing urbanization, rising participation in the paid labor force, and greater job instability mean that fewer parents are able to live close to their children, while more families are pushed to adapt to new types of economic and caregiving arrangements. More and more immigrant families are beginning to feel the intense pressures of resource competition and constraint, which are forcing women and children to take on even more burdens and responsibilities and families to concentrate on economic survival over emotional and physical welfare. These problems have been aggravated by various national trends, including the growing presence of immigrant children in overcrowded and underfunded schools, increasingly restrictive immigration policies that have divided and isolated immigrant families, the regional dispersal of immigrants into nontraditional receiving communities, and legislative attacks on welfare and social service programs servicing both documented and undocumented families.[7] It is apparent that the heightened demands of the global economy accompanied with these neoliberal reforms are having a devastating effect on the social and emotional fabric of overwhelmed migrant families.

AT THE CROSSROADS OF RACE AND ETHNICITY

The findings on the emotion work of Korean and Chinese Americans also have broader ramifications for the way we define racism in the United States and study its complex logic in the post–civil rights era. During the Jim Crow era of legalized segregation and discrimination, surveys on racial attitudes offered a relatively accurate assessment of people's social distancing from racial minorities, particularly blacks in America. In other words, what they said is what they did, for the most part. As Bobo and his coauthors assert, surveys indicate that we have clearly come a long way since the days when race presented an insurmountable barrier to racial integration.[8] However, numerous studies on racial formations after the disintegration of legal barriers have problematized the reliability of racial attitudinal surveys alone in assessing a social order where ideologies of color blindness and political correctness denounce open and blatant expressions of racism.[9] In most surveys, white Americans profess support for an equal and color-blind society in theory but are more ambivalent about crossing racial borders when it comes to issues of interracial marriage and residential preferences.[10] So indeed, what they (whites) say is often not necessarily what they do in reality.

What this study has uncovered however is the contradictory logic of emotion work and the social construction of self when it comes to racially liminal groups like Asian Americans who occupy an intermediary position in their relationship with blacks and whites. For one, what they say is sometimes what they do and sometimes not, depending on how they process their ethnic identities. But more central to the premise of this book, what they say and what they do are not necessarily how they feel. By using the concept of emotion work, I am referring to not only how Korean and Chinese Americans identify and where they find their sense of social belonging, but also what they feel as a result of the cumulative effects of daily racial microaggressions—and this despite the fact that they deny having experienced racism and express a desire to be part of the American mainstream.

Thus, the narratives of Korean and Chinese American participants in this study underline several critical insights about race and racism for nonblack/nonwhite Americans in the current era. The traditional assimilation literature tends to treat ethnicity as mutually exclusive from race and nationality and ignore how certain minority groups may experience both ethnic-based assimilation and racial subjugation. Voluntary immigrants to America are presumed to follow in the footsteps of their early twentieth-century European predecessors in temporarily maintaining ethnic distinctions and homeland cultures that eventually give way to American identities through the processes of generational assimilation. In contrast, the racial oppression of black Americans has been consistently treated as an exception to the classic assimilation story—one in which their skin color becomes the basis for discriminating against them as secondary citizens. Both narratives are examined within the American nationalist framework with little attention paid to the changing dynamics of contemporary race relations and growing transnationalization among ethnic groups.

When applied to contemporary immigrant groups from Asia and Latin America, the tendency is to conflate certain indicators of assimilation such as social mobility with racial equality. The argument goes, if you are assimilating then you are being socially accepted as equals and are thus not bound by the racial order. When taken to the extreme, assimilation is used to prove that racism does not exist at all, as it is in the model minority myth where Asian American "success" is touted as a sign that anyone—including African Americans—can overcome racial hurdles if they work hard enough.

However, contrary to how most traditional scholars have approached the issue of race, achieving assimilation does not necessarily negate the relevance of race and racial ideology, but rather it can operate parallel to or even reinforce the logic of racism for certain groups. At the crossroads of racism and assimilation, Asian American families experience racial othering differently than other minority groups and have relatively more leeway to negotiate their entrance into mainstream institutions. This is because ethnic groups that are immigrants (or children of immigrants) as well as racial minorities are exposed to two competing frames of reference: the first involves the ups and downs of the immigrant family experience fraught with tales of sacrifice, family honor, and an obligation to succeed. The other is premised on a long-established system of racial stratification that ranks social groups according to phenotype while rendering such unequal practices invisible. Although Asian Americans are valorized for their academic achievements, their incorporation into highly skilled professions, and their visibility in middle-class suburban neighborhoods, second-generation Korean and Chinese Americans sense that they are also excluded from full social citizenship in the American racial imaginary and stigmatized for those very same cultural features that supposedly aid in their assimilation. This contradictory practice of racial othering appears in the form of subtle insinuations to outright discriminatory practices from their romantic relationships to their workplace encounters.

As they transition into adulthood, most of the participants in the study were able to come to terms with the various tensions, burdens, and contradictions of living in an immigrant family, some better than others. What is clear however is that the ability to pass down ethnic pride and cultural value systems from immigrant to American-born children depends not only on the stability of the family but also on how the second generation strategically reconstructs, frames, and bridges the disconnected pieces of family around their ethnic-centered experiences as Korean or Chinese American women, gays or lesbians, working-class or middle-class children, and mothers or fathers. As opposed to viewing ethnicity as the outcome of uniform identities and experiences, ethnic-centered experiences refer to the increasingly diverse and intersectional ways in which individuals and groups find ethnicity as having some relevance in shaping their day-to-day lives so that identifying more strongly as a heterosexual Korean American mother means something different than relating to one's ethnicity as a working-class gay Korean American.[11]

Despite these class differences, the narratives also point to the way in which middle-class Asian Americans share a common fate and worldview with their working-class counterparts that is shaped by the absence of mainstream institutional support and their racial invisibility in mainstream society. For example, the inability of parents to communicate their family histories to their children stands in sharp contrast to the experiences of middle-class second-generation Jewish Americans who, although grappling with similar intergenerational and cultural conflicts, were more likely to be aware of the political history of their homeland, their parents' struggles with anti-Semitism, and their place within a heterogeneous Jewish community. The narratives suggest that relatively stronger verbal communication among family members, the institutional completeness of the Jewish community (e.g., Hebrew schools), the greater availability of mentors and role models, and perhaps the wider coverage of Jewish history in the media and urban public school systems all play a role in preserving family legacies. Some may argue that communication barriers between immigrant parents and American-born children are an inevitable part of the assimilation experience. But how society validates their ethnic roots and family histories through mass media and multicultural education, provides support for ethnic organizations and mentorship programs as well as ethnic studies programs, and encourages a wider range of art, books, and films on Asian Americans and Asian history can provide a strong emotional foundation for countering the psychological burdens and racial microaggressions they encounter both within and outside the family. The findings thus underline the need for more institutional support for Asian immigrant families that does not diminish the value of family culture as a resource against outside racism.

The Costs of the Family Myth

Both immigrant parents and their children embrace the myth of the Asian family (albeit with some ambivalence) because it provides a means to receive some degree of cultural validation for their lifelong sacrifices and gives them hope that they can follow the paths of Jewish immigrants before them. In trying to justify their family's hardships and praise their hard-won goals, some Asian Americans also fall into the trap of selectively reconstructing and streamlining their ethnic identities in a way that highlights how they best typify core American ideals on hard work, family values, and overall cultural superiority. As Park points out, references to the sacrifices and heroism of their parents allow children of Korean and Chinese immigrants to normalize their racial differences by framing their family experiences within the traditional narrative of the American Dream.[12] Taking the middle road in navigating racial formations allows Asian Americans to maximize the personal benefits and minimize the costs of being a racially liminal minority—that is by exerting their moral righteousness over their racial aggressors, while distancing themselves from these stereotypes and gaining some degree of acceptance from mainstream American society.

The book has shown that this stems not so much from a desire to be accepted as "honorary whites" as some pundits argue, but rather from the constraints of a social vocabulary and reference framework for understanding and articulating "racial liminality" in a society adverse to talking about racism. By racial liminality, I am referring to the in-between and structurally ambiguous positioning of post-1965 racial groups—namely, Asian Americans—at the crossroads of immigrant-driven aspirations and racial marginalization. As argued by Omi and Winant, racial formations manifest themselves not only through explicit languages, labels, and cultural practices but also through a variety of subtle behaviors and coded cultural repertoires learned from past family experiences.[13] Second-generation Asian Americans today experience racial liminality against the backdrop of color-blind or laissez-faire racism, where racism presumably does not exist and, if it does, exists only in the form of extreme Jim Crow–style racism, such as hate crimes, derogatory language, and legalized segregation. It has less to say about citizenship, the glass ceiling, ethnic entrepreneurship, and U.S. relations with Asia.[14] What these theories do not take into account is the possibility that Asian Americans may be adapting their ethnic differences as a means to counter their racialization as foreigners in American society in a way that is difficult to capture through the conventional language of race.

The stories of second-generation Korean and Chinese Americans reveal how these adaptive strategies however come at a considerable social and psychological cost. Contrary to the model minority myth of family order, discipline, and harmony perpetuated by American society, the children of immigrants conveyed profound feelings of sorrow, regret, anger, and guilt over losing their adolescence to care for themselves or other family members, witnessing volatile and at times violent conflicts between their parents, being subjected to abuse, neglect, and unequal treatment from parents and kin, and navigating life without any mentors, role models, or even close friends. From a sociopsychological standpoint, the Asian immigrant family myth obscures much of the emotional struggles, psychological stresses, and internal dysfunctionalism that can emerge within these families, while making Asian Americans vulnerable to both unreasonable expectations from their teachers and employers and social ridicule and resentment from their peers.

Much has been written about the economic barriers, cultural norms, and fear of family shame that discourage Asian immigrant families from seeking outside assistance with mental illness. These internal barriers are only aggravated by society's inability to acknowledge the problems of so-called model Asian immigrant families and adapt their methods to the specific needs and emotional dynamics of diverse family situations. The tragic consequences of inadequate mental health care services were demonstrated by the mass shooting rampage at Virginia Tech by Korean American college student Seung-Hui Cho, who did seek professional help but slipped through the cracks. The findings from this study indicate that we must also think beyond the generation gap and assimilation especially when it comes to mental health care for immigrant families. Addressing mental health issues in Asian American communities requires health care professionals to recognize the diverse ways these families are structured, to look beyond traditional Western modes of communication, and to provide support for those aspects of family culture and ethnic community that help members to adapt.

Until these problems are addressed, this unstable emotional environment is conducive to depression, suicide, delinquency, high school cheating and

dropout, teenage pregnancy, abuse, increasing divorce, and gang involvement, as it was for many of the participants and their siblings in this study.
National surveys consistently indicate that rates of mental disorder among
Asian Americans are similar to, or lower than, the national average, yet
their families continue to be viewed as paragons of stability and order.
Furthermore, these numbers may likely be lowered by underreporting as a
result of greater fear of stigma and greater underutilization of mental health
services among Asian Americans.[15] Asian American boys and girls especially
between the ages of fifteen and twenty-four exhibit some of the highest rates
of anxiety, depression, and suicide among all racial groups and are much
less likely than white youth to find proper assistance.[16] Especially among
U.S.-born Asians, women are much more likely than men to have higher rates
of depression, anxiety, and other mental disorders.

The book also shows how the nostalgic construction of the immigrant
family and ethnic community as authentic spaces for reproducing traditional
culture can be as emotionally debilitating for daughters and sons, even as
it is psychologically empowering against outside racial marginalization: for
example, antiquated and essentialist understandings of family impose restrictive roles and responsibilities onto daughters and reinforce heteronormative
masculine ideals that complicate the lives of sons of immigrant families. A
s they begin to establish their own families and careers, daughters will continue to face the same dual burdens as modern American women. Although
American-born daughters may have the capacity to challenge gendered
expectations as they grow older, many also struggle with rising standards on
marriage and motherhood despite juggling jobs and careers and lack the
social support to negotiate the work-life balance. Unlike their immigrant
mothers who could turn to their children for assistance, second-generation
mothers must cater to the growing needs of their priceless child even if it
means taking on the greater weight of household labor and ultimately giving
up their careers for their families.[17] Nevertheless, I find that the dynamics of
gender inequality are complex and negotiable especially as American-born
daughters achieve their independence and reconstruct their identities as
adults. Future research on the changing context of motherhood for second-
generation Asian Americans as compared with immigrant parents may provide
some more insights in this area.

Finally, as many Asian American scholars have emphasized, stereotypical
representations of the model minority Asian family may help secure short-
term gains for some but ultimately conceal the discriminatory practices and
institutions that sustain the broader system of racial inequality. Using white
middle-class families as a normative yardstick against which other families of

color are measured, the myth insinuates that Asian families trump black families in terms of their social stability and positive work values but remain inferior to white families in terms of their rigid hierarchy and lack of feeling and humanism. This "racial triangulation" of Asian Americans as both superior to blacks and inferior to whites is used to either highlight their unassimilability as perpetual foreigners or champion the need for the complete assimilation of Asians into the white Anglo-Saxon Protestant core; both serve to assert and legitimize white hegemony over all racial minorities.[18] The mainstream portrayal of the model Asian immigrant family is often juxtaposed against the good nurturing white mother and the bad welfare-dependent black mother in a way that idealizes heteronormative middle-class motherhood and stigmatizes the morality of poor minorities. As a result, the perpetuation of this stereotype means that all mothers and nontraditional parents lose, although in different ways and to different degrees depending on gender, class, sexual orientation, and race. For example, the belief that as compared with Asian Tiger Mothers, white mothers are more nurturing and attentive to the all-consuming needs of their children disregards the realities of the dual burdens of working white mothers and justifies mothering as women's natural responsibility. It also disregards the wide range of parents, parenting styles, and household structures that are emerging among American families across race, religion, class, and sexual orientation.

The argument that Asian Americans face less racism and fewer family problems than blacks and Latinos completely misses the fact that the effects of racism are relational. The same cultural myths about Asian American families that are used to justify the social stigmatization, blocked mobility, and negligence of Asian American needs are also used to defend the social stigmatization, poverty, and withdrawal of support for African Americans, just in different ways. Conversely, Asian Americans who perpetuate cultural myths about dysfunctional black families are reinforcing the salience of monolithic cultural explanations that are used to justify their own alienation and social exclusion from American society. Using the model proposed in this book, future research may expand on the works of Dreby and Menjívar by examining further the dynamics of emotion work among racially marginalized families who also struggle with unstable or undocumented legal status, such as Mexican Americans and Salvadoran Americans.[19] By attributing the problems of poverty and oppression to other "Third World" family cultures, white Americans divert attention from their part in perpetuating racial and gender marginalization and establish their moral superiority over other economic competitors in East Asia. Blaming the social problems associated with poverty, discrimination, and mental illness on the cultural values of racial minorities also relieves whites, policy makers, and corporations of the responsibility of rectifying the behaviors, practices, and institutional barriers that prevent minorities from achieving true parity with whites.

By racially distancing themselves from blacks, Latinos, and even other Asian Americans, Asian Americans succeed only in undermining potential collective solidarity and mobilization between foreign-born and native-born Asian Americans, between blacks and immigrant minorities, between hetero-sexual and LGBTQ Asians, between working-class and white-collar Asians, between white and Asian women, and even between Asian Americans on issues of mutual interest. In agreement with feminists of color, I advocate for a shift in the way we currently assess racial oppression not as relative but rather as relational—that is, paying attention to the way in which the inter-section of race, class, and gender can create hierarchies of oppression but also understanding how they derive meaning only in relation to the other. In other words, it is important to acknowledge how oppression can be worse for some, but we should use it not to ignore or exclude the plight of others but rather to build bridges where those inequalities intersect.

A New Asia, the Old Orient

The way second-generation Americans view their family and ancestral cul-ture is based on a selective reinterpretation of immigrant parents' values that help them make sense out of a combination of conflicting emotions. Along the same lines, Toro-Morn and Alicea argue that even the parents' under-standing of these cultural traditions are based on a nostalgic reinterpretation of a homeland that no longer exists.[20] Having immigrated when South Korea and China were still developing and recovering from political turmoil, Korean and Chinese immigrants remember a traditional culture that has since undergone dramatic changes. When I presented some of my findings on sibling roles to my Korean immigrant husband and also a first-generation Korean audience at a community-oriented conference, they expressed utter surprise at the outmoded ways in which these children were raised by parents who immigrated around the 1960s and 1970s. Many of the main cities from which most recent Korean and Chinese immigrants migrate have experienced such rapid modernization in their adaptation to a highly competitive global economy that some suggest even the generation gap between parents and children from the same homeland nation is almost as wide as that between immigrant parents and their children raised abroad. This is particularly true for newly industrialized countries with globally linked cities such as Seoul, Shanghai, and Taipei.

What this also means is that some of the specific cultural traditions and values that were passed down to second-generation Asian Americans are now remnants of a culture that no longer exist. On some issues, even second-generation Asian Americans hold onto ideals that are considered too old-fashioned and traditional for younger generations in Korea and China. In South Korea, for example, the tradition of delegating family traditions and caregiving responsibilities to the oldest son or oldest daughter-in-law has changed rapidly since the International Monetary Fund crisis in the late 1990s and the enactment of primogeniture laws. Some studies indicate that Koreans may be transitioning from a solely patrilineal line toward one that distributes resources and transfers rights and privileges along both patrilineal and matrilineal lines.[21] In addition, Korean and American media alike have been speculating on the rising preference for daughters in a political economy where being male no longer confers substantial advantages and a culture where daughters provide more emotional care for their parents in their old age.[22]

In countries like mainland China, political statutes such as the one-child policy, which mandated a limit of one child for most families, and the abolition of the pension system in urban areas have also reorganized family relationships and hierarchies within Chinese households. In the old multigenerational household, Chinese families were structured around the care and authority of elderly grandparents along patrilineal lines. However, greater dependency on children has reoriented the emotional, social, and financial center of the modern Chinese family toward the care and needs of the one child.[23] Concerned by the growing caregiving needs of its aging population, China has gradually relaxed its family planning laws over the years and in January 2016 enacted a landmark decision to allow Chinese families to have two children, instead of one. It remains to be seen what impact these developments will have on the filial expectations and primogenitary practices of Chinese immigrant families. As a result of postindustrial economic expansion, Taiwan has also witnessed rapid change in gender and family relations since the late 1990s. Research in this area suggests that as more young women enter the labor force, they are migrating away from the patrilocal family and forming their own nuclear families where they can bargain for a more equitable division of household labor.[24] Daughters, especially those with education and income, have also been assuming greater responsibility in supporting their parents, although traditional values of filial piety persist as a result of the dependency of the elderly on their children.[25] Taken together, the rapidly shifting context of these newly industrialized countries will invariably have an impact on parent-child relations in later waves of immigration.

The emotional dynamics of family roles and relationships may also play out differently in immigrant families that have strong substantive ties to their homeland such as South Asian Indian Americans, Mexican Americans, and Dominicans. In the case of second-generation Korean and Chinese Americans in the study, transnationalism did not appear to be a very significant influence on their identities in most cases, with some major exceptions among those who happened to do overseas business through their careers. This may be because, first of all, most of them were raised during the 1970s and 1980s, when transnationalism was just beginning to take root in these communities. More important, Korean and Chinese Americans are located far from their ancestral homelands, unlike immigrant groups from Latin America and the West Indies, many of whom have demonstrated stronger evidence of transnational activities.[26] Even children whose families were separated across borders made only sporadic visits to their parents' homeland and were more likely to reunite with family members in the United States. Perhaps the one exception to this general pattern among Asian Americans is South Asian Americans, on whom there has been many an increasing number of studies.[27] However, the cultural climate may be shifting with the globalization of Asian media and pop culture, growing economic opportunities for second-generation Asian Americans overseas, and the influx of younger, hipper Asian immigrants in metropolitan areas like New York, which may ultimately reshape the dynamics of racialized masculinities and femininities of Asian Americans. Future research should explore how transnational identities, networks, and cultures may help to mediate or complicate the emotional sense-making processes and support systems of children in Asian and Latino immigrant families.

The rapid economic expansion and modernization of Asian countries has also threatened the fundamental premise of Orientalism, which was based on the West's indomitable political, economic, and military control and subjugation of the East. Morley and Robins state that when Japan reached its economic peak in the 1980s, it stoked old racial fears and anxieties among Western powers about an imminent cultural and economic takeover by a rigid, hierarchical, and conformist society that threatened the very essence of American individualism, egalitarianism, and humanity. Underlying this ideological discourse was an intense fear that perhaps the economic expansion of these nations was "call[ing] into question the supposed centrality of the west as a cultural and geographical locus for the project of modernity."[28] Japan's growing lead in the technology sector prompted the rise of what the authors call "techno-Orientalism" which "reinforce[s] the image of a culture that is cold, impersonal and machine-like, an authoritarian culture lacking emotional connection to the rest of the world."[29] They state that "within the political and cultural unconscious of the West, Japan has come to exist as the figure of empty and dehumanised technological power. It represents the alienated and dystopian image of capitalist progress. This provokes both resentment and envy. The Japanese are unfeeling aliens; they are cyborgs and replicants."[30]

Although Japan has lost some of its stature as an economic superpower, the United States has employed a similar racial logic to reposition itself against the newly emerging economic powerhouses throughout East Asia especially China. Within a climate of increasing global economic competition, white Americans can reclaim their position of moral and cultural superiority over the East by acting as the voice of civility, humanism, and democracy in the face of totalitarianism, human rights abuses, political corruption, and environmental degradation in booming economies like China. Yet ironically, they do so even as they try to emulate the educational systems of Japan and Korea at the expense of humanistic education and creative professions, implement neoliberal cutbacks on social services, public education, and labor, and outsource all manufacturing industries to these very same countries in order to compete against them in the global economy. It is within this geopolitical context of economic competition, capitalist envy, and racial anxiety that the Asian immigrant family myth has been evolving. The extraordinary economic achievements of the stern patriarch, the education-obsessed Tiger Mom, and their robotic model minority children help to reconcile some of these contradictions by providing irrefutable proof of the American Dream, while reconstructing the Oriental figure and the modern nation as the emotionless and inhumane Other. Against this backdrop, it remains to be seen how the evolution of these racial myths will ultimately play out.

Presumably, the powerful influence of the immigration experience will eventually fade away as the next generation is raised by native-born parents, most of whom have acculturated to American society and established a communication channel through which to convey their histories and ethnic roots to their children, should they choose to do so. Much of this depends on if the flow of immigration from Asia continues. However, given that race relations are still structured around a system that orders ethnic families around myths of cultural superiority and inferiority, it is not clear where the fate of Asian Americans lies. Although the specific nature of cultural norms may be changing for Asian Americans, this study is still salient in showing how children of immigrants negotiate and make sense of the multiple strains and burdens that arise within and outside the family. If anything, the question of how emotion work conditions the processes of ethnic identity formation warrants a closer look given increasing economic pressures, rising standards of education, racial inequality, neoliberal reforms, and the transnational spread of families in the contemporary era. In so doing, we provide future generations of immigrant families with the tools to live healthy and productive lives and negotiate greater social inclusion in a multiracial and globally connected society.

Appendix A: Methodological Notes

I contacted interviewees through snowball sampling from my diverse personal contacts, Internet postings (e.g., Craigslist), various clubs and events I attended (e.g., book clubs and social networking groups), and select community-based organizations and events. I tried to find individuals who were in a similar stage of the life cycle where they were coming to grips with issues of marriage, family, and career, but I used maximum-variation sampling to include wide-ranging perspectives of individuals from diverse backgrounds.[1] In other words, I deliberately aimed to recruit a diverse sample of participants based on (1) individual characteristics (e.g., gender, ethnicity, current income, birth order), (2) social background characteristics (e.g., family income and structure while growing up, racial/ethnic composition of friends, schooling, and organizational involvement), and (3) current relationship status (e.g., marital status, race of partner, sexual orientation, and with or without children). I also trained a gay male research assistant to recruit and interview LGBTQ as well as married Asian Americans with children, and a white American graduate assistant to interview second-generation whites.

For the sample of second-generation white Americans, my native-born white research assistant and I drew on referrals from personal/professional networks, acquaintances of past interviewees, an advertisement on Craigslist, and nonprofit organizational contacts. In terms of ethnic breakdown, the Jewish interview sample was composed of seven Russian Jews, two Ukrainian Jews, and one Israeli Jew. The other white interviewees included individuals of Sicilian, Greek, Irish, Portuguese, and Italian ancestral heritage. As shown in Appendix B, the gender ratio for the Asian, Jewish, and other white sample was roughly similar. The median age of the Asian and Jewish participants was also comparable, while the median age of other whites was somewhat higher.

As compared with the Asian American participants, for the second-generation white sample a similar percentage were oldest children (40 percent), a greater number were only children (40 percent), and there were only two youngest children and no middle children. As with the Asian American sample, a large majority of the participants were reported to be single and heterosexual with no children, with the exception of two LGBTQ and four married individuals, and four participants with children.

There is one imbalance worth noting in this white American sample: despite efforts to diversify the sample, we ended up with a larger number of middle-class/professional interviewees than working-class participants, although several of them came from working-class family backgrounds. These interviews were conducted in the midst of the 2008 recession, which also explains why several of the interviewees were unemployed at the time of the interview. Such economic stability can potentially affect their interpretation of past events in a negative way, but their accounts instead seemed to reaffirm their unwavering faith in the American Dream. Taken together, I analyzed the narratives not as a representative comparison of white and Asian American perspectives but rather as a preliminary frame of reference for understanding Asian American racial positionality.

Whenever possible, I initially sent participants an introductory email with a brief description of the study, a copy of the consent form, and a short background questionnaire so that I could structure the interview around such details as their birth order, marital/child status, and family structure. I used a semistructured interview guide to conduct each interview, which lasted roughly an hour to an hour and a half. All were done in person, except for one telephone interview. During the interview, I explored four areas as they relate to familial roles, gender, and ethnicity/culture: (1) the interviewee's childhood and family's experiences as they shaped familial roles and responsibilities; (2) past and current relationships with parents, siblings, and romantic partners; (3) racial/ethnic experiences in the school, workplace, neighborhood, and ethnic communities throughout their lives; (4) and normative values about ethnicity and culture as expressed in views on identity, activities, and social relationships. I also took field notes on any additional conversation or comments made after the interview formally concluded and the tape was turned off, which sometimes led to interesting follow-up conversations.

The study uses a grounded theory approach by generating theory from the data themselves.[2] As opposed to merely verifying and testing based on a priori hypotheses and assumptions, grounded theorists are more interested in understanding the world from the perspectives of their participants and adapting the questions and concepts to fit what they discover throughout the course of collecting data. Conceptual themes that arise from the empirical data are compared with other groups and then either refined or revised to fit the patterns that emerge. Based on an inductive reading of the interviews, I coded and recoded each interview around such emerging themes as the effects of family roles and responsibilities; the meaning of family/ marriage/financial independence; the emotional dynamics of parent-child relationships; ways of carrying culture; gender/class differences in family relationships; communicating emotions; the role of alternative caregivers; and responding to racism. I used both a qualitative software program (NVivo) and manual coding to help me analyze the interview transcripts for repetitions, exceptions, and patterns. NVivo was useful in allowing me to openly code and categorize emerging themes, but manual coding offered more flexibility to develop and refine these themes and compare them across class, gender, and race lines. I also created brief memos on each participant so that I had a better sense of the individual situations within which these themes took shape; I used the memos to contextualize these key themes.

Through this arduous process, I found new and interesting categories that pushed me to recode many of the interviews around new themes. As one example, operating on the established assumption that family solidarity leads to strong ethnic identification, I initially set out to explore if views on parental sacrifice help strengthen the connection that second-generation participants feel with their parents' ancestral culture. I did not find there was any clear pattern since even those who had emotionally negative relationships with their parents still felt indebted to their parents for their sacrifice. Instead, as the study evolved, I began to notice the deep emotional impact that the specific family roles and responsibilities of interviewees had in not only informing their understanding of their parents' culture but also evoking different viewpoints on the relevance of ethnicity in their adult lives. This led me to the observation in Chapter 4 that cultural brokering and other atypical family roles informed the perspectives of participants on their parents' ancestral culture. I then sorted, grouped, and developed these mini-themes into common topics (memos) and constructed a broader theory on the effects of family roles on ethnic identities based on these themes (inclusive integration).[3]

Appendix B: Characteristics of Study Participants

	Asian (n, %)	White (n, %)	
	Total (N = 59)	Jews (n = 10)	Other Whites (n = 5)
Age			
Range	25–38	25–34	26–40
Median	29	28	33
Sex			
Male	19 (32.2)	4 (40.0)	3 (60.0)
Female	40 (67.8)	6 (60.0)	2 (40.0)
Ethnicity[a]			
Korean	21 (35.6)		
Chinese	31 (52.5)		
Taiwan	6 (10.2)		
Chinese-Taiwanese	1 (1.7)		
Class Status (current)[b]			
Upper class	23 (39.0)	4 (40.0)	1 (20.0)
Upper-middle class	2 (3.4)	1 (10.0)	1 (20.0)
Middle class	17 (28.8)	4 (40.0)	2 (40.0)
Lower-middle class	7 (11.9)		
Lower class	10 (16.9)	1 (10.0)	1 (20.0)
Family class status (childhood)			
Upper class	17 (28.8)	5 (50.0)	1 (20.0)
Upper-middle class	3 (5.1)		
Middle class	13 (22.0)	4 (40.0)	3 (60.0)
Lower-middle class	8 (13.6)	1 (10.0)	1 (20.0)
Lower class	16 (27.1)		
Mixed/unknown	2 (3.4)		

(continued)

	Asian (n, %)	White (n, %)	
	Total (N = 59)	Jews (n = 10)	Other Whites (n = 5)
Birth order			
Oldest	26 (44.1)	4 (40.0)	2 (40.0)
Middle	10 (16.9)	0	0
Youngest	17 (28.8)	2 (20.0)	2 (40.0)
Only child	6 (10.2)	4 (40.0)	1 (20.0)
Sexual orientation			
Heterosexual	52 (89.7)	10 (100.0)	3 (60.0)
LGBTQ	6 (10.3)	0	2 (40.0)
Marital status			
Married	15 (27.1)	2 (20.0)	2 (40.0)
Single^c	42 (62.7)	8 (80.0)	3 (60.0)
Divorced	2 (1.7)	0	0
Child status			
None	51 (86.4)	8 (80.0)	3 (60.0)
Pregnant	1 (1.7)	0	0
Have children	7 (11.9)	2 (20.0)	2 (40.0)

Note: Values are n and percentage unless otherwise indicated.

a. Ethnicity and sexual orientation are indicated as reported by the participant with the understanding that ethnicity is politically disputed in the case of China/Taiwan and sexual orientation might also be underreported.

b. I asked participants generally how they would categorize themselves in terms of class status, because of some difficulties getting income information in preliminary interviews. The reader should interpret the numbers with caution though since people have very different concepts of what constitutes lower/middle/upper class. In cases where people reported their income, I used the following categories: lower class = <$32,500; middle class = $33,000–149,000; and upper class = $150,000+. Many participants had only a very vague knowledge of their family class status growing up since their memories had been distorted over time, many parents did not discuss financial matters with their children, and income often fluctuated throughout their childhood.

c. This category includes those who are partnered or engaged. Several LGBTQ participants lived with long-term partners, but gay marriage was not legalized in most states, including New York, at the time of most of these interviews.

Notes

CHAPTER 1 — THE ASIAN IMMIGRANT FAMILY MYTH

1. Jeffrey Goldberg, "The Overachievers," *New York Magazine* 28, no. 15 (1995): 45.

2. Ibid., 43.

3. Ibid., 46.

4. In this study, I use the conventional sociological definition of generation based on the country where the individual was mostly socialized and educated. Thus, second generation refers to those who were born in the United States or immigrated before primary school age (age five); 1.5 generation includes those who immigrated sometime in the middle of their primary and high school years; and first generation refers to those who immigrated to the United States after high school.

5. Vivian Louie, *Compelled to Excel: Immigration, Education, and Opportunity among Chinese Americans* (Palo Alto, Calif.: Stanford University Press, 2004).

6. William Petersen, "Success Story, Japanese-American Style," *New York Times Magazine* 9 (1966): 20–21.

7. Stacey J. Lee, *Unraveling the "Model Minority" Stereotype: Listening to Asian American Youth* (New York: Teachers College Press, 1996).

8. Petersen, "Success Story," 73.

9. Amy Chua and Jed Rubenfeld, *The Triple Package: How Three Unlikely Traits Explain the Rise and Fall of Cultural Groups in America* (New York: Penguin, 2014).

10. Daniel P. Moynihan, *The Negro Family: The Case for National Action* (Washington, D.C.: Office of Policy Planning and Research, U.S. Department of Labor, 1965).

11. William Julius Wilson, *The Declining Significance of Race: Blacks and Changing American Institutions* (Chicago: University of Chicago Press, 2012).

12. Carol B. Stack, *All Our Kin: Strategies for Survival in a Black Community* (New York: Basic Books, 1975); Ronald L. Taylor, "Black Ethnicity and the Persistence of Ethnogenesis," *American Journal of Sociology* 84 (1979): 1401–1423.

13. Mary C. Waters, "Ethnic and Racial Identities of Second-Generation Black Immigrants in New York City," *International Migration Review* 28 (1994): 795–820, 795.

14. Daniel T. Lichter and Zhenchao Qian, "Marriage and Family in a Multiracial Society," in *The American People: Census 2000*, ed. Reynolds Farley and John Haaga (New York: Russell Sage Foundation, 2005), 169–200.

15. Ellen Wu, *The Color of Success: Asian Americans and the Model Minority* (Princeton, N.J.: Princeton University Press, 2013), 155, 169.

16. Ibid., 172.

17. National Commission on Asian American and Pacific Islander Research in Education and College Board, "Asian Americans and Pacific Islanders: Facts, Not Fiction—Setting the Record Straight" (2008), http://professionals.collegeboard.com/profdownload/08-0608-AAPI.pdf (accessed July 28, 2015).

18. Stanley Sue and Sumie Okazaki, "Asian American Educational Achievements: A Phenomenon in Search of an Explanation," *American Psychologist* 45 (1990): 913–920.

19. Rosalind Chou and Joe Feagin, *The Myth of the Model Minority: Asian Americans Facing Racism*, 2nd ed. (New York: Routledge, 2014); Timothy Fong, *The Contemporary Asian American Experience: Beyond the Model Minority* (Upper Saddle River, N.J.: Prentice Hall, 2002); Lee, *Unraveling the "Model Minority"*; Deborah Woo, *Glass Ceilings and Asian Americans: The New Face of Workplace Barriers* (Lanham, Md.: AltaMira, 2000).

20. Natalia Sarkasian and Naomi Gerstel, "Kin Support among Blacks and Whites," *American Sociological Review* 69 (2004): 815.

21. Masako Ishii-Kuntz, "Diversity within Asian American Families," in *Handbook of Family Diversity*, ed. David H. Demo, Katherine Allen, and Mark A. Fine (New York: Oxford University Press, 2000), 274–292.

22. Yen L. Espiritu, *Asian American Women and Men: Labor, Laws and Love* (Thousand Oaks, Calif.: Sage, 2007); Evelyn Nakano Glenn, "Split Household, Small Producer, and Dual Wage Earner: An Analysis of Chinese-American Family Strategies," *Journal of Marriage and Family* 45, no. 1 (1983): 35–46; Alejandro Portes and Ruben G. Rumbaut, *Legacies: The Story of the Immigrant Second Generation* (Berkeley: University of California Press, 2001).

23. William I. Thomas and Florian Znaniecki, *The Polish Peasant in Europe and America* (New York: Knopf, 1927).

24. Rubén G. Rumbaut, "Ties That Bind: Immigration and Immigrant Families in the United States," in *Immigration and the Family: Research and Policy on U.S. Immigrants*, ed. Alan Booth, Ann C. Crouter, and Nancy S. Landale (Mahwah, N.J.: Lawrence Erlbaum, 1997), 36.

25. Espiritu, *Asian American Women*; Nazli Kibria, *Family Tightrope: The Changing Lives of Vietnamese Americans* (Princeton, N.J.: Princeton University Press, 1993); Stack, *All Our Kin*; Pierette Hondagneu-Sotelo, *Domestica: Immigrant Workers Cleaning and Caring in the Shadows of Affluence* (Berkeley: University of California Press, 2007).

26. Espiritu, *Asian American Women*; Kibria, *Family Tightrope*.

27. Mia Tuan, *Forever Foreigners or Honorary Whites? The Asian Ethnic Experience Today* (New Brunswick, N.J.: Rutgers University Press, 1998).

28. Douglas Massey, "International Development and Economic Development in Comparative Perspective," *Population and Development Review* 14 (1988): 383–414.

29. Saskia Sassen, *The Mobility of Capital and Labor: A Study in International Investment and Labor Flow* (New York: Cambridge University Press, 1990).

30. Portes and Rumbaut, *Legacies*; Alejandro Portes and Min Zhou, "The New Second Generation: Segmented Assimilation and Its Variants," *Annals of the American Academy of Political and Social Science* 530 (1993): 74–96; Carola Suarez-Orozco and Marcelo M. Suarez-Orozco, *Children of Immigration* (Cambridge, Mass.: Harvard University Press, 2001).

31. Desiree B. Qin, "Doing Well vs. Feeling Well: Understanding Family Dynamics and the Psychological Adjustment of Chinese Immigrant Adolescents," *Journal of Youth and Adolescence* 37 (2008): 22–35; Ruben G. Rumbaut, "The Crucible Within: Ethnic Identity, Self-Esteem and Segmented Assimilation among Children of Immigrants," *International Migration Review* 28 (1994): 748–794.

32. Pyong Gap Min, *Changes and Conflicts: Korean Immigrant Families in New York* (Boston: Allyn & Bacon, 1998); Suarez-Orozco and Suarez-Orozco, *Children of Immigration*.

33. Rhacel Salazar Parrenas, *Children of Global Migration: Transnational Families and Gendered Woes* (Palo Alto, Calif.: Stanford University Press, 2005).

34. Miri Song, *Helping Out: Children's Labor in Ethnic Businesses* (Philadelphia: Temple University Press, 1999).

35. Maura I. Toro-Morn and Marixsa Alicea, "Gendered Geographies of Home: Mapping Second- and Third-Generation Puerto Ricans' Sense of Home," in *Gender and U.S. Immigration*, ed. Pierrette Hondagneu-Sotelo (Berkeley: University of California Press, 2003), 194–214.

36. Amy Chua, *Battle Hymn of the Tiger Mother* (New York: Penguin, 2011).

37. Robert E. Park, *Race and Culture* (Glencoe, Ill.: Free Press, 1950).

38. Milton Gordon, *Assimilation in American Life: The Role of Race, Religion, and National Origins* (New York: Oxford University Press, 1964).

39. Richard Alba and Victor Nee, *Remaking the American Mainstream: Assimilation and Contemporary Immigration* (Cambridge, Mass.: Harvard University Press, 2009).

40. Herbert J. Gans, "Symbolic Ethnicity: The Future of Ethnic Groups and Cultures in America," *Ethnic and Racial Studies* 2, no. 1 (1979): 1–20.

41. Joane Nagel, *American Indian Ethnic Renewal: Red Power and the Resurgence of Identity and Culture* (New York: Oxford University Press, 1997), 949.

42. Elisabetta Zontini, "Continuity and Change in Transnational Italian Families: The Caring Practices of Second-Generation Women," *Journal of Ethnic and Migration Studies* 33, no. 7 (2007): 1116.

43. Lisa Lowe, *Immigrant Acts: On Asian American Cultural Politics* (Durham, N.C.: Duke University Press, 1996), 63.

44. Gillian Stevens and Hiromi Ishizawa, "Variation among Siblings in the Use of a Non-English Language," *Journal of Family Issues* 28, no. 8 (2007): 1008–1025.

45. Karen Pyke, "'Generational Deserters' and 'Black Sheep': Acculturative Differences among Siblings in Asian Immigrant Families," *Journal of Family Issues* 26 (2005): 491–517.

46. Pierette Hondagneu-Sotelo, *Gendered Transitions: Mexican Experiences of Immigration* (Berkeley: University of California Press, 1994); Espiritu, *Asian American Women*; Kibria, *Family Tightrope*.

47. Karen K. Dion and Kenneth L. Dion, "Gender, Immigrant Generation, and Ethnocultural Identity," *Sex Roles* 50, nos. 5–6 (2004): 347–355.

48. Anita Ilta Garey and Karen V. Hansen, "Introduction," in *At the Heart of Work and Family*, ed. Garey and Hansen (New Brunswick, N.J.: Rutgers University Press, 2011), 5.

49. Arlie Hochschild, "Emotion Work, Feeling Rules, and Social Structure," *American Journal of Sociology* 85 (1979): 551–575.

50. Arlie Hochschild, *The Second Shift* (New York: Penguin, 2003).

51. Arlie Russell Hochschild, *The Time Bind: When Work Becomes Home and Home Becomes Work* (New York: Macmillan, 2001); Jerry Jacobs and Kathleen Gerson, *The Time Divide: Work, Family and Gender Equality* (Cambridge, Mass.: Harvard University Press, 2005).

52. Grace J. Yoo and Barbara W. Kim, *Caring across Generations: The Linked Lives of Korean American Families* (New York: New York University Press, 2014).

53. Erving Goffman, *The Presentation of Self in Everyday Life* (Norwell: Anchor, 1959).

54. Arlie Hochschild, *The Commercialization of Intimate Life: Notes from Home and Work* (Berkeley: University of California Press, 2003).

55. Nadia Kim, *Imperial Citizens: Koreans and Race from Seoul to LA* (Stanford, Calif.: Stanford University Press, 2008).

56. Pseudonyms are used to protect the confidentiality of the interviewees.

57. Erik H. Erikson, *Identity: Youth and Crisis* (New York: Norton, 1968).

58. From here on, I will refer to East Asian (Americans) as Asian (Americans) throughout the book.

59. Readers should be mindful of the heated political dispute over whether or not Taiwanese should be included under the label of Chinese. Although most Taiwanese consider themselves ethnically Chinese, they make critical distinctions about their culture and political sovereignty from China. I've used the specific term "Taiwanese Americans" to refer to the identities or experiences of specific participants whenever reported, but use the generic term "Chinese" to refer to the entire sample when referring to their racialization, immigrant perceptions, and family structures.

60. Yu Xie and Kimberly Goyette, *A Demographic Portrait of Asian Americans* (New York: Population Reference Bureau/Russell Sage Census 2000 Series, 2004).

61. LGBTQ refers to lesbian, gay, bisexual, transgender, and questioning (their sexual orientation) individuals.

62. See Appendix A for a detailed discussion on the data and methodology.

63. After I had completed the interview and written a rough draft of an article that I disseminated to all the participants, one of the interviewees asked to withdraw from the study because she felt uncomfortable about revealing her personal life and also disagreed with my interpretation of her experiences. I returned the interview tape to her and withdrew her from the study.

CHAPTER 2 — EDUCATION, SACRIFICE,
AND THE "AMERICAN DREAM"

This chapter is a revised version of an article originally published as Angie Y. Chung and Trivina Kang, "Reassessing the American Dream: Family, Culture, and Educational 'Success' among Korean and Chinese Americans," in *Second-Generation Korean Experiences in the United States and Canada*, ed. Pyong Gap Min and Samuel Noh (New York: Lexington Books, 2014), chap. 10. Reprinted with permission from Lexington Books.

1. Amy Chua, "Why Chinese Mothers Are Superior," *Wall Street Journal*, January 8, 2011, http://www.wsj.com/articles/SB10001424052748704111504576059713528698754.

2. Richard R. Pearce, "Effects of Cultural and Social Structural Factors on the Achievement of White and Chinese American Students at School Transition Points," *American Educational Research Journal* 43, no. 1 (2006): 75–101; Barbara Schneider and Yongsook Lee, "A Model for Academic Success: The School and Home Environment of East Asian Students," *Anthropology and Education Quarterly* 21 (1990): 283–299.

3. Betty Lee Sung, *The Story of the Chinese in America* (New York: Collier Books, 1971), 124–125.

4. Thomas Sowell, *Race and Culture: A Worldview* (New York: Basic Books, 1994), 9.

5. John U. Ogbu and Herbert D. Simons, "Voluntary and Involuntary Minorities: A Cultural-Ecological Theory of School Performance with Some Implications for Education," *Anthropology & Education Quarterly* 29, no. 2 (1998): 155–188.

6. Oscar Lewis, *The Children of Sanchez: Autobiography of a Mexican Family* (New York: Random House, 1961).

7. Herbert J. Gans, "Second-Generation Decline: Scenarios for the Economic and Ethnic Futures of the Post-1965 American Immigrants," *Ethnic and Racial Studies* 15, no. 2 (1992): 173–192; Alejandro Portes and Ruben G. Rumbaut, *Immigrant America* (Berkeley: University of California Press, 2014).

8. Cynthia Feliciano, "Does Selective Migration Matter? Explaining Ethnic Disparities in Educational Attainment among Immigrants' Children," *International Migration Review* 39, no. 4 (2005): 841–871.

9. Stephen Steinberg, *The Ethnic Myth: Race, Ethnicity, and Class in America* (Boston: Beacon, 1989).

10. Jamie Lew, *Asian Americans in Class: Charting the Achievement Gap among Korean American Youth* (New York: Teachers College Press, 2006).

11. Andrew Sanchirico, "The Importance of Small Business Ownership in Chinese American Educational Achievement," *Sociology of Education* 64 (1991): 293–304.

12. Philip Kasinitz, John Mollenkopf, Mary Waters, and Jennifer Holdaway, *Inheriting the City: The Children of Immigrants Come of Age* (New York: Russell Sage Foundation, 2008), 110.

13. This chapter is based mostly on the interview data from my research study, with one exception, but I draw on revised key conceptual themes identified in Kang's study of thirty Korean American college students and graduates between the ages of nineteen and twenty-seven from New York City.

14. Pyong Gap Min, "From White-Collar Occupations to Small Business: Korean Immigrants' Occupational Adjustment," *Sociological Quarterly* 25, no. 3 (1984): 333–352.

15. Pyong Gap Min, "Problems of Korean Immigrant Entrepreneurs," *International Migration Review* 24, no. 3 (1990): 436–455.

16. Portes and Rumbaut, *Legacies.*

CHAPTER 3 — LOVE AND COMMUNICATION
ACROSS THE GENERATION GAP

This chapter is a revised version of an article originally published as Angie Y. Chung, "From Caregivers to Caretakers: The Impact of Family Roles on Ethnicity among Children of Korean and Chinese Immigrant Families," *Qualitative Sociology* 36, no. 3 (2013): 279–302. Reprinted with permission of Springer Science+Business Media.

1. Karen Pyke, "'The Normal American Family' as an Interpretive Structure of Family Life among Grown Children of Korean and Vietnamese Immigrants," *Journal of Marriage and Family* 62, no. 1 (2000): 240–255.

2. Kim Wong Keltner, "Tiger Moms: Don't Turn Your Kids into Robots," May 10, 2013, *CNN*, http://www.cnn.com/2013/05/10/opinion/keltner-tiger-mom/.

3. Jennifer Van Hook and Jennifer Glick, "Immigration and Living Arrangements: Moving Beyond Economic Need versus Acculturation," *Demography* 44, no. 2 (2007): 225–249.

4. Espiritu, *Asian American Women*; Suarez-Orozco and Suarez-Orozco, *Children of Immigration*.

5. Fictive kin refers to friends who are not related by blood or marriage but assume the roles and responsibilities of extended kin in terms of providing support, guidance, and caregiving needs.

6. Min, *Changes and Conflicts*.

7. Espiritu, *Asian American Women*.

8. In-Sook Lim, "Korean Immigrant Women's Challenge to Gender Inequality at Home: The Interplay of Economic Resources, Gender, and Family," *Gender & Society* 11, no. 1 (1997): 31–51; Nazli Kibria, "Power, Patriarchy, and Gender Conflict in the Vietnamese Immigrant Community," *Gender and Society* 4, no. 1 (1990): 9–24.

9. Espiritu, *Asian American Women*.

10. Lim, "Korean Immigrant Women's Challenge"; Kibria, *Family Tightrope*; Min, *Changes and Conflicts*.

11. Min, *Changes and Conflicts*.

12. Kasinitz et al., *Inheriting the City*.

13. Parrenas, *Children of Global Migration*.

14. Yoo and Kim, *Caring across Generations*.

15. Espiritu, *Asian American Women*; Kibria, *Family Tightrope*.

16. The phrase enclosed in brackets was translated from Korean.

17. Parrenas, *Children of Global Migration*.

18. Thomas and Znaniecki, *Polish Peasant in Europe and America*.

19. Edward T. Hall, *Hidden Differences: Doing Business with the Japanese* (Garden City, N.Y.: Anchor, 1990).

20. Susan Chan and Cynthia W. Leong, "Chinese Families in Transition: Cultural Conflicts and Adjustment Problems," *Journal of Social Distress and the Homeless* 3, no. 3 (1994): 263–281.

21. Ishii-Kuntz, "Diversity within Asian American Families."

22. Min Zhou and Carl L. Bankston, *Growing Up American: How Vietnamese Children Adapt to Life in the United States* (New York: Russell Sage Foundation, 1998).

23. Kibria, *Family Tightrope*; Stack, *All Our Kin*.

24. Carol B. Stack and Linda M. Burton, "Kinscripts: Reflections on Family, Generation, and Culture," in *Mothering: Ideology, Experience, and Agency*, ed. Evelyn Nakano Glenn, Grace Chang, and Linda Rennie Forcey (New York: Routledge, 1994), 33–44.

25. Stack, *All Our Kin*, 62.

CHAPTER 4 — CHILDREN AS FAMILY CAREGIVERS

1. Won Moo Hurh and Kwang Chung Kim, "The Success Image of Asian-Americans: Its Validity, and Its Practical and Theoretical Implications," *Ethnic and Racial Studies* 12, no. 4 (1989): 512–538.

2. Joanna Dreby, *Divided by Borders: Mexican Migrants and Their Children* (Berkeley: University of California Press, 2010); Vikki S. Katz, *Kids in the Middle: How Children of Immigrants Negotiate Community Interactions for Their Families* (New Brunswick, N.J.: Rutgers University Press, 2014); Marjorie F. Orellana, *Translating Childhoods: Immigrant Youth, Language, and Culture* (New Brunswick, N.J.: Rutgers University Press, 2009).

3. Suarez-Orozco and Suarez-Orozco, *Children of Immigration.*

4. Katz, *Kids in the Middle;* Orellana, *Translating Childhoods;* Lisa Park, *Consuming Citizenship: Children of Asian Immigrant Entrepreneurs* (Stanford, Calif.: Stanford University Press, 2005); Abel Valenzuela, Jr., "Gender Role and Settlement Activities among Children and Their Immigrant Families," *American Behavioral Scientist* 42 (1999): 720–742.

5. Suarez-Orozco and Suarez-Orozco, *Children of Immigration.*

6. Dreby, *Divided by Borders;* Parrenas, *Children of Global Migration.*

7. I make a distinction between the terms "caretaker" and "caregiver." The term "caretaker" implies that someone is taking care of the home in the owner's absence, whereas the term "caregiver" focuses on the act of a person providing care for another person. Autonomous caretakers may also act as caregivers for their siblings, but their experience and emotional environment are largely shaped by the absence of parental figures, unlike cultural brokers who engage with their parents and provide care for the entire family.

8. Portes and Rumbaut, *Legacies;* Valenzuela, "Gender Role and Settlement Activities."

9. Park, *Consuming Citizenship;* Song, *Helping Out.*

10. Maria W. L. Chee, "Migrating for the Children: Taiwanese American Women in Transnational Families," in *Wife or Worker? Asian Women and Migration,* ed. Nicola Piper and Mina Roces (Lanham, Md.: Rowman & Littlefield, 2003), 137–156; Yean-Ju Lee and Hagen Koo, "'Wild Geese Fathers' and a Globalised Family Strategy for Education in Korea," *International Development Planning Review* 28 (2006): 533–553.

11. Orellana, *Translating Childhoods;* Park, *Consuming Citizenship;* Valenzuela, "Gender Role and Settlement Activities."

12. Min Zhou, "Conflict, Coping, and Reconciliation: Intergenerational Relations in Chinese Immigrant Families," in *Across Generations: Immigrant Families in America,* ed. Nancy Foner (New York: New York University Press, 2009), 21–46.

13. Lee and Koo, "'Wild Geese Fathers.'"

14. Pyke, "'Generational Deserters' and 'Black Sheep.'"

15. Kasinitz et al., *Inheriting the City.*

16. I considered those who identify with their panethnic or Asian American identity and not with their specific ethnic identity as Korean, Chinese, or Taiwanese Americans as more Americanized and distanced from their parents' homeland culture since the racial lumping of heterogeneous Asian cultures makes sense only within the American context of race relations.

17. Dreby, *Divided by Borders;* Valenzuela, "Gender Role and Settlement Activities"; Orellana, *Translating Childhoods.*

CHAPTER 5 — DAUGHTERS AND SONS CARRYING CULTURE

1. Maxine Hong Kingston, *The Woman Warrior: Memoirs of a Girlhood among Ghosts* (New York: Knopf, 1976).

2. Amy Tan, *The Joy Luck Club* (New York: Penguin, 1989).

3. Yuko Kurahashi, *Asian American Culture on Stage: The History of the East West Players* (New York: Routledge, 1999).

4. Frank Chin, "Come All Ye Asian American Writers of the Real and the Fake," in *A Companion to Asian American Studies*, ed. Kent A. Ono (Hoboken, N.J.: Wiley-Blackwell, 2005), 134–135; Frank Chin and Jeffrey Paul Chan, "Racist Love," in *Seeing through Shuck*, ed. Richard Kostelanetz (New York: Ballantine Books, 1972), 65–79.

5. Sau-ling Cynthia Wong, "'Sugar Sisterhood': Situating the Amy Tan Phenomenon," in *The Ethnic Canon: Histories, Institutions, and Interventions*, ed. David Palumbo-Liu (Minneapolis: Minnesota University Press, 1995), 174–210.

6. King-Kok Cheung, "The Woman Warrior versus the Chinaman Pacific: Must a Chinese American Critic Choose between Feminism and Heroism?," in *Conflicts in Feminism*, ed. Marianne Hirsch and Evelyn Fox Keller (New York: Routledge), 244.

7. Elaine Kim, *Asian American Literature: An Introduction to the Writings and Their Social Context* (Philadelphia: Temple University Press, 1982).

8. Raymond Buriel and Terri de Ment, "Immigration and Sociocultural Change in Mexican, Chinese, and Vietnamese Families," in Booth, Crouter, and Landale, *Immigration and the Family*, 165–200; Ishii-Kuntz, "Diversity within Asian American Families"; Laura Uba, *Asian Americans: Personality Patterns, Identity, and Mental Health* (New York: Guilford, 1994).

9. Karen D. Pyke and Denise L. Johnson, "Asian American Women and Racialized Femininities: 'Doing' Gender across Cultural Worlds," *Gender and Society* 17, no. 1 (2007): 33–53.

10. Sarah Deutsch, "Women and Intercultural Relations: The Case of Hispanic New Mexico and Colorado," *Signs: Journal of Women, Culture and Society* 12, no. 4 (1987): 719–739; Betty Lee Sung, *Chinese American Intermarriage* (Staten Island, N.Y.: Center for Migration Studies, 1990).

11. Bic Ngo, "Beyond 'Culture Clash': Understandings of Immigrant Experiences," *Theory into Practice* 47, no. 4 (2008): 4–11.

12. Ibid., 5

13. Patricia Hill Collins, "Shifting the Center: Race, Class and Feminist Theorizing about Motherhood," in Glenn, Chang, and Forcey, *Mothering: Ideology, Experience, and Agency*, 48–49.

14. Espiritu, *Asian American Women*; Kibria, *Family Tightrope*.

15. Monisha Das Gupta, "'What Is Indian about You?': A Gendered, Transnational Approach to Ethnicity," *Gender and Society* 11, no. 5 (1997): 572–596; Espiritu, *Asian American Women*; Toro-Morn and Alicea, "Gendered Geographies of Home."

16. See, respectively, Zhou and Bankston, *Growing Up American*; Das Gupta, "'What Is Indian about You?'"; Toro-Morn and Alicea, "Gendered Geographies of Home."

17. Espiritu, *Asian American Women*, 268.

18. Min, *Changes and Conflicts*.

19. Ibid.; Zhou and Bankston, *Growing Up American*.

20. So Jin Park and Nancy Abelmann, "Class and Cosmopolitan Striving: Mothers' Management of English Education in South Korea," *Anthropological Quarterly* 77, no. 4 (2004): 645–672.

21. Dion and Dion, "Gender, Immigrant Generation, and Ethnocultural Identity."

22. Pyong Gap Min and Chigon Kim, "Patterns of Intermarriages and Cross-Generational In-Marriages among Native-Born Asian Americans," *International Migration Review* 43, no. 3 (2009): 447–470.

23. Nazli Kibria, "The Construction of Asian American: Reflections on Intermarriage and Ethnic Identity among Second-Generation Chinese and Korean Americans," *Ethnic and Racial Studies* 20, no. 3 (1997): 523–544, 530.

24. Pyke and Johnson, "Asian American Women."

CHAPTER 6 — THE RACIAL CONTRADICTIONS OF
BEING ASIAN AMERICAN

1. Jean S. Phinney and Anthony D. Ong, "Conceptualization and Measurement of Ethnic Identity: Current Status and Future Directions," *Journal of Counseling Psychology* 54, no. 3 (2007): 271–281.

2. Eduardo Bonilla-Silva, "From Bi-racial to Tri-racial: Towards a New System of Racial Stratification in the USA," *Ethnic and Racial Studies* 27, no. 6 (2004): 931–950; Andrew Hacker, *Two Nations: Black and White, Separate, Hostile, Unequal* (New York: Scribner, 2003); Jonathan W. Warren and France W. Twine, "White Americans, the New Minority? Non-Blacks and the Ever-Expanding Boundaries of Whiteness," *Journal of Black Studies* 28, no. 2 (1997): 200–218.

3. See the Chapter 1 and Appendix A for a discussion on methodology.

4. Lucie Cheng and Yen Espiritu, "Korean Businesses in Black and Hispanic Neighborhoods: A Study of Intergroup Relations," *Sociological Perspectives* 32, no. 4 (1989): 521–534.

5. Kibria, "Construction of Asian American"; Park, *Consuming Citizenship.*

6. Claire Jean Kim, *Bitter Fruit: The Politics of Black-Korean Conflict in New York City* (New Haven, Conn.: Yale University Press, 2003); Nadia Kim, "Critical Thoughts on Asian American Assimilation in the Whitening Literature," *Social Forces* 86, no. 2 (2007): 561–574; Tuan, *Forever Foreigners or Honorary Whites?*

7. Joel Perlmann and Roger Waldinger, "Second Generation Decline? Children of Immigrants, Past and Present—A Reconsideration," *International Migration Review* 31 (1997): 893–922.

8. Lawrence Bobo, James R. Kluegel, and Ryan A. Smith, "Laissez-Faire Racism: The Crystallization of a 'Kindler, Gentler' Anti-black Ideology," in *Racial Attitudes in the 1990s: Continuity and Change*, ed. Steven A. Tuch and Jack K. Martin (Westport, Conn.: Praeger, 1997), 16–42.

9. Kim, *Bitter Fruit.*

10. Evelyn Nakano Glenn, *Unequal Freedom: How Race and Gender Shaped American Citizenship and Labor* (Cambridge, Mass.: Harvard University Press, 2009).

11. Kim, "Critical Thoughts on Asian American Assimilation."

12. Although Ukraine, along with other nations like Georgia, achieved independence from the former Soviet Union in 1991, second-generation participants still refer to their ethnocultural identity as "Russian" or use the terms interchangeably.

13. Kasinitz et al., *Inheriting the City.*

14. Mary C. Waters, *Ethnic Options: Choosing Identities in America* (Berkeley: University of California Press, 1990).

15. Joe R. Feagin, Hernán Vera, and Pinar Batur, *White Racism: The Basics*, 2nd ed. (New York: Routledge, 2001).

16. Eduardo Bonilla-Silva, *Racism without Racists: Color-Blind Racism and the Persistence of Racial Inequality in the United States* (Lanham, Md.: Rowman & Littlefield, 2006), 233.

17. Derald Wing Sue, *Microaggressions in Everyday Life: Race, Gender, and Sexual Orientation* (Hoboken, N.J.: John Wiley, 2010), 5.

18. Chou and Feagin, *Myth of the Model Minority.*

19. Anthony Chen, "Lives at the Center of the Periphery, Lives at the Periphery of the Center: Chinese American Masculinities and Bargaining with Hegemony," *Gender and Society* 13, no. 5 (1999): 584–607; Gina Marchetti, *Romance and the "Yellow Peril": Race, Sex and Discursive Strategies in Hollywood Fiction* (Berkeley: University of California Press, 1994).

20. The glass ceiling and bamboo ceiling refer to the invisible institutional barriers that exclude and prevent women and minorities from moving up at the workplace beyond a certain point based on discriminatory and subjective criteria beyond job performance, such as leadership and communication skills.

21. Ashley W. Doane and Eduardo Bonilla-Silva, *White Out: The Continuing Significance of Race* (New York: Routledge, 2003).

22. John Horton, *The Politics of Diversity: Immigration, Resistance, and Change in Monterey Park, California* (Philadelphia: Temple University Press, 1995), 187.

23. Kevin Keogan, "A Sense of Place: The Politics of Immigration and the Symbolic Construction of Identity in Southern California and the New York Metropolitan Area," *Sociological Forum* 17, no. 2 (2002): 223–253.

24. Like Sebastian, some American-born children referred to themselves as "first generation" because they are the first generation to be born in the United States. However, sociologists tend to categorize the American-born/American-raised children of immigrants as "second generation" because they are the second generation to live in the United States.

25. Steven Vertovec and Robin Cohen, "Introduction: Conceiving Cosmopolitanism," in *Conceiving Cosmopolitanism: Theory, Context and Practice*, ed. Steven Vertovec and Robin Cohen (Oxford: Oxford University Press, 2002), 1–22.

26. Joe R. Feagin, "The Continuing Significance of Race: Antiblack Discrimination in Public Places," *American Sociological Review* 56, no. 1 (1991): 101–116; Michael Omi and Howard Winant, *Racial Formation in the United States* (New York: Routledge, 2014).

27. Kim, *Imperial Citizens.*

CHAPTER 7 — BEHIND THE FAMILY PORTRAIT

1. Barrie Thorne and Marilyn Yalom, eds., *Rethinking Family: Some Feminist Questions* (Boston: Northeastern University Press, 1992); Kathleen Gerson, *The Unfinished Revolution: Coming of Age in a New Era of Gender, Work, and Family* (New York: Oxford University Press, 2011).

2. Kamini Maraj Grahame, "'For the Family': Asian Immigrant Women's Triple Day," *Journal of Sociology & Social Welfare* 30, no. 1 (2015): 65–90.

3. Naomi Gerstel, "Rethinking Families and Communities: The Color, Class, and Centrality of Extended Kin Ties," *Sociological Forum* 26, no. 1 (2011): 1–20.

4. Ishii-Kuntz, "Diversity within Asian American Families."

5. Portes and Rumbaut, *Legacies.*

6. Nancy Foner, "The Immigrant Family: Cultural Legacies and Cultural Change," in *The Handbook of International Migration: The American Experience*, ed. Charles Hirschman, Philip Kasinitz, and Josh DeWind (New York: Russell Sage Foundation, 1999), 257–264; Portes and Rumbaut, *Legacies.*

7. Michael Fix and Wendy Zimmerman, "The Integration of Immigrant Families in the United States" (Washington, D.C.: National Conference of State Legislatures, Urban Institute, 2001), http://www.urban.org/sites/default/files/alfresco/publication-pdfs/410227-The-Integration-of-Immigrant-Families-in-the-United-States.PDF (accessed January 18, 2016).

8. Lawrence D. Bobo, Camille Z. Charles, Maria Krysan, and Alicia D. Simmons, "The Real Record on Racial Attitudes," in *Social Trends in American Life: Findings from the General Social Survey since 1972*, ed. Peter V. Marsden (Princeton, N.J.: Princeton University Press, 2012), 38–83.

9. Ibid.

10. Lawrence Bobo, "Racial Attitudes and Relations at the Close of the Twentieth Century," *America Becoming: Racial Trends and Their Consequences* 1 (2001): 264–301.

11. Angie Y. Chung, *Legacies of Struggle: Conflict and Cooperation in Korean American Politics* (Palo Alto, Calif.: Stanford University Press, 2007).

12. Park, *Consuming Citizenship.*

13. Michael Omi and Howard Winant, *Racial Formation in the United States: From the 1960s to the 1990s* (New York: Routledge, 1994).

14. Taeku Lee, "Racial Attitudes and the Color Lines at the Close of the Twentieth Century," in *The State of Asian Pacific America: Transforming Race Relations. A Public Policy Report*, ed. Paul Ong (Los Angeles: Asian Pacific American Public Policy Institute, LEAP and UCLA Asian American Studies Center, 2000), 103–158.

15. Seunghye Hong, Emily Walton, Emi Tamaki, and Janice A. Sabin, "Lifetime Prevalence of Mental Disorders among Asian Americans: Nativity, Gender, and Sociodemographic Correlates," *Asian American Journal of Psychology* 5, no. 4 (2014): 353–363.

16. Ibid.; Qin, "Doing Well vs. Feeling Well."

17. Zontini, "Continuity and Change in Transnational Italian Families."

18. Kim, *Bitter Fruit.*

19. Dreby, *Divided by Borders*; Cecilia Menjívar, *Fragmented Ties: Salvadoran Immigrant Networks in America* (Berkeley: University of California Press, 2000).

20. Toro-Morn and Alicea, "Gendered Geographies of Home."

21. Jaerim Lee and Jean W. Bauer, "Motivations for Providing and Utilizing Child Care by Grandmothers in South Korea," *Journal of Marriage and Family* 75, no. 2 (2013): 381–402; Sanghui Nam, "The Women's Movement and the Reformation of the Family Law in South Korea: Interactions between Local, National, and Global Structures," *European Journal of East Asian Studies* 9, no. 1 (2001): 67–86.

22. Sang-Hun Choe, "South Koreans Rethink Preference for Sons," *New York Times*, November 28, 2007, http://www.nytimes.com/2007/11/28/world/asia/28iht-sex.1.8509372.html?_r=1&; Sung So-young, "After a Long Preference for Sons, It's a Girl Generation," *Korea Joong Ang Daily*, November 21, 2012, http://koreajoongangdaily.joins.com/news/article/article.aspx?aid=2962687.

23. Xiao-Tian Fend, Dudley L. Poston Jr., and Xiao-Tao Wand, "China's One-Child Policy and the Changing Family," *Journal of Comparative Family Studies* 45, no. 1 (2014): 17.

24. Chin-Ju Lin, "Identity Differences among Women in Patrilineal Families: A Cross-Generational Comparison of the Division of Domestic Labor of Middle-Class Working Women," *Taiwan: A Radical Quarterly in Social Studies* 68 (2007): 1–75.

25. Lei Lei, "Sons, Daughters, and Intergenerational Support in China," *Chinese Sociological Review* 45, no. 3 (2013): 26–52.

26. Rubén G. Rumbaut, "Severed or Sustained Attachments? Language, Identity, and Imagined Communities in the Post-immigrant Generation," in *The Changing Face of Home: The Transnational Lives of the Second Generation*, ed. Peggy Levitt and Mary C. Waters (New York: Russell Sage Foundation, 2002), 43–95.

27. Bandana Purkayastha, *Negotiating Ethnicity: Second-Generation South Asian Americans Traverse a Transnational World* (New Brunswick, N.J.: Rutgers University Press, 2005).

28. David Morley and Kevin Robins, *Spaces of Identity: Global Media, Electronic Landscapes and Cultural Boundaries* (New York: Routledge, 1995), 160.

29. Ibid., 169.

30. Ibid., 170.

APPENDIX A: METHODOLOGICAL NOTES

1. John Lofland, David Snow, Leon Anderson, and Lyn Lofland, *Analyzing Social Settings: A Guide to Qualitative Observation and Analysis* (Thousand Oaks, Calif.: Sage, 2006).

2. Barney G. Glaser and Anselm L. Strauss, *The Discovery of Grounded Theory: Strategies for Qualitative Research* (Chicago: Aldine, 1967).

3. Lofland et al., *Analyzing Social Settings*.

Index

About the Author

ANGIE Y. CHUNG is an associate professor in the Department of Sociology at the University at Albany and former visiting professor at Yonsei and Korea University. She is the author of *Legacies of Struggle: Conflict and Cooperation in Korean American Politics* (2007) on intergenerational relations among ethnic organizations in Koreatown, Los Angeles. She has published on the topics of ethnic politics, interethnic coalitions, immigrant families, ethnic enclaves, and second-generation youth in various journals such as *Ethnicities, Urban Affairs Review, Journal of Ethnic and Migration Studies*, and *Qualitative Sociology*. She is currently working on a new project on redevelopment politics in Koreatown and Monterey Park.

CPSIA information can be obtained
at www.ICGtesting.com
Printed in the USA
LVOW04s0834050816

498807LV00005B/7/P